China and Latin America:

Paths to Overcoming the Middle-income Trap

Edited by Fudan Development Institute

Paths International Ltd

中国社会科学出版社
CHINA SOCIAL SCIENCES PRESS

Plan: Fudan-Latin America University Consortium (FLAUC)

Fudan University (China)

Monterrey Institute of Technology and Higher Education (Mexico)

University of Buenos Aires (Argentina)

National University of La Plata (Argentina)

University of Campinas (Brazil)

University of Sao Paulo (Brazil)

University of Chile (Chile)

Pontifical Catholic University of Chile (Chile)

University of Los Andes (Colombia)

Del Rosario University (Colombia)

National Autonomous University of Mexico (Mexico)

ESAN University (Peru)

National University of San Marcos (Peru)

Contents

Introduction
The Middle-income Trap: A Puzzle from Different Perspectives

Daniel Lemus-Delgado, Miguel A. Montoya B., Mauricio Cervantes-Zepeda

The 'middle-income trap' (MIT) is a concept employed to discuss the phenomena of growth slowdowns of developing economies (Pruchnik and Zowczak, 2017). However, this concept habitually refers to those countries "that have experienced rapid growth, which enabled them to reach the status of a middle-income country but have not been able to finally catch up to the developed countries and achieve high-income status—instead they became caught in the middle-income range" (Glawe and Wagner, 2016).

Gill and Kharas (2007) defined the MIT concept for the first time. Indeed, Gill and Kharas, through the analysis of the development of the economies of East Asia, proposed a definition of the MIT as the case of middle-income countries being squeezed between low-wage poor-country competitors that dominated in mature industries and rich-country innovators that dominated in industries undergoing rapid technological change. In this sense, they foreground that middle-income countries in East Asia could experience three transformations: "first, diversification will slow and then reverse, as countries become more specialized in production and employment; second, investment will become less important, and innovation should accelerate; third, education systems will shift from equipping workers with skills that allow them to adjust to new technologies to preparing them to shape new products and processes". (Gill and Kharas, 2007). In consequence, these transformations would be the observable outcomes connected with a successful move in strategy as countries progress through middle-income position.

Regarding the concept of MIT, Pruchnik and Zowczak (2017) have proposed three types of definitions. The first group consists of non-empirical, descriptive interpretations of what the MIT is. In general, they defined the trap as a situation when a country is no longer able to maintain the pace of firm convergence by continuing to use basic growth engines, most notably low wages. On the one hand, such a country is unable to compete with advanced nations that are not price-competitive but rather quality-competitive, which requires a high level of innovativeness. On the other hand, it is also unable to compete with low-income countries that have even lower wages. As a result, it finds itself stuck in the middle—hence, in the MIT. The second group suggests a fixed threshold for the MIT. For example, Spence (2011) proposed a range of between 5,000 USD and 10,000 USD per capita (PPP) income because he thinks that this is the phase of development at which the shift to higher-income levels becomes puzzling. Finally, the third group of interpretation is based on the concept of growth slowdowns. Eichengreen, Park, and Shin (2013) analyzed middle-income countries that in the past half-century had enjoyed average GDP growth of at least 3.5% for several years. In this way, MIT is the sudden economic slowdown as a decline in the 7-year average growth rate of at least 2 percentage points. As Woo affirms: "Possibly the most important consideration in defining the analytical metric to classify a country as high-income, or middle-income, or low income is that the definition of income categories must have a built-in dynamic element to take into account that the income of the world's richest countries has been rising steadily over the last two hundred years. In the context where the highest potential level of income (output per person) internationally is increasing… the boundaries of the income categories should not be drawn on the basis of absolute levels of income" (Woo, 2014).

Beyond the definition of MIT what it is, more important is to establish how the countries can escape from this trap. Naturally, the academic literature suggests many different factors that influence a country to remain inside of the MIT. Eichengreen, Park, and Shin (2013) proposed that the principal factor whereby the countries stagnate in the rout of the development is the slowdown of productivity growth; in consequence, the governments need to boost productivity. Agenor and Canuto (2014) accentuated the role of access to finance and product innovation to escape from MIT. On the other hand, Egawa (2013) argued that income inequality is also a cause that increases the possibility of being stuck in the trap. Jankowska, Nagengast, and Ramon (2012) suggested that the absence of aptitude to adjust to fast urbanization could increase the probability of a country becoming trapped in the MIT.

Other approximations propose no critical factor that makes countries caught in the trap because of a multiplicity of conditions that contribute to this problem. Among other factors, it is possible to identify a limited diversification of the economy; an inadequate level of human and physical capital; a weak legal and institutional framework; the prevalence of low sectoral development relationships with other sectors, and a little diversification of exports and export of goods with a little value added (Felipe, Abdon, and Kumar, 2012). Ayiar et al. (2013), consider that it is necessary to propose multiple approaches to solve the puzzle of the MIT. These approaches must keep in mind factors as institutions, infrastructure-communication and roads regional integration, demography, macroeconomic environment, economic structure, low quality of the legal system and property rights, excessive growth of the public sector, low share of high-tech goods in exports, and unfavorable demographics tendencies. Finally, Pruchnik and Zowczak (2017) point out seven factors that determinates how a country can fall into MIT. These factors are unfavorable demographics, low level of economic diversification, inefficient financial market, insufficient advanced infrastructure, low level of innovation, weak institutions, and inefficient labor market.

It is a fact that the different factors previously presented have strong relationship with the national competitiveness. In consequence, it is logical to observe how the capacity of the countries to be successful in a global competitive environment goes hand in hand to possibility that eventually a country can leave of the MIT. In the case of the Latin America and the Caribbean countries (LACs) it is palpable the countries with a better competitiveness are nations more developed, too.

Table 1 shows the Global Competitiveness Index (2017–2018) for Latin American countries of the World Bank and in it we can see that most of the Latin American nations are located from 50th place and down, which shows a low competitiveness and therefore a (theoretical) lower preparation to circumvent MIT.

Table 1. Global Competitiveness Index 2017–2018 for Latin American countries

Country	Global Position
Chile	33
Costa Rica	47
Panama	50
Mexico	51

(Contd.)

Country	Global Position
Colombia	66
Jamaica	70
Peru	72
Uruguay	76
Brazil	80
Guatemala	84
Argentina	92
Nicaragua	93
Honduras	96
Ecuador	97
Dominican Republic	104
El Salvador	109
Paraguay	112
Venezuela	127
Haiti	128

Source: The Global Competitiveness Report 2017–2018.

On the other hand, Ginsburg (2014) proposes a different perspective of the MIT. For him, "Middle-income countries face a particular set of challenges that are, ultimately, political rather than technical or purely economic. The basic problem is one of path dependencies. Institutions that are suitable for growth at the early stages of development may not be able to work for later stages. Instead, the regime that gets the country to middle-income status may stick with the strategies and institutions that have worked to date. After all, early-stage economic growth underpins regime legitimacy and may generate increasing political returns that lock in particular structures. The challenge for the political leadership in middle-income countries is how to reform the political and institutional bases of growth at the right time to avoid what the economists call a "local maximum". (Ginsburg, 2014) According to this thought, Doner and Schneider (2016) affirm that most studies of MIT identify the need for some minimal political conditions for enacting necessary policies. These requisites include political determination, long time horizons on the part of political leaders, broad societal consensus, business-government collaboration, and some degree of inclusive politics.

Despite the search for a conceptual precision about the term of MIT and how the countries can escape from this trap, the reality of the Middle Income Countries (MICs) is overwhelming. The concept of MICs reflects a variety of countries with specific and diverse contexts. The world's MICs have been defined by the group of countries that have a per capita gross national income of US$1,026 to $12,475 (2011). Thus, these nations are a diverse group by size, population, and income level. The table 2 shows the evolution of the GDP Per Capita of the most important countries of LACs in comparison with Developed Countries. The evidence shows us two crucial considerations. In the last twenty years, the growth in the GDP Per Capita is not enough to guarantee a better life for the majority of people of this region. Second, inside the LACs exists an enormous diversity both in the current income levels as well as the possibilities to scape to MIT.

Table 2. GDP Per Capita (Current USD)

Country	1996	2006	2016	MIC at 2016*
Latin America and Caribbean countries				
Argentina	7,684	5,879	12,440	yes
Barbados	9,069	15,440	15,892	
Bolivia	959	1,234	3,105	yes
Brazil	5,157	5,860	8,650	yes
Chile	5,383	9,485	13,793	
Colombia	2,554	3,709	5,806	yes
Costa Rica	3,230	5,245	11,825	yes
Dominican Republic	2,258	3,837	6,722	yes
Ecuador	2,159	3,351	6,019	yes
El Salvador	1,819	3,063	4,224	yes
Guatemala	1,472	2,257	4,147	yes
Haiti	365	506	740	
Honduras	688	1,438	2,361	yes

(Contd.)

Country	1996	2006	2016	MIC at 2016
Mexico	4,153	8,768	8,209	yes
Nicaragua	917	1,241	2,151	yes
Panama	3,530	5,349	13,680	yes
Paraguay	2,010	1,810	4,078	yes
Peru	2,261	3,172	6,049	yes
Uruguay	6,316	5,878	15,221	
Venezuela	3,014	6,736	-	yes
Jamaica	2,539	4,313	4,879	yes
Latin America and Caribbean	4,172	5,877	8,311	
Selected Asian countries				
China	709	2,099	8,123	yes
Hong Kong	24,818	28,224	43,681	
Republic of Korea	13,138	20,888	27,539	
Singapore	26,263	33,580	52,963	
Selected Western countries				
United States	30,068	46,437	57,638	
Spain	16,069	28,483	26,640	
Ireland	20,861	54,307	63,862	
Germany	30,564	36,448	42,070	
Portugal	12,185	19,821	19,840	
OECD Members	22,818	32,592	36,864	

* *Middle Income Countries (MIC) classification by World Bank.*
Source: The World Bank (2018), World Development Indicators.

The challenge of MIT has been analyzed both in China and in Latin America Countries (LACs). Specifically, in Chinese case, according to Woo (2014), there are three classes of failures that could conduct this country to fall in MIT. He calls these failures hardware failure; software failure; and power supply failure. The first case includes the breakdown of an economic mechanism, for example, a banking crisis that origins a credit crunch that could dislocate production economy-wide, and a budget crisis that necessitates reductions in essential infrastructure and social expenditure, generating high inflation, and balance of payment difficulties. The second failure refers to a flaw in governance that creates common, widespread social disorders that disrupt production economy-wide and discourage private investment. This failure is linked to inequality and corruption. Finally, a power supply failure denotes to the economy being unable to move forward because it hits either a natural limit or an externally-imposed limit, for example, an environmental collapse.

The World Bank with the collaboration of Development Research Center of the State Council presented a complementary approach. The World Bank Report established that China is at risk of being caught in the MIT. To evade the trap, China needs to explore new ways to encourage the development. These actions include "increased efficiency in input use, higher human capital investments, increased innovation, and a shift to high-value services" (World Bank 2012). Therefore, the proposal establishes some strategic directions for China's future: First, completing the transition to a market economy and accelerating the pace of open innovation. Also, going 'green' to transform environmental stresses into green growth as a driver for development; expanding opportunities and services such as health, education and access to jobs for all people. At the last, modernizing and strengthening its domestic fiscal system; seeking mutually beneficial relations with the world by connecting China's structural reforms to the changing international economy (World Bank 2012).

Talking about middle-income LACs, Kharas and Kohli(2011), 284 propose that these countries have been through several cycles of growth based on credit extended during commodity booms, followed by crisis, and then recovery. "This stop—go cycle has prevented Latin American countries from becoming advanced economies even though they have enjoyed several episodes of fast growth" (kharas and kohli, 2011). To Kharas and Kohli it is evident that the story of LACs is a sharp contrast with successful countries in the region of East Asia, specifically Japan, Hong Kong, Taiwan, Singapore, and South Korea, nations that have been able to sustain high growth over some 50 years.

Although there is no single formula to overcome the challenge of the MIT, a multidisciplinary vision is indispensable that considers economic, political and social aspects related to the factors that can help to escape this trap. In this regard, both the public and private sectors can contribute to a country moving forward in the development path and, therefore, find a way to help nations to advance to high incomes. Consequently, it is necessary to observe, from different angles, the different edges of this complex reality.

This book is a multidisciplinary analysis of the theme of MIT recovering experiences from both China and LACs. The different authors reflect from a different and complementary perspective this problem, such as the fight against income inequality, the promotion of trade agreements, financing for development and the role of multinational companies about MIT. The ultimate intention of the authors has been to increase the analysis in this topic from analyzing and contrasting the cases of China and LACs.

In the first chapter, Cortés discusses how the region can leverage from a post-commodity boom development strategy with China, as it transforms itself towards a more consumption-based economy, to generate a long-run productive and competitive growth in the region adequate to overcome the MIT. Secondly, Feldmann emphases the role of a large company in creating technology. For him, to overcome the middle-income trap, it is necessary to be an essential developer of innovations and technology and the massive local companies are the best way to get it. Thus, LACs need to find a way to base a group of important domestic large multinationals in order to enter the very restricted group of developed nations.

Borquez analyses the case of Chile and the agreements signed with the U.S. and China. Borquez notes that both agreements were signed practically in the same period and have developed release procedures for goods, services, and investment. However, differences in the development of additional agreements are detected. The U.S.-Chile FTA practically included no significant change. Instead, China-Chile FTA transformed into a more complex instrument thanks to new clauses incorporated gradually, emphasizing developing financial, technological and scientific research cooperation with the focus on sectors where mutual and complementary interests exist. In this context, the China-Chile FTA emerge as an alternative to cooperation that allows small economies such as Chile to advance on the road to development.

Binetti signalizes how since the early 2000s, China has become a key economic partner for countries of the Common Market of the South (Mercosur). He analyzes the evolution of Mercosur-China relations with a focus on the development of Mercosur members (Brazil, Argentina, Uruguay, and Paraguay). In this way, he highlights Mercosur's strengths and shortcomings as an integration mechanism, and proposes ways in which members can reform the bloc to boost integration, build a common policy towards China, and take advantage of present opportunities to break out of the middle-income trap.

Zhou, Valderrey, and Montoya analyze a potential scenario where Mexico and the People's Republic of China (PRC) collaborate through liberalizing bilateral trade. In this sense, they take a glance at their bilateral commercial rapport before we reveal areas of potential benefits from cooperation under a welfare perspective. Their approach shows the benefits and limitations of using trade to raise the welfare of societies.

In a complementary way, Cervantes and Hartmann deal with the expansion of multinational companies(MNEs) from an emerging economy to another country that is very distant, both physically and culturally, namely the activities of Mexican multinational companies in China. This chapter introduces the challenges of the puzzle of the MIT not only from a governmental issue but also from the private sector. Likewise, Regalado-Pezúa, Zapata, and Montoya explain the strategies for the construction and internationalization of Chinese brands aimed at the Latin American market. Both chapters offer experiences about how the business environment also can contribute to solving the MIT problem.

González and Lemus observe that LACs are losing competitiveness with poor economies on manufactured exports. At the same time, these nations are also incapable of competing with flusher economies in high-skill innovation. In consequence, these countries are "stuck" in the middle-income category. In consequence, they explain the model of creative cities in China as a possible way to escape from the MIT.

Hernández analyzes the China's international cooperation and how in recent years Beijing has significantly increased international cooperation aid, foreign direct investment, and trade, especially in Asia, Africa, and Latin America. Hernández affirms that specifically, Latin America has become a strategic destination for China's international cooperation. From the perspective of Hernández, despite the China's cooperation is not exempt from geo-economic interest, it includes commercial objectives and direct foreign investment, which could contribute to releasing Latin American countries from the middle-income trap. Lemus and Cerda show the other side of the coin when they analyze the Chinese funding for development in LACs. They explore how new actors for financing development are emerging in LACs; specifically, they examine how the Chinese model has operated in Latin America and if this model can contribute to scape to middle-income trap. They explain the context of the financing by Chinese institutions to support the economic growth and discuss the characteristics and scope of the financial aid during the years between 2006 and 2016. Finally, they conclude with the idea of the Western, and the emerging models mean risks and opportunities for development.

The last two chapters refer the case of Brazil and China. As Hase, Tjong, Werner, and Junqueira observe, China and Brazil, as emerging countries, share many challenges and opportunities for development. However, despite their similarities concerning territorial dimension and income level, it is necessary to consider the specificities of each context to address the needs for sustainable development. Specifically, Brazil was considered a typical case of an economy stuck in the middle-income trap and the country's difficulties to move up the value chain, and its extreme income inequality has a negative impact on economic growth and poses a severe threat for sustainable development. China, after decades of rising living standards and wealth generation, also has to deal with the increasing problem of inequality. Recently, both countries have been investing in domestic consumption as a way to prevent an economic slowdown. In this context, they assume a comparative analysis on the policies adopted by each government to stimulate consumption and on their impacts on growth and income distribution.

Finally, Barbieri, Ferreira, and Barbi analyze the global climate change and the economic development. They propose that environmental governance must be promoted at different levels (local, national and global) with the participation of several society extracts in the search for responsible environmental development. In this sense, Brazil and China, significant emitters of greenhouse gases, have a fundamental role in the formulation and implementation of public policies for adaptation and mitigation, thus contributing to a sustainable future being as overcoming the MIT, thus to adopt a global sustainable vision of development in the present as in the future.

Chapter 1
Post-China Boom Development: Policy Priorities for Latin America in the Way Out of the Middle-income Trap

Silvia Cortés C.

Economic vulnerability and underlying structural flaws are barriers towards the achievement and maintenance of sustainable and inclusive growth that most countries around the world face. Some countries may present outstanding economic growth for a certain period and then experience a slowdown, due to-among other reasons — a commodity price boom or inward financing and foreign direct investment (FDI). These two reasons explain the economic growth some Latin American countries experienced with the China boom from 2003 to 2013. Since China's consumption of Latin American commodities made these products more scarce, prices scaled up in the global marketplace, allowing the region to enjoy a massive commodity boom, as it was also looked at as an opportunity to diversify trade relationships away from its traditional dependence on the United States. The levels of trade and Chinese FDI into the commodity sector reached by the region were simply remarkable.

However, around 2014, China started to experience an economic slowdown, and along with that, prices in a range of key commodities started to plunge as China's appetite for raw materials slowed, while supply, especially of oil and iron ore, increased. The combination of a global surplus of output in many commodity markets and the slowdown in demand from China reinforced market weaknesses and drove prices down. This declining growth represented a commodity and investment shock on commodity-intensive exporting countries, such as those in the Latin American region. The subsequent fall also hit demand for manufacturing goods, further reducing the value of exports across most of the region. The negative terms-of-trade shock resulted in a large trade deficit, which also turned into current account and government budget deficits (Gómez, 2016). Income windfall[①] from the China boom in Latin America was both unforeseen and unprecedented. Nonetheless, despite this windfall, the region showed a weak economic and social performance, due to the lack of capital investment into the economies to develop productive capabilities, as well as deficiencies in the capture of tax and royalty revenues (Gallagher, 2016).

Furthermore, the China commodity boom masked the need to make urgent progress on pending competitiveness gaps. Large inflows of FDI coming from China, oil prices above USD 100, and the resulting export and government revenue increases, all lessened the urgency of advancing on a competitiveness agenda that would allow new sectors and innovative processes to emerge and develop (Gómez, 2016). The deficiency of strictness towards the administration of the windfall profits received from China generated a growth slowdown and lengthened the stay of many Latin American countries within the middle-income trap (MIT). According to Paus (2017), MIT is a concept used to describe a situation in which a middle-income country can no longer compete internationally in standardized, labor-intensive commodities as wages have become too high, but it can also not participate in higher value added activities because competitiveness is too low. From Latin America, only Chile and Uruguay are classified as high-income countries, but it is important to note that notwithstanding this classification, these two states still face similar development challenges to the rest of Latin American countries categorized at the middle income level (Paus, 2017).

Economic growth can only be achieved in middle-income states if the main factor of economic activity shifts from commodity production into more sophisticated and value-added processes. This productive transformation is at the heart of the transition from middle-income to high-income status (Paus, 2014). The core of the middle-income trap consists in the poor development of productive and innovative competences in a globalized scenario where the pressure to innovate has become bigger and heavier. Thus, the "trap" currently faced by Latin American countries, is that their economies need to make the transition up the productivity ladder by proactively producing more innovative and knowledge intensive goods, and retooling workers from manufacturing and

① Windfall profits are unexpected profits that occur due to fortuitous or unpremeditated circumstances, such as the price increase of certain strategic export products.

production to services and other value-added industries.

Latin America needs to work on advancing a growth strategy based on innovation capabilities to ensure their international competitiveness and find a way out of the MIT. This chapter is based on the premises of the Overlapping Generations Perspective model formulated by Agénor and Canuto (2012), which focuses on human capital accumulation and access to advanced technological infrastructure. Since the main barriers to climbing the economic ladder for middle-income countries are education, technical skills and innovation, this approach will be used to identify in which phase Latin American countries are currently positioned and what needs to be done in terms of policy and institutional adjustments to avoid what happened with the windfall profits from the China commodity boom.

Incidentally, Latin American countries need to identify the opportunities and scenarios in which the economic partnership with China and the region can be reshaped, considering and accepting that the China boom has passed already, and that the eventual first global economy has shifted from an export-led economy towards a consumer-based one. As well as it offered trade and investment opportunities in the region's commodities, China is also keen to offer prospects of development programs and foreign aid in areas that Latin American countries need the most, such as innovative capabilities and human capital development, but first, the region must implement proper policy reforms to advance its path in innovation and technology, in order to prevent these opportunities from being squandered as it happened with the China boom's profits.

This chapter begins with an overview of China's economic slowdown and its impact on Latin America's economies and their middle-income status. It continues with the overview of the Overlapping Generations Perspective Model to identify the policy adjustments in terms of innovation and human capital accumulation that Latin America needs to focus on in order to sustain a high growth rate and generate renewed competitiveness agendas to eventually lose the middle-income label. It then concludes with the opportunities for both China and Latin America to improve their economic partnership after the commodity boom period.

1. China's Slowdown and its Impact on Latin America

Latin America's history of reliance on exports as its comparative advantage dates back to colonial times, which also goes hand in hand with foreign exploitation of its natural resources, according to dependency theory. To prevent vulnerabilities caused by the international marketplace's elasticities and to somehow respect their sovereignty, during the 1950s Latin American states adopted strategies based on economic nationalism, which favored policies emphasizing the domestic control of the economy, such as the import-substitution industrialization model. However, these strategies left the region further behind the development level and economic prosperity reached by many other states during that time, such as Japan, South Korea, and Singapore (Watson, 2017). Although in the 1970s the region experienced a slight improvement in the economy, massive debt and crisis were experienced in the 1980s, and as a result, the export-oriented industrialization model became the "prevailing orthodoxy" for developing economies around the world within the Washington Consensus framework (Gereffi, 2014). This neoliberal model was acclaimed for representing a new development paradigm. As stated by Gereffi (2014), it would give developing countries the opportunity to benefit from scale economies and to learn from exporting with larger trade partners. Nevertheless, by the end of the Cold War, Latin America still struggled with economic problems consequent with its inexorable dependence on natural resources and raw materials exports.

It was until the first years of the 21st century that the region started to catch up and undergo certain success with free trade and foreign investment. Although the United States has long exercised dominant influence in Latin America, after the 9/11 events in 2001, U.S.-Latin American relations lost strength, as Washington was absorbed by the war on terrorism, with Latin America becoming a less urgent priority. This situation happened to coincide with an increasing integration of China into the world economy, which was fundamentally driven by the fast expansion of its international trade and large FDI inflows. Using as foundation Beijing's diplomatic successes achieved in Asia since the 1990s when the "Going Out" was officially implemented—to bring investments in while also "going out" to take advantage of both domestic and foreign markets, former Chinese President Hu Jintao designed a policy of cross-regional diplomacy in 2003, seeking to expand diplomatic and mostly trade driven ties beyond the Asia-Pacific, including Latin America among other regions (Lanteigne, 2013). China pursued in Latin America deals for regional commodities and energy. Simultaneously, China began to develop its role as an alternative to the United States, both in political and economic partnerships, and was notoriously active in materializing different types of diplomatic and economic initiatives to build and reinforce relations with different countries across the region.

Up to the late 1990s, China had established rapprochements with 19 Latin American nations and began to develop affairs with regional bodies such as Rio Group and Mercosur, establishing dialogue and consultation mechanisms with them. Starting in the 2000s, Sino-Latin American relations went to a new stage in which development was much more rapid. It was in 2003 that China's trade demand improved trade terms with Latin America, boosting the region's economies and helping them to experience a new growth period (Lanteigne, 2013). China's demand for raw materials and energy to boost its vast economic development was directly translated into large economic gains for Latin America, with China providing a large market to this commodity-based region. Bilateral trade between China and Latin America increased outstandingly since the early 2000s—from USD 12 billion in 2000 to USD 289 billion in 2013 (Elson, 2014), with China already surpassing the European Union as the region's second import market since 2011, according to the United Nation's Economic Commission for Latin American and the Caribbean (2016). Such exploding trade brought a game changing effect for Latin American economies. In 2011, China became the first export market for Brazil, Chile and Peru, and the second for Argentina, Cuba, Uruguay, Costa Rica and Venezuela (Economic Commission for Latin America and the Caribbean, 2016b).

In addition, even closer political and economic relations resulted in free trade agreements between China and three Latin American countries: Chile, signed in 2006; Peru, in 2009; and Costa Rica, in 2011. Momentarily, Colombia is the only country from the region that is negotiating this kind of commercial agreement with China since 2015. It is important to mention that there has always been an evident and growing imbalance between the region and China in favor of the last one, demonstrating that China is considerably a more significant trading partner for Latin America than Latin America is for China. Besides trade, China's presence has also been noticed by its investments in the region. In the early 2000s Chinese investments in Latin America were still modest; however, by 2013 they became larger and were based fundamentally on the extraction of natural resources, energy and infrastructure projects. China's large-scale investments in Latin America were meant to represent an incentive for the local economies, since this projects of infrastructure upgrading would favor and increase Latin American countries' competitiveness and productivity.

In 2014 China found itself in the midst of a progressive economic slowdown process, which drove growth rates down from double-digits percentages to 7.4%—the lowest in 24 years. Along with this situation, the Asian giant developed a new economic focus on consumption and services, which are less intensive in natural resources and energy. As such, China's economic slowdown began having serious implications for economic growth at a global level. Latin America, a region highly dependent on commodities, reaffirmed its vulnerability to these types of slowdowns, now coming from China. Yet again, a world power sneezed and Latin America caught the flu. In 2014, trade between Latin America and China decreased by 2% in value terms, compared to 2013, signaling the first fall since 2009 (Economic Commission for Latin America and the Caribbean, 2016b). The decline in the region's exports to China since 2014 reflects the contraction on the demand of the raw materials that make up most of the region's basket of exports to that country, putting a lot of pressure on Latin American economies.

It is well-known that economic growth based primarily on natural resources leads to a resource curse, or in other words, to the harmful consequences of large increases in a country's income as a result of the profits generated just by commodities. During commodity booms, windfalls pour into the commodity sector, but does not contribute to job creation. It also causes the exchange rate of countries to appreciate, making non-commodity exports more expensive and hence less competitive. However, the region has not learned the lesson. Latin America's economic wellbeing has come to the point of directly depending on China's economic performance, and this is particularly concerning, considering that governments have not yet created clear linkages between the commodity-export sectors and other areas of the economy, and even more worrying, they did not managed well the profits resulting from the China boom. Bearing this in mind, Gallagher (2016) compiled the following findings from different international organizations data regarding Latin America's use of these profits:

Latin American policy-makers should have used some of the benefits of the Chinese commodity boom to diversify into other sectors and industries, as well as environmental protection, by building institutions to oversee these profits in a socially inclusive way. Moreover, many countries had the opportunity to invest in innovation and human capital, which could have resulted in reaching a higher income level and becoming competitive enough to leave the MIT. As Economic Commission for Latin America and the Caribbean (2016b) has pointed out, given the slower pace of economic growth forecasted for the next few years both in China and in Latin America, bilateral trade is unlikely to expand at the pace seen in the last decade and a half. This is the reason why the region must work towards policy strategies that can boost economic development without heavily relying on commodity booms to be competitive. Fleeing the MIT is possible if policy adjustments are consciously made.

Table 1.1 Latin America's misuse of China boom's windfall profits according to international organizations

International Monetary Fund	World Bank	ECLAC
The China boom was among the most lucrative booms the region had ever experienced, and yet most Latin American countries saved less of these windfalls than they had in past booms. Governments did not invest in productive capital investments to generate innovation and industrialization in thc long term.	During the China boom, investment in capital formation amounted to 19.6% of GDP, whereas from 1980 to 2002 (Washington Consensus period) investment averaged 18.8%. Latin America had one of the lesser China booms in the world—South Asia grew by 7.1% the sub-Saharan region by 5.2%, and Latin America by 3.6%	The region did not capture tax and royalty revenues from commodities exports in proportion with the perceived upsurge in the windfalls. Additionally, nations were more oriented to quickly spend the windfalls rather than to invest them into innovation and industrialization.

Source: Author based on Gallagher (2016).

2. Innovation as the Way Out of the MIT

The end of the China boom and the decline of commodity prices it entailed took its toll on Latin America's economic growth. Although there were evident development opportunities derived from the windfall profits, the region failed to achieve prosperity levels seen in industrialized countries and its economic performance was disappointing during the boom period. Nonetheless, economic slowdowns like this one can be turned into opportunities for governments to plan the required strategies in order to guarantee their citizens a better future. After all, only Latin America can and must take responsibility to advance its own economic and social development, and avoid both the MIT and its dependence to an external source of financing. Following this line, it is important to point out that growth towards reaching a higher income status cannot be tenable unless policies are considerably redesigned to activate a country's full potential to internalize innovation.

Many countries in Latin America were ranked as middle-income economies as early as the 1960s and 1970s, with the great majority of them having remained there ever since. As mentioned before, just Chile and Uruguay within the region have risen enough to become high-income economies since then, and still have not had it easy: underneath their development levels, both economies show symptoms of being in the middle-income trap. In the case of Chile, and similar to other Latin American countries, it has had difficulties in advancing its productivity, increasing its value-added exports or undertaking an economic upgrade in value chains (Dingemans, 2016). The region's stance in the long term strongly depends on the extent to which it can accomplish a structural transformation of the economy. For this matter, it is crucial to begin by understanding and facing the causes of the MIT challenge.

As it has been stressed throughout this chapter, the MIT is mainly characterized by a drastic deceleration in growth and in the pace of productivity. There are important lines of theoretical research that help understand how the MIT works. The elementary explanation for development slowdowns in this topic is the Lewis Turning Point. In this model, an economy first becomes industrialized and grows rapidly with the unskilled labor from rural areas. Following what Agénor, Canuto and Jelenic (2012) state, at first, low-income countries can compete in international markets by producing labor-intensive and low-cost products using foreign technology, attaining large productivity gains. But after a while, wages start to rise: this is the turning point, where firms become less profitable and they have to come up with new sources of growth to maintain sustained increases in per capita income. The comparative advantage then begins to weaken, thus causing a fundamental shift in the structure of the labor market, and forcing the economies into the MIT (Shambaugh, 2016). The trap is that the countries need to reinvent its development strategies to transition up the productivity ladder.

Some other characteristics that define the MIT in the Latin American region are misallocation of talent and innovation stagnation. There is a more recent alternative elucidation of economic slowdowns developed by Agénor and Canuto (2012) that focuses on these problems. According to their Overlapping Generations Perspective, a number of factors may impact productivity growth, including individual decisions to acquire abilities, access to different sorts of public infrastructure, and knowledge network externalities which are defined as the possibility that a higher share of workers with advanced levels of education will have a positive output on the economy. This model focuses on human capital accumulation, in which advanced skills can be developed by dedicating a given amount of time to higher education in early adulthood (Agénor and Canuto, 2012).

In this model, individuals with either basic or advanced skills can both work in manufacturing, while only those with advanced skills can perform in innovative processes. The model also assumes that individuals decide to invest in education only if remunerations in the innovation sector are high enough, compared to manufacturing. The combination of a knowledge spillover and a learning-by-doing effect, will result in an increase of the marginal productivity gain associated with the stock of ideas, which is important for countries at low levels of development (Agénor and Canuto, 2012). Regarding the access to public infrastructure, the model considers two types: basic infrastructure, consisting of roads, electricity and basic telecommunications; and advanced infrastructure, which entails advanced information and communication technologies (ICTs), as well as high-speed communications networks. It is now well-known that access to advanced infrastructure simplifies the expansion of domestic and international knowledge networks, research and innovation (Agénor and Canuto, 2012).

The main contribution of this model is that if the marginal benefits associated with non-rival knowledge depend in a non-linear approach on the share of the population working in innovation activities, as a result of a knowledge network effect, then multiple equilibria may arise, with the lower growth equilibrium being equal to MIT. Agénor and Canuto (2012) conclude that this low-growth equilibrium would be characterized by a misallocation of talent, since skilled people, who could be highly productive in innovation processes, end up working in manufacturing or other transactional tasks. This approach to the MIT challenge is the one that best suits Latin America's situation. Growth that depends on natural resources sooner or later comes to a halt, and other alternatives need to be contemplated to undertake the policy reforms needed to boost the region's growth potential. Innovation through a proactive industrialization policy has proven to be a solution to escape the MIT in Asian economies such as Singapore, Japan and South Korea (Ohno, 2009), as well as a useful tool for other developing countries in the quest of moving up the income ladder and reaching high-income status.

Policy prioritization to encourage endogenous innovation and hence economic development is urgently needed in Latin America. There are a number of public policies that governments can pursue, all implemented within a framework where human capital and technological infrastructure are fundamental to advancing innovation. Starting with those related to human capital, it is clear that improving long-term growth projections and productivity requires raising the skill level of the workforce. Many Latin American countries face a lack of adequately educated labor force, considering that inequality in access to education is one of the main challenges in the region (OECD/CAF/ECLAC, 2017). These human capital and technological constraints restrict the ability of countries to diversify and increase their economic productivity. Another major problem in the region is the completion of tertiary education.

According to the OECD (2017), although enrolment in universities has improved, graduation rates are still low, and in addition, a small share of students focus on science, technology, engineering and mathematics (STEM) degrees, which are key to develop more value-added processes. For the economy not to end up in a lower-growth equilibrium, it is necessary to internalize skills and competences by accumulating human capital, either by public means alone, or in collaboration with the private sector and other non-profit actors, when the levels and types of competences are perceived to be insufficient. By training the workforce with the required skills demanded by the global market in terms of innovation, it might be easier for the region to push the technological frontier and move from imitating and importing foreign technologies to innovating technologies of their own (Agénor and Canuto, 2012) and "graduate" from the middle-income status to become high-income economies.

As well as developing the skills necessary to undertake indigenous innovation activities, the region should reconsider its investment in advanced infrastructure to facilitate these processes and enhance productivity while fostering a knowledge-driven economic growth, particularly in high-speed communications networks. These efforts should develop into public policies able to guarantee citizens affordable and good-quality internet access, acknowledging ICTs as enablers of socio-economic development and inclusion. ECLAC (2016a) indicates that in 2015, on average, 43% of households in Latin America were connected to the internet.[①] Digital connectivity is vital for enabling socio-economic inclusion. Following Agénor and Canuto's model

---

① According to Economic Commission for Latin America and the Caribbean (2016a), there is a great difference in access levels among the countries of the region: of the 24 countries analyzed in 2015, three had household Internet penetration that was below 15%; fifteen were between 15% and 45%; another three were between 45% and 56%; and only Chile, Costa Rica and Uruguay reached 60%.

(2012), if productivity in innovative activities is low because of a limited access to advanced infrastructure, jobs will lack complexity and wages will continue to be low, which thus implies that individuals will choose not to invest in the advanced skills needed to work in that sector.

Economic upgrading cannot be achieved without promoting technological upgrading and innovation capacity. The availability of good-quality ICTs plays a significant role in encouraging innovation by facilitating the rapid diffusion of knowledge flows, becoming crucial to economic efficiency and international competitiveness. As Gallagher (2016) points out, a twenty-first-century infrastructure is needed in the region to expand not only ICTs, but also energy and electricity, as well as roads, ports and railways, in order to increase regional trade and investment and better connect Latin America with the rest of the world. Predominantly, infrastructure projects in the region have been designed only at a national level and with extractive purposes—such mentality is typical of a commodity-dependent economy.

Human capital accumulation and advanced technological infrastructure appear to be the top priorities for Latin America in order to achieve capabilities based on innovation that will boost its productivity and improve its economic situation. In addition to what has been previously mentioned, government institutions may need to take the lead in this process by leveraging macroeconomic policies, tax incentives for activities involving innovation, and protection of intellectual property (Stiglitz and Lin, 2013). Moreover, along with increasing profits in these areas, the region needs to expand the tax base to the engines of the economy, as well as to invest the proceeds into more diversification and social improvement, to avoid what happened during the China boom. Besides advancing the region's economies, the right application of these measures might also open up the possibilities to redesign the economic relations with China, following a new development model that does not rely solely on commodities nor windfall revenues resulting from them, but in the diversification of competitive industries based on innovation.

3. Rebuilding the Sino-Latin American Economic Partnership

As previously stated on this chapter, it is necessary for the Latin American region to come up with a new development strategy for the post-China boom era able to both reshape the economic relation with China as well as help the region's economies escape the MIT. A new development approach more focused on industrialization policies like the ones aforementioned will certainly be attractive enough to catch China's attention, and will also be useful to ensure a more balanced economic relationship with the Asian giant than the one based on commodities trade that resulted during the China boom period. Latin America should take advantage of its strategic measures in innovation to leverage when engaging with China in this sense. Considering a new industrialization pattern from Latin America, China might be keener to advance its leading companies abroad and provide financing to governments in emerging markets such as those in the region in order to diversify its assets.

According to Gallagher (2016), there are three areas where China may buy into a new development strategy in Latin America. First, it is important to know that in terms of demand for Latin American commodities and beyond, China is not going away. It will not be like during the boom, but it will continue to be a source of demand for the region's products and possibly for a more diversified array of products beyond the commodities sector as well. As China revamps itself towards a more consumption-based economy, it will eventually require more consumer goods. Although the Latin American manufacturing sector has lost competitiveness during the commodity boom, Chinese transformation offers a second opportunity. If Latin American nations put an actual effort on innovation, industrialization and export competitiveness, they may find openings in the Chinese economy that may be impossible to find anywhere else in the world.

Second, China may have an even larger presence in terms of FDI in Latin America than it has nowadays. China can also continue to be a constant source of FDI into the region not only in the commodity sectors if Latin American countries get their policies right. Since companies in the infrastructure, construction and manufacturing sectors in China saturate the markets that led China's transformation in those sectors, they will be looking to expand overseas. Chinese national companies are currently looking to merge with or acquire Latin American companies that had economic difficulties due to the slowdown, lower prices, and bloated balance sheets because of exchange rate depreciation. As the exchange rate and wages rise in China, Latin America may not only be a destination for FDI in the primary commodities sector, but will also be an option for other industries with more complex activities, thus enabling knowledge transfer in different areas.

Third, China and its ever growing set of development banks and funds can be a source of much-needed finance for infrastructure and industrialization. In terms of finance, there is no sign that China is pulling the plug from Latin American governments, though it may begin to be redirected to other extents. In 2015, China hosted the first China-CELAC (Community of Latin American and Caribbean States) summit. This meeting launched a new dialogue platform and joint forum that intends to link China and Latin America. China pledged to increase FDI in the region to USD 250 billion by 2020, committing also to support billions of dollars in regional projects and almost double bilateral trade to USD 500 billion by 2025. To thrust its commitment, China established a number of funding arrangements totaling USD 35 billion, including USD 20-billion special loans for China-Latin America infrastructure cooperation, the USD 10-billion preferential loans for Latin American countries, as well as the USD 5-billion China-CELAC Cooperation Fund that China previously pledged (Gallagher, 2016).

The China-CELAC Forum offers a great opportunity for a regional dialogue with China to further bilateral economic relations. If managed properly, this platform could be useful to allow the region to reach common goals for regional infrastructure and industrialization. At the China-CELAC summit leaders from Latin America drew up a *China-CELAC Cooperation Plan (2015–2019)*. The comprehensive plan covers a wide range of thematic areas of work-13 in total, including policy and security; international affairs; trade, investment and finance; infrastructure and transportation; energy and natural resources; agriculture; industry, science and technology; education and human resources training; culture and sports; press and media; tourism; environmental protection; and people-to-people friendship (China-CELAC Forum, 2015). The possibilities for potential cooperation are therefore extremely broad and wide-ranging.

The Cooperation Plan is an exceptional opportunity for Latin America to upgrade its industrial competitiveness. In addition to assuring the increase of trade and investment and to create a number of funding means to facilitate them, China and CELAC pledge to stimulate the promotion and facilitation of investment, including through joint ventures and partnerships; to boost collaboration to promote in CELAC countries' high-technology and value-added goods production; and to support the internationalization and presence of small and medium-sized enterprises in global value chains. Furthermore, regarding science and technology, the plan also commits to explore initiatives to the joint construction of industrial parks, science and technology, special economic zones and high-tech industrial parks between China and CELAC countries, especially in research and development activities in order to improve industrial investment and the creation of industrial value chains. It also refers to improving mutually beneficial cooperation in fields such as electronics, ICTs and the transfer of technology and know-how between the two parties (China-CELAC Forum, 2015).

Taking into account the top priorities Latin America has in order to enhance productivity and competitiveness—human capital accumulation and development of advanced infrastructure, China also commits to making major investments in these areas. Regarding human resources training and education, the plan contemplates exchanges, research mobility programs and cooperation between education departments and institutions. It also envisages capacity building and collaboration in different areas, by providing CELAC countries with 6,000 governmental scholarships, 6,000 training opportunities and 400 opportunities for on-the-job master degree programs in China between 2015 and 2019.

With respect to infrastructure, the Cooperation Plan promotes infrastructure development in areas such as transportation, ports, roads and warehouse facilities, business logistics, ICTs, broadband, radio and television. It also encourages experienced Chinese and CELAC's enterprises to participate in key projects for the improvement of connectivity and intercommunication between China and CELAC countries. There are other initiatives put into infrastructure projects, such as the China-LAC Cooperation Fund, the China-LAC Special Loan for Infrastructure, concessional loans offered by China as well as other financial sources, to support the key cooperation projects between China and CELAC countries, in a manner consistent with the social, economic and environmental development requirements of the CELAC region, as well as with a sustainable development vision. (China-CELAC Forum, 2015).

This agenda offers a unique opportunity for Latin America's economic development along with the possibility to transform its partnership with China. Although the thematic areas propose only general goals and lines of action, these can be deepened and translated into specific initiatives and projects needed by each country and additionally, China has created a technical secretariat for the continuing progress evaluation in these areas. The plan also reveals that both Chinese and Latin American leaders have already observed the need to diversify this relationship and explore other economic sectors apart from primary commodities. Partnering up in new and strategic spheres with such a global power can only bring benefits to the region's growth. As it has been depicted,

China offers several post-commodity boom opportunities to assist Latin America into becoming an industrialized and competitive region based on innovation and a second chance to flee out of the MIT; however, it only depends on Latin America to make the proper policy and institutional adjustments to overcome the obstacles that might keep the region from taking advantage of this plan.

4. Conclusions

After enjoying approximately a full decade of relatively high growth due to the China commodity boom and the windfall profits received from it, Latin America is going through another economic slowdown. This situation has forced the region to face the challenge of diversifying its economies and reassess what has always been its only development strategy: depending on primary commodities. This has open an array of options that the region can consolidate into a plan B to achieve economic growth, and most of them are based on innovation.

Innovation has proven to be the driver of development in high-income countries that escaped the MIT. Only those middle-income countries that have firmly taken the decision to actively and properly build and advance their own national system to pursue innovation will break free from the MIT. Following the Overlapping Generations Perspective, policies are fundamental to advancing technological infrastructure, training a talented workforce into innovation activities, and encouraging the escalation of local, national and international knowledge networks. Latin American countries must attain abilities and knowledge that the global markets demand, take part in innovative and value-creating activities, and build a national mindset focused on an ongoing training and upgrading of its human capital to boost innovation processes.

Since Latin America is such a heterogeneous region, it is central to determine the right upgrading of these policies. Past attempts to industrialization in the region were general in all senses: industrialize in all sectors at all costs. It is important for policymakers along with the private sector of every country to discover the areas in which they struggle the most to achieve economic growth. Governments and private companies need to act early and strengthen national innovation systems as one of the main purposes of any policy to thoroughly reinforce competitiveness, involving both the public and private sectors. Companies dedicated to producing goods and services must deepen their commitment to implement new technologies and develop their own, being able to easily find government funding and sponsoring to carry out research and development activities. Government must also be better organized with the revenues derived from this new development model, in order to prudently invest them in a socially inclusive manner, and avoid the misuse and mismanagement that happened with the China boom's income windfalls.

China recognizes the strategic nature of its ties with Latin America, as witnessed by the development agenda set on the China-CELAC Cooperation Plan. The Asian giant has also recognized the need to reshape this relation by identifying new areas of growth in which Latin America fits in, besides the trade of commodities that used to be the corner stone of this partnership. These new working areas proposed by China entail various aspects of innovation and capacity building the region can leverage from to boost its competitiveness and productivity in the global economy. This opportunity might develop the region enough to find a way out of the MIT and finally reach a high income status.

As Garret (2004) has stated, middle-income countries must find ways to "tech up" and enter the global knowledge economy, in order to escape the trap of having to "dumb down" to compete in standardized manufacturing. Perhaps the end of the China commodity boom will end up being a blessing in disguise for the region. Perhaps it represents the opportunity the region has long been waiting for to begin a new era of economic development based on innovation as the main engine of growth.

Chapter 2
The Lack of Large Local Enterprises as an Important Explanation for the Middle-income Trap in Latin America

Paulo Roberto Feldmann

The majority of Latin American countries have overcome the barrier of 5,000 dollars per capita as income but they have not yet surpassed the ceiling of 30,000 in order to be considered a very developed country. Unfortunately, for Brazil, Colombia, Argentina, Chile, Mexico and the other Latin American countries there is no ready and easy formula to reach the level of the rich world. However, there is a kind of an indication of the road that must be taken. The countries that have managed to join the group of developed countries were able to generate large and very competent international companies that have their headquarters located inside their borders.

The importance of the local large companies is related to the fact that normally they are more productive then the small ones. Not only economy of scale explains this fact but also the aspect that large companies have more capacity to invest in R & D—Research & Development and consequently they can introduce innovations in a much higher velocity then medium or small companies. Large companies have also the capacity of hiring the most qualified labor resources.

In the present chapter we intend to highlight the role of a large company in generating technology and to indicate how its absence is a fact that makes it difficult to produce more technology in Latin America.

1. Main Hypothesis

The main hypothesis of this chapter is that the production of innovations and technology is increasingly originating in large companies and consequently the countries that are important producers of technology are the countries that are home to a greater number of very large-sized companies. This hypotheses and respective findings are important because they can serve as guidance for countries and governments to encourage the formation of large companies and conglomerates in order to increase their production of technology, mostly in case of Latin America where this is an important issue. This region has a few powerful companies, and worst, almost always performing in sectors that were important in the nineteenth century, but became irrelevant in this twenty-first century. Being a global player in industries such as drinks, cement, mining, agriculture, fish or steel is not bad, but it is not enough.

2. The Chinese case

Although China is still stucked in the middle-income trap, it is important to understand a fact that accompanies its explosive growth in this 21st century. The table below shows the evolution achieved by this country in some indicators and its relation with investments in R & D and the growth of the number of large companies. We can easily notice that the growth of China has been very similar to the growth of the number of large companies and to the amounts that have been spent in R & D by this country.

Table 2.1 Investment of China in R & D, 2005–2016

YEAR	GDP (trillion of dollars)	Income per capita (dollars)	Investments in R & D (billion of US$)	Number of companies among the 2000 list of the largest companies of the world FORBES
2005	2.6	2000	34	25
2016	21.3	15400	232	200
Growth in the period	8.2	7.7	6.8	8

Source: The Global Innovation Index (2016).

It is sure that it is extremely difficult to separate cause and effect but the truth is that the per capita income growth of China has taken place in a virtually unprecedented way in the world, and if China has maintained the same pace, it will reach the per capita income of the richer countries by the end of the next decade when China will finally be free of the trap of the middle income. We can not fail to recognize that this growth has been accompanied by the R & D investments and also that the large Chinese companies have a great responsibility on these expenses.

These facts serve to confirm our central thesis that Latin America will not be able to break free from the trap of the average income without a significant set of big companies because they are the ones that make investments in R & D as we will discuss later.

3. Literature Review

Almost 40 years ago Galbraith pointed to the fact that the large companies were always increasing their supremacy and power over the economy because only they have the conditions to sustain the expenses demanded by innovation. "The small company does not have the conditions to sustain the expenses demanded by innovation" said Galbraith in "The New Industrial State" (Galbraith, 1978: 26). In his ironic and didactic way of analyzing the large problems of the economy, Galbraith would say that the enemy of the market system was not the ideology but the engineer. As he was increasingly working in favor of the large companies and generating innovations in processes and products that contributed increasingly more to increase the difference between the large and the small companies. In all of his books Galbraith emphasized the advantages of a large organization: "The large organization can tolerate the uncertainty of the market, which a smaller company cannot do…All, with the exception of the pathologically romantic, now recognize that this is not the era of the small ones" (Galbraith, 1978).

More recently Stiglitz (2003)[①], explained somewhat more the reasons why technological innovation is increasingly a subject restricted to the large company. When he commented on the proximity between technological change and imperfect competition Stiglitz pointed out four reasons that made it difficult for the small companies to generate technology:

---

① Nobel Prize of Economy in 2001.

> *First, so that the expenditures with research and development can be compensated, and thereby stimulate innovation, the inventions are protected by competition through patents. Patents are specifically destined to limit the competition. Second, industries in which technological change is important normally have elevated fixed costs. This implies that the average cost is decreasing to levels of quite elevated production costs—another characteristic which limits competition. Third, the industries that are characterized by rapid technological change are also those where the advantages of an experiment with new production techniques can lead to rapidly decreasing costs. Finally, why is it so difficult to raise funds for new and small companies? Because banks generally don't finance research and development. All of this makes it difficult to enter the market and to reduce the competition in the sense as defined by the basic model of competition (Stiglitz, 2003).*

According to Besanko, Dranove, Schanley and Schaefer (2006), the expenses with research and development exceed 5% of the total sales in many companies and numerous sectors, citing as examples Intel, Microsoft, Pharmacia and GE. According to them, "...Research and Development involve significant invisibilities. The nature of scientific research and engineering suggest that there exists a minimum size viable for a project of research and development just as for an R & D department" (Besanko et. al., 2006). In other words, in the Research & Development activity there also occur significant scale economies. Even so, Besanko et. al., highlight that despite the presence of a scale economy in Research & Development there is no way to conclude that there is a direct relation between size and innovation emphasizing that the economic theory and the empirical evidence are too ambiguous to say that the large companies are more innovative than the small ones. The authors point out that, generally, large companies are more able to motivate their researchers.

Quijano (2007) points out numerous authors that defend the existence of the positive correlation between size of company and innovation. Among these, Schumpeter (1934) for whom the innovations are products of the long efforts of research and with the uncertain results at the beginning and which need strong investments, in such a way that only large companies with strong technical teams and solid and elevated cash flows are able to bank on them. Quijano also cites Davis (1979) for whom the large-sized firms have a greater disposition that the middle and small-sized ones to incorporate new process technologies because of scale, the technological indivisibility, management resources and the absorption capacities. But Quijano calls attention to the fact that there are sectors where the role of the small and medium-sized companies is relevant as far as the appearance of innovations. He exemplifies with the cases of software and biotechnology where the small companies have had an outstanding role.

Sbragia (2006) cites a Fapesp[①] study done in 2005 where they analyze the relation between the size of the company and sources of innovation, and they found that there is a greater diversity of the sources of innovation to the degree that size of the company increases and concluded that "... the greater the size of the company, the greater their capacity to access useful information coming from institutions (universities, research institutes, consulting companies, etc.) to use them in the process of innovation".

Arbix (2007) emphasizes that the process of innovation is a result of the growth of interactions among individuals, firms and other producer of knowledge institutions, on local national and international. But he emphasizes that "... The fundamental agent of the process of innovation continues to be the company, especially the large one..." (Arbix, 2007).

Brito Cruz (2004) calls attention to the role of the company, in general, in the production of technology, highlighting that if the place for Science and Education is the University, the place for Development and Technology is, par excellence, the company. He cites the case in the Unites States where in 2001 there were one million people working in R & D—Research & Development, being that 80% of these same worked for companies and only 20% for universities or government research centers. Brito Cruz states that unfortunately this fact is not the reality in Brazil. In Brazil, in 2004, there were 125 thousand people working in R & D, of which only 23% worked in companies. South Korea has a population four times less than Brazil, but has a greater number of researchers: 160 thousand people and approximately 59% of them work for private companies.

With these data in hand Brito Cruz (2004) referring to Brazil said that contrary to what is imagined, technological innovation is created much more in the company than in the university. In Brazil there has lately been a tendency to attribute to the university the responsibility for the innovation that would make the company more competitive. This is a serious mistake which, if taken seriously, could cause great damage to the Brazilian university system, taking it away from its specific mission, that of educating professionals and generating fundamental knowledge.

It is about this theme that Sbragia (2006) comments that Japan and Korea currently present a corporate participation in expenditures with R & D above 70% of the total. This occurs because these countries, wanting to increase

① A Brazilian agency destined to finance R & D projects.

the competitiveness of their companies, and in the case of Korea, industrial penetration in more dynamic markets, need to privilege corporate participation in the efforts of technological innovation (Sbragia, 2006).

Sbragia (2006) continues saying that in Brazil only 23% of the scientists and engineers are in private enterprise; this number goes up to 79% in the case of the United States. His conclusion is that although the number of researchers has increased in Brazil, they were allocated outside of the productive sphere (companies) which has caused the number of scientific papers to increase, whereas the number of patents continue to be low, especially when considering the number of patents in the USA.

4. The Technological Backwardness of Latin America

At the beginning of the sixteenth century some of the inhabitants of Latin America, mainly the Aztecs, Mayas and Incas, had scientific and technological knowledge many times superior to that of Europe or China. In some fields, such as astronomy, botany, pharmacology, and metallurgy the Spanish assimilated the knowledge acquired in the region and spread this throughout Europe.

Today, however, Latin America has stopped being an important provider of scientific and technological knowledge, despite representing approximately 9% of the world's population, the region as a whole corresponds to merely 3,0% of the total investment in Science and Technology. In the year 2016, the world invested approximately $1,948 billion in this area of which only 3% of this total came from Latin America. This represents approximately 0.65% of the accumulated GDP of the continent which, compared to Europe (2,0%) and U.S.A (3,0%) is too low (Riemschneider, 2016).

Different statistical studies indicate that Latin America, its countries and local companies, invest very little in Research & Development. This is, indeed, an important fact as it could compromise the entire future economic development of the region. Hobsbawm (1999) upon analyzing the end of the twentieth century commented that "...two areas that visibly generate few scientists in absolute and relative terms: Latin America and Africa" (Hobsbawn, 1999).

We intend to highlight the role of a large company in generating technology and to indicate how its absence is a fact that makes it difficult to produce more technology in Latin America.

Below Table 2.2 indicates how much some countries invested in R & D in

2016 according to Riemschneider. Looking at this table you can see that even in the country that spends the most with R & D, which is Brazil, it is much less than what the developed countries spend. This is a chronic problem in the region which has only become accentuated with time. The importance of Latin America in the area of Science and Technology in the world is increasingly less.

Table 2.2 Expenditures in Science and Technology relative to GDP in 2016

Country	Expenditures with Science and Technology relative to GDP—in%
Israel	3.93
Japan	3.39
Germany	2.92
U.S.A.	2.77
U.K.	1.78
China	1.98
India	0.85
Latin America median	0.65
Brazil	1.21
Argentina	0.62
Mexico	0.45

Source: OECD (2016).

Why isn't Latin America a region that produces more technology? And, what is the reason, except for a few distinguished exceptions, for that there are no companies originating from this continent that stand out globally in the areas of more advanced technology? This is an age-old discussion, but a very important one, which, deep down, is the attempt to answer the question: "What makes some places in the world more oriented to innovation than others?"

The abundance of natural resources in Latin America has been pointed out as an important explanation for having little concern with the innovation that predominates in the region. Fairbanks and Lindsay (2000) state that the local businessmen tend to presuppose that the advantages in natural resources, abundant raw material and cheap labor will proportion positions of leadership in the export markets and, because of this, do not create the conditions for such innovation. Furthermore, Fairbanks and Lindsay point out another important reason for the lack of innovations: It is the deficient cooperation among the companies. According to them there is no culture of cooperation among the companies of the region. Contrary to countries such as Italy, where they have "clusters", also referred to as industrial groups, promoting cooperation and encouraging the companies to unite, for example, and jointly seek external markets, launch a new brand or even invest jointly in R & D—Research & Development, whereas in Latin America, almost invariably, the businessmen see the competitor as an enemy that should be knocked down.

This contributes to creating a climate of mistrust and suspicion in every sector that always destroys any possibility of cooperation. An honorable exception is the automobile industry and their relations with the suppliers of auto parts in Brazil or in Mexico. But this is the exception to the rule, probably due to the fact that these are sectors where there is a predominance of foreign money.

This lack of business cooperation also explains the small number of *clusters* in the region and as Fairbanks and Lindsay state: "...we note a profound absence of clusters in correlated or support sectors, and a corresponding lack of innovation: companies that do not cooperate amongst themselves are not capable of learning from one another" (Fairbanks and Lindsay, 2000).

In 1998, the British magazine *Nature* published a special supplement called "Science in Latin America" with an interesting article by its editor Colin Macilwain in which he analyzed the conditions of Science & Technology on the Latin American continent at the end of the twentieth century, but which continues to be totally valid. In the beginning of this twenty-first century: "The intellectuals and Latin American scientists lament the extinction on the non-competitive industrial base that existed behind the commercial barriers of the old Latin American economy (pre-Neo Liberalism). In that economy the role of Science & Technology was clear: Science would help technology build a domestic industrial base that would take the region to the developed world. However, says Macilwain, a large part of this industry, due to non-competitiveness, collapsed when this became evident during its peak, in the 1990's, and the neo-liberal doctrine brought international competition. As such, factories and companies were sold to multinational corporations who are modernizing them, with technology imported from abroad. Macilwain concludes that science and technology in Latin America need to redefine their role in this new configuration.

Larrain (2014) explaining why Latin America has not advanced as much as

Asia in the last 20 years, has attributed much of this backwardness to a closed market and to the protectionism that predominated in our region during the 1970s and 1980s; this because this suspension did not expose the region to international competition, and ended up delaying building the infra-structure necessary for local researchers to develop their projects.

Freeman and Soete (1997) give a historic retrospective of what happened in the region, commenting that until the beginning of the 1950's the industrial development throughout Latin America was characterized by the reduced degree of technological sophistication and by the simple importation of technology, mainly from the United States and Germany, that was incorporated to capital goods. From the second half of the 1950's various countries introduced measures of protection to their respective national markets trying to eliminate or substitute the importations.

It was during this time that countries of the region began to manufacture middle and high-end items having greater technological complexity. The strategy employed mainly by Brazil, Argentina and Mexico was to seek investments from foreign companies, mainly in the automobile segment. The respective governments also invested, but in the segments with a longer maturation period, such as raw material and infra-structure, but not in the sectors of media and high-density technology. What happened is that explicit technological importation increased without the necessary internal effort to absorb these technologies.

For Malecki (1997) the general panorama of technology in Latin America shows that institutions are weak and political considerations predominate, which end up costing more due to the lack of long-term strategies for science and technology and the lack of involvement of the private sector.

Peter Dicken (1998) emphasizes that an important characteristic in the development of third-world countries, Asian or Latin American, is the strong presence of the State. Nonetheless, this author points to the fact that in Latin America the governments were not as successful as the Asians. According to him, the main reason for this lack of success was the absence of concern with increased internal empowerment aiming to increase exportations. While in Asia, the greatest concern was increasing exportations of industrialized products and in Latin America the emphasis was in substituting importations.

Dicken calls attention to the fact that the old division of labor, when the developed countries produced manufactured goods and the developing countries sold their commodities, minerals or agricultural products, is not valid any longer.

Today the flow of merchandise throughout the world is extremely complex and has become possible because of the fragmentation of the commodity chain. However, what we see is the existence of some commodity chains which extend throughout numerous countries of Latin America, but that they are almost entirely headed by companies with headquarters in countries of the developed world. As examples of these chains we could cite the automobile, pharmaceutical, data processing and telecommunication equipment, finished consumer electronic goods, and the chemical sectors. Generally speaking, the companies of these sectors have North American, European or Japanese capital and are in Latin America in search of a profitable market, the size of which is not small, and also with the intention of obtaining cheap labor to employ in their production lines, which most times is limited to finished goods. Any phase of the vast process of the value chain of global companies will not be realized in the respective subsidiaries in Latin America if in that phase there is a need for some technological development. In this hypothesis, it will certainly be realized in the headquarters of these companies which can be found exactly in North America, Europe or Japan.

Freeman and Soete (1997) upon comparing the economic development of some nations in Asia, specifically South Korea and Taiwan, with the progress in Latin America during the decade of the 1980's, called attention to the importance of the differences that exist in some few aspects. According to the authors, decisive facts in explaining the enormous growth of the Asian tigers and the stagnation of the Latin American nations during that period were the three deficits listed below. Here are the main problems of the continent when compared to the Asian tigers.

(1) Deteriorated Educational System with few graduating engineers.

(2) Much transference of technology, especially the United States, with low absorption capacity due to little investment of local companies in Research & Development.

(3) Weak infra-structure of Science & Technology.

And also when we compare to South Korea and Japan, conceding subsidies or fiscal incentives for projects of research and development receives low priority on the agendas of most of the governments of Latin American countries.

It should be noted that Porter and Stern (2002) mentioned Latin America and emphasized as great vulnerabilities in the region, referring to increased innovations, the lack of a link between the universities and the companies. According to them "the system of higher education in Latin America has little to do with the companies and little involvement with the national policies related to science and technology" (Porter & Stern, 2002). This is confirmed by other authors who have dedicated themselves to analyze the question of science and technology of the continent. Sagasti (1981) points out that one of the chronic problems of Latin America is the enormous distance between producing science and the generation of technology which, according to him, is a consequence of the non-existence of the University-Company relationship.

This same aspect is placed by Millanand Concheiro (2000) when he analyzes the reasons for Mexico's backwardness in the questions of Science & Technology. He goes beyond, mentioning that an additional reason for the country's delay in this question is the lack of an industrial policy that would define the priority areas for investment; and it is very clear that contrary to the more developed countries where the companies invest in research and development, in Mexico this expenditure is largely done by the government. Thus, while in Japan, Germany and the United States the private companies are responsible, respectively for 67.1%, 61.1% and 58.4% of the total expenditures with R & D, in Mexico this amount is merely 17.6%.

As we have previously mentioned, in 1999 the British magazine *Nature* produced a special edition called "Science in Latin America". In the article dedicated to Mexico there is an important analysis about the fact that helps to explain the numbers above and that is repeated throughout the continent:

> *Part of the problem is cultural. Mexico inherited the European tradition of the scientist as an academic and not the North American model of scientist-inventor and businessman. For a university researcher to have a link with industry is considered prostitution by his colleagues. On the side of industry, there is not a strong tradition in R & D investment. Until the beginning of the 80's, Mexico had an industrial policy defined by the state and protectionism which resulted in little incentive to invest in innovation. Now the companies want to modernize their technology, but they turn more to foreign companies for help, and are not willing to wait the time necessary for national science and technology to find the answers to their needs* (Millan & Concheiro, 2000).

Since the middle of the 1960s, in all of these countries, we assisted the creation of numerous institutes and centers of Research and Development of a public character. However, few were the ones that deserved funds and special attention of the respective governments. Despite this, some of them were decisive for the creation of quality research in the economic sectors in which they perform. And today they exercise a fundamental role. Only to mention two Brazilian examples, we have the outstanding TCA—Technological Center of

Aeronautics (Centro Tecnológico da Aeronáutica), which is considered as the main reason for the success of Embraer; and EMBRAPA—Brazilian Company of Agriculture (Empresa Brasileira de Agropecuária) responsible for the greater part of the studies that resulted in the enormous increase of productivity in Brazilian agriculture during the last few years. Malecki (1997) considers that what happened in Brazil in these two areas should be a model to be followed by other Latin American countries.

We cannot conclude this analysis of why there is little involvement with innovation and technology without speaking of the vulnerability of the patent system existing in many of the Latin American countries: Many local companies see their investments in research paralyzed by the absence of mechanisms that guarantee the propriety of the research results. As all research activity consists of risk for the companies it would be vital for the existence of such a mechanism. Nonetheless, to obtain a patent in Latin America is something very difficult and slow.

5. Methodology

In this line, we intend to prove that the great inducer of R & D in the world is the large company. According to Steven Markovich (2012) statistics about R & D expenses encompass 3 activities : basic research, applied research and development. He also mentions that in countries with very intensive activities like U.S.A., Japan, South Korea, Germany and China we can assume that 60% of the total R & D expenditures has been done by large business companies. This assumption is fundamental for what we will following do in our methodology.

We sought to do a statistical analysis that would establish the relation between the large companies and technological development of the respective nations where they are headquartered. We considered two indices that allowed us to evaluate one nation in terms of research and development; they are the number of patents registered in the United States, at USPTO and the expenditures in science and technology according to what was pointed out in the report of 2017 Global R & D Funding Forecast according to Riemschneider (2016). We obtained the respective values for approximately 100 nations. For these same nations we verified the number of companies that each one had among the 500 largest companies in the world, according to those listed by *Fortune* Magazine 2016. In other words, what was done was a comparison of approximately 22 countries or regions in terms of the number of large companies classified among the 500 largest of the world with expenditures in the country or region in R & D and the number of patents requested at USPTO in 2016. The table below is the result of this study. Finally, we calculated the coefficient of the linear correlation among the various columns and we verified a very high value. So, the correlation between the number of companies of each country or region and the respective expenditure in Research & Development reached 98.2%. The correlation between the number of large companies against the number of patents in each country reached 81.2%; and finally, the correlation between expenditures in R & D in each country or region against the number of patents presented a correlation of 82.0%. In other words, the conclusion that we can infer is that there is an important correlation among the three sets of data which brings us to believe that the more large companies existing in a given country or region, the more that country will spend on R & D and, likewise, the greater the number of patents registered at USPTO.

Table 2.3 Large companies and expenditures in R & D, 2016

	Country or region	Number of companies in the FORTUNE 500 (2016)	Expenditures with R & D in US$ billion (2016)	Patents per country or region
1	U.S.A.	134	496	181069
2	China	103	372	14065
3	Japan	52	165	63536
4	France	29	59	8651
5	Germany	28	107	20075
6	U.K.	25	44	6463
7	South Korea	15	75	26097
8	Switzerland	15	13	5142
9	Netherlands	12	17	4685
10	Canada	11	29	6610
11	Italy	9	26	2647
12	Spain	9	20	1056
13	Australia	8	27	1896

(Contd.)

	Country or region	Number of companies in the FORTUNE 500 (2016)	Expenditures with R & D in US$ billion (2016)	Patents per country or region
14	Brazil	7	37	379
15	India	7	66	1712
16	Taiwan, China	7	25	15983
17	Russia	5	51	469
18	Singapore	3	12	1937
19	Sweden	3	15	4257
20	Belgium	2	11	1331
21	Ireland	2	14	904
22	Mexico	2	10	968
OTHERS	12 countries	12	–	–
TOTAL	34 countries and regions	500	–	–

Source: Author's compilation of *Fortune* Global 500 and *The Global Innovation Index* (2016).

As we have already mentioned before the conclusion here is that not only production of innovations but also the expenditures of a country or region in Research and Development are basically done by large companies. A country that doesn't have an expressive group of large companies won't never have an important role as a developed country.

6. Final Considerations

Latin America is very wealthy in natural resources and, generally, the labor is cheap, and these are the main ingredients that stimulate large companies of the region, with very rare exception. Why a region so blessed with natural resources and gifts of nature has failed in developing and industrializing in the same way that other regions have had success? We have sought to explain and, in our opinion, this is due to the fact that the region is not managing to generate an expressive number of global companies and this is very much due to the non-professional way of leading the companies that predominate on the continent and this has been changing in the last twenty years, but not at the desired speed. Due to these factors, Latin America has a few powerful companies, but almost always performing in sectors that were important in the nineteenth century, and became irrelevant in this twenty-first century. Being a global player in sectors such as drinks, cement, mining, agriculture, fish or steel is not bad, but it is not sufficient. As we have seen, more developed countries have companies in sectors that dominate the world economy, such as communications, software, hardware, medical equipment or pharmaceuticals. In other words, we can say that the big Latin American companies are generally out of the high technology sectors with very rare exception, such as the Brazilian, manufacturer of planes, or the Mexican Mabe, in electronics. Companies from our continent, when they achieve size and projection, are in low technology sectors, most of the time producing "commodities". Petrobras and Cemex are excellent examples.

It is clear that no country can survive, with dignity, exporting only their agricultural and mineral "commodities" to pay, for example, for the importation of pharmaceuticals or computers, as is today the rule in almost all of the countries of Latin America. Increasingly, the wealth of natural resources of the region is being consumed as currency, instead of, at least, being administered as a basis for sustainable development. Basing development in raw materials is never the solution. All you need to do is to look at the countries of OPEC, who supposed that they could achieve higher stages of development at the cost of petroleum when the exact opposite is what happened.

Furthermore, the recent globalization of Latin American countries together with the growth of the population is radically affecting the environment of the continent. The growth of exportations has been mainly in the sectors of agriculture, fish and mining. This means more deforestation for the exportation of wood and making more lands available for agriculture and livestock.

But it is important to make this very clear that the solution of the aspects mentioned in this paper cannot be exclusively up to the Latin American companies: Some measures of governmental support are necessary. For example, the small investment in education, and the little infra-structure destined to research are very important to explain the little presence of Latin America in all that is relevant today in science and technology. Generally, the fragility of the infra-structure is a serious problem for all the countries of the region. It is fundamental to have excellent infra-structure in order to facilitate a more competitive flow of material, machines and goods. The way things are, the inefficient infra-structure greatly increases the operational costs and makes it very difficult for the companies to become globally competitive. In fact, this is not the only point where the various governments from the countries of the region fall short. The Latin American companies need to operate in a legal system but sometimes they are politicized and, frequently, they are corrupt and with markets of weak capital and very low levels of savings. Credit is very difficult, and mechanisms for long-term financing are rare. Interest rates are very high and in some countries like Brazil the tax load already surpasses one-third of GDP.

Another important measure that should involve government and society is the stimulation to form big conglomerates as was done in Korea and Japan, and to support the formation of "clusters" as is done in the United States and Italy.

The treatment of this question is extremely difficult for the various governments of the region, and because of this reason the society and the legislators have to be involved. There is no other alternative: Without big groups, strong and healthy, and without professional administration there is no way to compete in the difficult scenario of globalization. Without horizontal and vertical groupings of related companies, in other words, "clusters", you cannot achieve even economies of scale, nor technological development. A typical example is what happens with exportations. The companies will only increase, sustainably, their exportations when they are more productive and more competitive, and this depends very much on them. It has taken Brazil a long time to perceive this mistake, but it seems that now it is clear for its businessmen and government. Nonetheless, it is still a chronic mistake throughout the region, with different shades, to think that increasing exportations is merely a question of macroeconomic policy and that it is enough to change the exchange rate or the interest rate or play with inflation goals. Not that the governments have been wrong. A good part of the governments has acted correctly, from a macroeconomic point of view but the positive results were short-lived, as the problem, truthfully, is with the companies, in the way that they define their strategies and in their management. Solving the macroeconomic problems could be a necessary condition, but it is not enough to increase competitiveness. It is fundamental that attention is also given to the problems of the company, examining them up close, actuating as soon as they appear and assisting in what makes it difficult to increase international competitiveness. As incredible as it may seem, in spite of being specific and individual problems, the governments have very much to do, especially because they are responsible for increasing the competitiveness of the countries as a whole.

Chapter 3
Free Trade Agreements as Mechanisms of Wide-ranging and Multi-layered Cooperation: China and the Deepening of Relations with Chile

Andres Borquez

More and more countries are using the mechanism of FTA to encourage economic and political cooperation. According to data published on the official website of WTO, around 300 FTAs were signed, with more than 90 participating countries. Among the most active countries are Singapore 33 FTAs, Switzerland 28 FTAs, South Korea 25 FTAs, Chile 23 FTAs, China 21 FTAs and United States 20 FTAs (WTO, 2017).

The WTO defines FTAs as international treaties both with individual countries and groups of countries that reduce barriers to trade, services and investment. There is a widespread consensus that this type of agreement allows better access to markets, improved competitive position for exports, reduced import costs and increased two-way investment (WTO, 2017). However, in practice the signatory countries tend to move their relations beyond these commercial features, and into aspects such as environmental regulations, labor issues and financial cooperation. In this regard, the signing of a FTA is only the beginning of a deepening of trade and political relations between the signatory countries. Therefore, attention should not only be paid to the trade impacts of the initial agreement, but also to the subsequent negotiations. This allows a more complete dimension of the evolution of the relationship and shows each country's direction regarding its policy of international cooperation. The following chapter addresses this perspective for the case of Chile and the agreements signed with the U.S and China. In this context, when the initial status of the FTA is compared to the status 10 years later, is it possible to identify substantial changes which explain the development of a specific cooperation strategy that goes beyond the WTO FTA model? Why are the United States and China following different paths in their approach to FTAs-what lies behind these decisions? And which "model"-American or Chinese-is more beneficial for Chile to advance in the development paths?

This chapter argues that although both superpowers (the United States and China) use the same initial instrument of cooperation based on the parameters of WTO, after a period of operation, each country will introduce its own characteristics. On the one hand, the NAFTA (North American Free Trade Agreement) model puts more attention on formal technical issues of cooperation. On the other hand, the Chinese FTA model is more ambitious, and based on concerted power and mutual stimulation, transforming the agreement into a mechanism of wide-ranging and multi-layered cooperation. The secondary argument is that FTAs have a structure that provides a balance between security and flexibility. This allows it to operate as a complex instrument that includes the transfer of non-commercial influence and the articulation with other kinds of bilateral strategic associations. Finally, this chapter argues that FTAs can balance one of the four development traps identified by Paul Collier (2008), the natural resource trap. Chile is a country that highly depends on the extraction of natural resources and it has been affected by the volatility of the primary products market. Nevertheless, the Chile-China FTA is on the road to development, since this instrument has not only served to encourage commercial exchange but has also become a comprehensive cooperation mechanism which includes long-term initiatives focused on encouraging scientific research, the transfer of technologies and the generation of a culture that is more prone to innovation and added value.

To demonstrate this, first, theoretical elements are discussed that support the Chinese influence and cooperation model. In this section, the concept of transmission of influence is revised, emphasizing its new role where the cooperation between countries work under the logic of co-actor or co-author (win-win approach). Second, the major elements of the signed initial agreements are compared. Third, the progress and new scope of the agreements signed after ten years of implementation are compared. Finally, some remarks and discussions are presented.

The originality of this chapter is based on the fact that the analysis stands out from the studies on ex ante and ex post trade impacts of the FTAs, paying attention to the political evolution of the agreements after their entry into force and how these become complex mechanisms of bilateral cooperation.

In addition, this chapter can be considered as a particular case of learning for future FTAs signed between China and Latin American countries: First, due to the pioneering role that Chile carried out more than a decade ago, being the first country in Latin America to sign this type of agreements with China, and second, because this research reveals the growing and balanced relationship between China and Chile, which translates into a series of positive impacts for both nations.

1. Theorizing the Political Economy of Trade Agreement and International Influence

1.1 Trade Agreements and Global Integration

The processes of global integration and market liberation can not be thought of in this way without considering the influence of trade agreements. Despite the resurgence of some protectionist currents in Western countries, every year there is a multiplication of trade agreements at an international level. Countries have understood that agreements allow the institutional and security framework to be delivered, but it also allows systematizing cooperation always under the principles of mutual benefit and reciprocity.

First, it is important to distinguish between bilateral and multilateral free trade agreements. Although both agreements are designed to eliminate commercial and non-commercial barriers and reduce transaction costs, multilateral agreements have a more political-economic role and seek to establish the basis for global governance in terms of foreign trade. At present, there are a series of multilateral initiatives, among which the most active are the Association of Southeast Asian Nations (ASEAN), the North American Free Trade Agreement (NAFTA) and the Asia-Pacific Economic Cooperation (APEC). On the other hand, bilateral agreements play a more technical role and focus on the specific interests of the two signatory nations. The most common bilateral agreements or partnerships are the Free Trade Agreement (FTA), the Economic Partnership Agreement (EPA) and the Strategic Partnership Agreement (SPA).

In this context, bilateral trade cooperation agreement (FTA) is defined as an instrument to enhance trade by reducing policy-imposed barriers, while promoting different levels of integration in as economic, financial, political, cultural, scientific and other areas. This definition incorporates two approaches, the first–promoted by the World Trade Organization (WTO)–delimits these agreements as instruments designed to remove trade barriers and tariffs. In this sense, the more technical role and the creation of binding trade policies are emphasized to strengthen international trade. World Trade Organization (WTO) members are encouraged to notify the WTO when new agreements are formed. Until the year 2016, 243 FTAs have been notified to the WTO, only considering the list of agreements in force (WTO, 2017). The second approach incorporates the first, but also highlights the political-economic issues of these agreements. Zissimos (2004) and Krugman (2012) opened the door to discuss the difficulties of economic integration and later on the strategic nature of agreements, specifically their role in the processes of comprehensive integration.

In operational terms, in this chapter two FTA approaches are distinguished. The first is called comprehensive agreement approach (CA) that includes most of the aspects of the bilateral economic relationship from the beginning (goods, services, investment, environment, labor issues, etc.). This format is used mainly by the United States and other Western superpowers such as the European Union. The second is known as gradual integration agreement approach (GIA), which starts with the signing of a specific agreement to liberalize the exchange of goods and services, but includes clauses that allow continuing progressive negotiation concerning the incorporation of new elements of cooperation. This kind of agreement is used mainly by China. Both cases are consistent with WTO requirements and are under the framework of General Agreement on Tariffs, Trade and Services 1994 (GATT-GATS).

1.2 Foreign Influence

Influence on international politics has been studied and categorized for a long time, and its definition has been changing over time. From the beginning, states are active actors in their environments (local, regional and global), just like individual level, they create, transform, preserve and even destroy. In turn, this behavior is often motivated by the need to adapt to internal or external conditions and to the pursuit of specific objectives beyond national boundaries. In this context, it is generally understood as an international influence on the ability to orient or influence government policy in third countries. This influence can be made through multiple forms and tools. The most common are through bilateral relations or multilateral associations such as international institutions (e.g. United Nations).

One of the first contemporary works that addresses the problem of influence in theoretical terms was Hans Morgenthau (1960) who works on the idea of obtaining and maintaining political power. In his book *Politics Among Nations* he deepens these ideas assuming that the desire to dominate is a constituent element of all human associations, therefore, regardless of the goals and objectives of a government, any action of the state is related to obtaining and maximizing power. In this configuration, international influence acts as the capacity of a country to exercise certain control over the power of another nation. For the author, the aspiration for power is the characteristic element of international politics. However, Morgenthau being a classical realist does not consider that a centralized global authority or supranational actor limits sovereign states. His vision of international influence has to do with a logic centered between nation-states as the great legitimate actors of global interactions. In this sense, the author dimensions the balance of power as a global dynamic where power is distributed among several nations with approximate equality. The realistic perspective claims that the international system has a minimum of rules to establish the bases, but that the states retain their national interests. At this point, Morgenthau assumes that conflicts of interest are inherent in the international system (as well as they are inherent in individual and state level), so the use of containment instruments such as alliances and the creation of institutions allow to maintain an international coexistence.

Beyond the fact that at the time there was a relative consensus that the international system was a space in which several actors interacted considering their capabilities and interests, there were other positions that indicated that control should be channeled by a great power in order to maintain a stability in the system. This nation should play a role of hegemony, which transmits its influences through coercion or persuasion with the aim of establishing the rules and agreements of the international system. These ideas formed the basis of the well-known theory of hegemonic stability (HST) and one of the authors that most participated in its debate was Robert Gilpin (1987), who argued that the influence of the United States has played a key role in the fostering international cooperation, especially in the establishment of post-Second World international organizations. The defenders of HST argue that international politics is characterized by the succession of hegemonies, where a single nation operates as a pivot modifying the rules and where cooperation between states is strongly influenced by the presence of the hegemonic country. However, the presence of a hegemonic country is not enough to ensure the stability of the system. As Stephen Krasner (1976) identifies, there are periods when the hegemonic state and the global tendency do not coincide, since the hegemonic country acts differently on the basis of its own interests.

In this scenery, another contemporary author named Kenneth Waltz (1979) takes distance from classical hegemonic approach, he opens up to consider new actors influencing the international scheme and explains how systemic forces influence the interactions among states. He anticipates the growth of international institutions, and also that their origin does not necessarily respond completely to the interests of the states. In this sense, institutions can be seen not only as effects of national interests but also as causes, that means, that institutions not only operate as a regulating entity as a constituent element of new processes. In this sense, Waltz opens a door to new theories that allow to consider the change in the course of time (unlike the realist assumptions: human nature is plain bad and does not change in the course of time). The author considered the founder of neorealism focuses its analysis on explaining the international system (third level, also called systemic level) in which it presents the relation of a dominant structure (which is called anarchy) that defines the interaction of the units (states that seek survival) and that this is concretized by means of the distribution of power (each country has its own capacity for power). In the works of Waltz, international politics is presented as a system that, through its structure, allows for the stability and continuity of the system (international system as an independent variable). It must be considered that Waltz's ideas were established in the cold war, where the world operated in a bipolar way, however, they set a pattern to understand that the hegemonic powers would need other forces than mere military power. The balance would tend towards the power that establishes a certain degree of global leadership where the influence should take place in a more complex way including political, economic and cultural aspects.

After the end of the cold war, liberal and neoliberal principles begin to take more force in international events. An idea arises that the balance between two superpowers is not an immutable law of nature, but rather a way of constructing realities about the world. A more multipolar world begins to be assimilated, first in Europe and then with the nations of the BRICS. In this new scenario, the idea that nations are more interconnected and economically interdependent begins to take hold. It emphasizes that beyond this new international order, interdependence contributes to peace between countries (Copeland, 1996;

Gartzke, Li and Boehmer, 2001). According to Copeland's theory, economic interdependence is the only factor that plays a key causal role in the liberal and realist arguments. Considering the relation of cost and risk, trade is more beneficial than war, making the trading option more rational. Even when current trade is low or non-existent, expectations for future trade will produce positive expectations, and therefore an incentive for continued peace (Copeland, 1996).

In this same line, the idea that economic interdependence allows to institutionalize cooperation between nations and to build a formal structure to the interactions between market and politics begins to be considered (Haggard & Simmons, 1987; Cohen, 1990; Alt, Frieden, Gilligan, Rodrik, and Rogowski, 1996). In this new scenery, there is a new increase in the use of the concept of foreign influence in the field of international relations. Following Keohane and Nye (1977, 1987), Haugaard (2012, 2015) and Hast (2014), International Influence is conceptually defined as the ability of an organization or state to apply indirectly, through strategic and concerted interactions, in other regions or specific countries economic, political or cultural influence. In this definition, Keohane's perspective is considered, which puts more emphasis on issues of the international political economy than on issues of international security, in the same way that this view emphasizes international cooperation rather than international conflict. In addition, this definition incorporates the form of concerted power proposed by Haugaard that focuses on the capacity to act in concert and mobilized countries to act together in the pursuit of common goals or in support of common values (shared goal and win-win strategy). Finally, the definition of International Influence introduces the ideas of Hast, who proposes a reconsideration of the concept of sphere of influence. This new approach must include a post-Cold War vision, where international influence plays a more consensual (power to) and bargaining-commitment (power with) role than coercive role (power over).

In this process of transmission of influence, not only the country that promotes power or influence participates, but also the country that receives it. In this context, many countries participate more actively at the international level in the presence of other nations than when they have to propose or generate something on their own. This behavior is one of the explanations to the question why the majority of countries choose to participate in international organization such as the WTO or the United Nations. Obviously not all cases operate with these logics, but these logics are applied in activities where competition or collaboration with others takes place. This phenomenon is known as the effect of the co-actor or co-author in the theory of social facilitation (Zajonc, 1965). If this theory is extrapolated to the international system, the principle is maintained that stimulation increases the likelihood of a country reacting by improving the implementation of some commitments. This approach supports the idea of mutual teaching and learning, with ways of learning and working towards a common goal and effectively exchanging resources. The principles of this theory are that the country that receives the influence can recognize it, as well as that it has the possibility to negotiate the rules and initiate evaluation processes. The second principle is that countries can endorse the norms that govern behavior among members.

David Baldwin (1980) suggests an approach between dependency relationship theories and social power literature, arguing that this allows to have a multidimensional nature of power. The author deepens this relationship by introducing the theory of stable social relation of Wrong (Baldwin, 1980), which claims that the control of one person or group over another with respect to a particular scope is balanced by the control of the other in a different scope. By extrapolating this theory, economic dependence and / or interdependence become a form of influence relation, where the interdependence operates as a power resource for a different form of influence. In other words, the author argues that states may also simultaneously depend on each other with respect to different kinds of scopes. Baldwin suggests that any particular economic power resource can usually be converted into another kind of economic power resource.

In synthesis, this chapter integrates elements of neo-realist and neoliberal theories with a foreign influence expansion model that identifies the conditions under which a sort of equilibrium is produced in the cooperation between an emerging power and small economy. This study tries to articulate the ideas of transmission of foreign influence via strategic and concerted interactions and the revised extrapolation of the theories of facilitation and stable social relation on an international level. In this case, China influences Chile to collaborate taking advantage of the simultaneous dependence (economic complementarity) through the FTA, which allows working strategically and institutionally towards a common goal, and including the effective exchange of resources (regional hub). This format of cooperation allows small economies such as Chile to advance on the road to development since they aim not only to trade primary products, but also to give them added value. For example, Chile has the main global reserves of saltpeter, key component for the manufacture of batteries for electric cars and for storing solar energy. China, through the benefits of having an FTA, proposes extracting the natural resource and transforming it into batteries to supply the Latin American market. The same happened when China proposed to strengthen Chile's financial services so that it becomes the regional platform of the RMB.

2. Comparative Analysis

This research is an ex-post comparative analysis focusing on the non-commercial impacts and which has three objectives: 1) identify the similarities and differences of the policies and structures of two FTAs signed with Chile (the first with United States and the second with China); 2) get clues that help to understand the strategies of cooperation of two superpowers with developing countries and 3) identify variables that can be useful when making a comprehensive assessment of the impacts (Ragin, 2014). To achieve this, it is first necessary to identify the main indicators that compose each FTA. This allows an X-ray of the document at the time of signature. In this process, only the indicators that have specific measures and policies of implementation are considered, which excludes the variables that are only mentioned as potential development units or in a status of future initiatives.

Then, changes and new indicators of cooperation after a period of 10 years of FTA are identified. With this new information, the progress of each agreement is compared with the progress undertaken by the other agreement analyzed. In total, 14 indicators of cooperation are studied, separated into four categories of analysis: a) three trade factors by default (Free trade in goods, Free trade in services and Free investment flow); b) three indicators of trade guaranties (Intellectual property rights, Dispute settlement and E-commerce); c) three factors of political coverage (Environmental & labor regulation, Immigration Policy and Government procurement) and d) five factors promoting non-commercial cooperation (Small & medium enterprises cooperation, Research & technology cooperation, Telecommunication cooperation, Cultural cooperation and Financial cooperation). Finally, the policies and institutionality that support these indicators and that are created after the signing of the agreements are compared.

2.1 FTA Key Indicators

Formally, FTAs focus on removing trade barriers between the signatory countries. It is assumed that these measures include conditions for a fair and flexible competition, and at the same time encourage investment (Zeng, 2016). Together with these measures, FTAs can provide investment protection, intellectual property right and mechanisms to solve controversies.

In the table 3.1, the main clauses of the analyzed trade agreements are defined. To establish a reference framework, a generic definition for each variable is used. The first three variables are considered as the basis of the FTA, since they are included by default in each agreement of this type, although its implementation depends on the negotiations conducted in each specific agreement. The following three variables (4, 5 and 6), operate as a complement to the first three variables and aim to provide guaranties for the implementation and regulation of trade between private and state enterprises. The variables 7, 8 and 9 of the table follow the same logic, but contain elements related to regulation of local policies and search for equivalent standards on environment, employment and movement of people. Finally, the last five indicators respond to the search for new bridges to enhance cooperation between the contracting parties and to extend the agreements as a platform comprehensive or to develop regional initiatives towards third countries, for example: financial hub initiative and hub of regional connectivity.

Table 3.1 Key FTA indicators definitions

1) Free trade in goods	Create a freer flow of goods, allow the partners to give each other preferential market access (remove tariff and non-tariff barriers)
2) Free trade in services	Create a freer flow of services to enhance their market access (remove tariff and non-tariff barriers)
3) Free investment flows	Remove the barriers to investment between FTA signed countries
4) Intellectual property rights	Provide protection for intellectual property and commitment to control piracy of copyrighted works
5) Dispute settlement	Provide competition laws and control the anticompetitive business practices
6) E-commerce	Ensure protection for trademarks, copyrighted works and internet domain names, at the same time promote the digital economy

(Contd.)

7) Environmental & labor regulations	Ensure that domestic labor and environmental laws provide high levels of protection
8) Government procurement	Provide anti-corruption rules in government contracting, firms are guaranteed transparent procurement procedures to sell goods and services to government entities
9) Immigration policy	Agreements about the transit of people across its borders into the country, especially those that intend to visit, work and do business in the country
10) Small & medium enterprises cooperation	Promote a favorable environment for the development of small and medium-sized enterprises
11) Research & technology cooperation	Promote cooperation in research and technological sectors with focus on industry where mutual and complementary interests exist
12) Telecommunication cooperation	Facilitate the cooperation on regulatory and policy aspects of telecommunications, including promotion and dissemination of new information and communication technologies
13) Cultural cooperation	Promote cultural exchange between the countries. Special attention is paid to promoting joint activities, including translation of literary works, mutual information exchange programs and promotion of local culture
14) Financial cooperation	Facilitate the use of the Chinese currency in international transactions between both countries and promote setting up financial hubs

Source: Author's compilation.

2.2 FTAs Scope

The Chile-U.S. FTA is a comprehensive agreement (CA approach) that includes most of the aspects of the bilateral economic relationship from the beginning (goods, services, investment, electronic commerce, environment, labor issues, etc.). To the contrary, the format of the Chile-China FTA includes progressive negotiation that will gradually incorporate new elements or instrumentalize the clauses written in the initial agreement (GIA approach). Although each treaty has its own logic and system of application, both propose from the beginning on the same principles to liberalize and instrumentalize the bilateral trade: market access, customs administration, safeguard, antidumping, etc.

In the table 3.2, initial indicators signed by both agreements are listed. Both the Chile-U.S. FTA and the Chile-China FTA considered from the beginning to liberalize products under the multilateral trading system embodied in Marrakesh Agreement, also known as the WTO Agreement (1994). This system includes chapters and articles referring to rules of origin, sanitary and phytosanitary measures and technical barriers. Both agreements also ensured intellectual property rights and dispute settlement under the General Agreement on Tariffs and Trade (1994). The main differences are detected in complementary or supplementary areas to stimulate exchange and cooperation. For example, the agreement with the United States emphasized the possibility of equal treatment for U.S companies to participate in requests for bid of the Chilean government. The same logic is visible concerning the encouragement and protection of digital commerce industry and telecommunications. In the case of the agreement with China, the initial agreement emphasizes the exchange of goods and bases are established to intensify cooperation on economic issues as well as cooperation to strengthen small and medium enterprises (see articles 106, 107, 109 and 113 of the treaty).

Table 3.2 Chile-China & Chile-U.S. FTAs Scope (entry into force)

Indicators	Chile-U.S. (2004) "AC"	Chile-China (2006) "AG"
1) Free trade in goods	×	×
2) Free trade in services	×	×
3) Free investment flows	×	×
4) Intellectual property rights	×	×
5) Dispute settlement	×	×
6) E-commerce	×	
7) Environmental & labor regulations	×	×
8) Government procurement	×	
9) Immigration policy		

(Contd.)

Indicators	Chile-U.S. (2004) "AC"	Chile-China (2006) "AG"
10) Small & medium enterprises cooperation	—	×
11) Research & technology cooperation	—	—
12) Telecommunication cooperation	×	—
13) Cultural cooperation	—	—
14) Financial cooperation	—	—

Source: Author's compilation of official FTAs articles of agreements.

2.3 Continuous Negotiation and Progressive Implementation

After having signed the agreements, the negotiations are continuing, and the treaties are gradually implemented. This is the point where significant differences between an agreement and another can be observed. It begins with an initial standard document, proposed by the WTO, but after 10 years of existence, the agreements show new nuances. Mainly, the agreements include new articles that extend the impact ratios (note that it is considered progress if the countries have reached an agreement on how to instrumentalize the variable through a specific policy or project). With regards to these perspectives, it is claimed that countries distance themselves from the initial format and end up developing their own model of cooperation with specific mechanisms and emphasis.

In the table 3.3, the current state of trade agreements after 10 years of implementation is described. This table includes all new articles incorporated after the negotiations under the framework of the FTA. With regards to these new clauses, only two new indicators are observed in the Chile-U.S. FTA (small and medium enterprises cooperation and free visa access), while seven new clauses appear in the Chile-China FTA with special emphasis on promoting non-commercial cooperation (E-commerce, Government procurement, Immigration policy, Research & technology cooperation, Telecommunication cooperation, Cultural cooperation and Financial cooperation).

Table 3.3 Chile-China & Chile-U.S. FTAs Scope (after 10 years entry into force*)

Indicators	Chile-U.S. (2014) "AC"	Chile-China (2016) "AG"
1) Free trade in goods	×	×
2) Free trade in services	×	×
3) Free investment flows	×	×
4) Intellectual property rights	×	×
5) Dispute settlement	×	×
6) Ecommerce	×	×
7) Environmental & labor regulations	×	×
8) Government procurement	×	×
9) Immigration policy	×	×
10) Small & medium enterprises cooperation	×	×
11) Research & technology cooperation	—	×
12) Telecommunication cooperation	×	×
13) Cultural cooperation	—	×
14) Financial cooperation	—	×

Source: Author's compilation of official FTAs articles of agreements.

The Chile-U.S. FTA has a progressive negotiation to operationalize the technical clauses. So far, this could have been observed in three occasions: (1) Free Trade Agreement of goods (signed in 2003); (2) Free visa access agreement also kwon as visa waiver program (signed in 2014). Also during 2014 both countries signed the patent cooperation treaty (PCT) and (3) Memorandum to promote the growth of SMEs (signed in June 2015).

In the case of the Chile-China FTA, the progressive negotiation is reflected in seven major milestones: (1) Free Trade Agreement on goods signed in November 2005; (2) Memorandum of understanding for labor and social security cooperation, signed in November 2005; (3) Supplementary agreement on trade in services, signed in April 2008; (4) Supplementary agreement on investment, signed in September 2012; (5) Financial cooperation agreement, signed in May 2015; (6) Also during 2015 both countries signed the visa facilitation agreement to promote tourism and business trips and (7) development of multiple cultural cooperation and scientific research initiatives, for example: The South American Astronomic Research Center of the Chinese Academy of Sciences (2016), Chinese Culture Center in Santiago (2016) and Traditional Chinese Medicine Association Chilean branch (2017).

2.4 FTAs Policies

Both agreements were signed practically at the same time. When these agreements were signed, the U.S. was the major trade partner of Chile, representing 18% of the Chilean foreign trade (DIRECON, 2003). Currently, the U.S. is the second commercial partner of Chile, with an average annual growth of 12% since the signing. On the other hand, when China signed the FTA, China was third Chile's largest commercial partners, coming after the U.S and Europe. However, China is today's Chile's largest trading partner and largest export destination, representing 23% of Chile's foreign trade. Since the signing of the treaty, the exchange with China has expanded with an average annual rate of 17%, compared to an 8% of growth when looking at Chile's relation to the whole world (DIRECON, 2015).

These changes of tendency are no coincidence and can't either be explained by the demand of each country. Behind the signing of this type of agreement lies a political will to deepen the cooperation in certain aspects. Both in the first and in the second White Paper on policy toward Latin America and the Caribbean, the People's Republic of China (PRC) announces the intention to expand cooperation with the region across a broad range of areas, maintaining a win-win relationship (The State Council the People's Republic of China-SCPRC, 2008, 2016). As the professor Jiang Shixue claims, after high-level exchanges became more frequent, bilateral trade volume increased and cooperation began in other fields (2010). In the same vein, professor Haibin Niu presented the strategic dimensions between China and Latin America, and how the Asian giant has updated its economic strategy toward the region by focusing on investment, financial and industrial cooperation, besides commercial transactions. He also explained that the rapid development of China-LAC relations is an important part of the changing international system and suggested that the political ties should serve to create mutual beneficial and sustainable economic relations (2015). This pre-disposition mentioned can be found in this case study. During the 10 last years, not only containers were moved from one place to the other, also a series of policies that seek to expand the levels of impacts have been developed.

The tables 3.4 and 3.5 review the policies and initiatives that have resulted from the negotiations carried out after the entry into force of the agreements. These policies support the instrumentalization of the clauses established in the original agreement. In turn, these policies represent the seek for consolidation of the strategic partnership.

In the case of the Chile-U.S. FTA, it is more complex to identify policies or specific instruments for each variable or indicator, since many of the clauses were developed around the time of signing. Afterwards, there are records of regular meetings, but few have announced specific policies that lead to a clause. For example, in 2015 a policy was established to encourage travel between citizens of both countries. Other examples are the Patent Cooperation Treaty (PCT) which seeks to protect industrial property, to strengthen innovation and the cooperation. Also, the Small Business Development Centers policy which seeks to promote the mutual support to small companies.

Table 3.4 Chile-U.S. FTAs policies (after 10 years entry into force)

Policies or instrument	United States
Intellectual property rights	Intellectual property rights policy (2004), Patent Cooperation Treaty (2014)
Government procurement	Government procurement procedures (2004)
Environmental regulations	Development of Pollutant Release and Transfer Register (PRTR) in Chile, similar to Toxic Release Inventory in the U.S. (2004)
Labor regulations	Both parties reaffirm their obligations as members of the International Labor Organization (ILO) (2004)
Immigration policy	Visa-free access, Mobility for Highly Trained Personnel (2015)
Small & medium enterprises cooperation	Small Business Development Centers (2014)

Source: Author's compilation of official FTAs articles of agreements.

In the case of the Chile-China FTA, more dynamism is observed related to the creation of specific policies after the signing. The initial policies are related to the cooperation of work and exchange of services. Concerning the services policies, a specific agreement that covers 60 industries and sub-industries was signed. China put emphasis on computer, consulting, mining and transport services, while Chile focuses on building and designing, engineering, mining and tourism services (MOFCOM, 2008).

In 2012, both countries agreed to promote their bilateral relationship to the status of strategic association. This status positions Chile and China as two complementary countries that need each other's products and services. The result of this upgrade is reflected two years later with the agreement on reciprocal promotion of investments. One year after, a double taxation agreement was signed that avoids the levying of tax by two jurisdictions on the same income (this agreement includes income taxes, asset or financial transaction). This is a symbol for a new step towards boosting mutual investments.

2015 has been the most active year in signing new agreements. In May 2015, in the framework of the visit of Premier Li Keqiang of China, to Chile, financial cooperation agreements between the central banks were signed, with the aim to facilitate the use of the Chinese currency in international transactions between both countries. To operationalize this point, the currency swap agreement and Clearing agreement (currency clearing bank) were signed, positioning Chile as the first country in Latin America and the second of America (after Canada) to join the Renminbi Qualified Foreign Institutional Investor program (RQFII). With this, the Yuan's first financial hub in Latin America was set up and Chile became a financial platform for its internationalization. In addition, the agreement of visa facilitation for promoting tourism and business travel was signed in 2015, as well as the cooperation agreement between China's Academy of Sciences, the Chilean branch of Huawei, and the Technical University Federico Santa Maria, aiming to establish one of Latin America's largest data centers in Chile. Also, during the last three years, fruitful results were reached in scientific, technological and cultural cooperation, e.g. the Chinese Culture Week celebrated every year in Chile and the opening of the Chinese Culture Center in Santiago (see table 3.5). These measures can be interpreted as a key to understand the next steps of Chinese integration in the Latin American region.

Table 3.5 Chile-China FTA specific policies (after 10 years entry into force)

Policies or instrument	China
Free trade in services	Supplementary Agreement on trade in services of the FTA (2008).
Free investment flows	Agreement on reciprocal promotion and protection of investments (2012), Double taxation agreement (2015).
E-commerce	New Chapter of e-commerce businesses-Memorandum of understanding (MOU) FTA upgrade (2017).
Immigration policy	Elimination of visa fees (2015).
Government procurement	Pacific Hydro renewable energy project (2016), Participation in bidding of lithium batteries (2017), New Chapter Government Procurement-Memorandum of understanding (MOU) FTA upgrade (2017).
Labor regulations	Memorandum of understanding (MOU) for labor and social security cooperation (2005).
Small & medium enterprises cooperation	China-Chilean free trade zone—Chile is seeking to encourage the smaller companies to tap Chinese market through Shanghai free trade zone (2015).
Research & technology cooperation	The Chinese Academy of Sciences and the National Commission for Scientific and Technological Research of Chile signed an MOU on astronomic cooperation (2015), The China National Space administration and the Chilean Agriculture Ministry signed and MOU to open a Center for Agricultural research (2016), The South American Astronomic Research Center of the Chinese Academy of Sciences (2016)-Regional science hub, Traditional Chinese Medicine Association Chilean branch (2017).
Telecommunications cooperation	Chinese-Chilean Big Data Center project-Regional telecommunications hub (2015). China-Chile Astronomical Data Center (2015).
Cultural cooperation	Chile Week in China (2014), Chinese Culture Week (2015), Chinese Culture Center in Santiago (2016).
Financial cooperation	Currency swap agreement, Renminbi clearing bank, Renminbi Qualified Foreign Institutional Investor program (RQFII)-Regional RMB clearing hub (2015).

Source: Author's compilation of official FTAs articles of agreements.

2.5 FTAs Institutionality

Both agreements have introduced institutional framework that allows to implement and evaluate new ways to deepen the cooperation. In the Chile-U.S. FTA two types of institutionality are presented. On the one hand there are two types of technical committees: technical barriers and sanitary measures. These committees allow a regular exchange of information and discussion of the difficulties arising in the implementation process. On the other hand, there are two mixed commissions: The joint commission for environmental cooperation and the small and medium business working group. These groups meet to exchange experiences and collaborate to implement specific regulations. For example, the small and medium business working group, exchanges experiences with regards to the implementation of business development centers focused on small companies.

Table 3.6 Chile-China and Chile-U.S. FTAs Institutionality (after 10 years entry into force)

Institutions	United States	China
1) Free trade committee	—	Ensure the implementation, administration and deepening of FTA
2) Technical committees	Technical barriers committee, Sanitary measures committee, Small & Medium Business Working group	Goods committee, technical barriers committee, sanitary measures committee
3) Mixed commission	Joint commission for environmental cooperation	Working groups in mining, infrastructure, agriculture and energy.

Source: Author's compilation of official FTAs articles of agreements and official reports.

In the case of the Chile-China FTA, three types of institutions are distinguished: Free trade commission, technical committees and mixed commission. The first is considered to be the highest authority of consultation and permits to meet periodically for the implementation and administration of the treaty. The second type of institution is similar to the agreement committees of the Chile-U.S. FTA, which are in charge of the periodical information exchange and discussion of specific difficulties. Finally, there are mixed committees that meet to expand the coverage of the agreements or seek new forms of cooperation. Currently four groups are working under the principle to strengthen ministerial meetings, foster the exchange of information on projects and investment opportunities in energy, mining and infrastructure, and to widen industrial cooperation and technology transfer in areas of mutual interest.

3. Discussion

3.1 United States and China: Different Paths toward FTAs Enforcement

In theory, the FTAs were conceived so that the nations can both harmonize their commercial relations and establish a more complex cooperation that includes diverse areas such as culture, environment and economy.

In this configuration, the FTAs have a balance between flexibility and security so that developing nations can establish complex linkages with great or emerging powers. These elements constitute a pillar for countries to advance in a comprehensive cooperation based on complementarity, standardization of certain procedures and mutual encouragement. However, in practice it is observed that not all great powers use FTAs as a mechanism to deepen their relations beyond commercial interests. On the one hand, there is the case of countries such as the United States, which choose to use FTAs as a strictly commercial instrument, focusing efforts on harmonizing standards and reducing technical barriers to trade. This approach reflects the classic model of north-south relationship, where it is assumed that industrialized countries sells manufactured products and non-industrialized countries commercialize raw materials and natural resources. This distribution of power in the international system has remained practically unchanged in the western regions since the 1960s and reflects more than a geographical order, an installed perception of the status quo. In this context, FTAs are seen as a mechanism that is part of a structure in which international cooperation is established by northern countries, based on the logic of comparative and competitive advantages. This translates into a lack of incentive for nations to deepen their cooperation beyond the mere exchange of goods. In this sense, there is a certain predisposition to see the relationships vertically and, as Marianne Marchand (1994) point out, the countries of the south end up being defined according to the characteristics and needs of the industrialized countries, omitting in the discussion the heterogeneity that represent the cataloged countries of the South. This lack of new impulses in the cooperation between the United States and Latin America has become even more plausible after the election of the new president of the North American nation.

It is pertinent to consider that, during the last century, the most influential country in the American subcontinent have been the United States. Its geographical proximity, its economic-military power and its influential popular culture have made it the center of attention of the countries of Latin America and the main trading partner after the processes of European colonization. However, this picture is gradually changing. During the last decade, it is observed how the United States have given ground at the expense of their own regressive policies. Perhaps two symbolic elements that exemplify this new scenario are the wall that the United States builds in front of Mexico, a country which represents the door between Latin American and North America and the self-exclusion of the United States from the TPP.

On the other hand, there is the case of China, which uses the FTAs as mechanisms of wide-ranging and multi-layered cooperation. During the past decade China began to use this type of agreements selectively, only a handful of nations established an agreement of this type (in Latin America only China signed three FTAs with Chile, Peru and Costa Rica). The rest of the strategic partnerships in the region were established based on diplomatic channels such as strategic partnership (characterized by a high level of investment and loans for projects related to the extraction and transport of raw materials).

At the beginning, as seen in the case of the Chile-China FTA, they focused on addressing commercial interests. It is observed that the initial steps of China in the region had similarities to those that historically have made large Western powers, since China is identified as a large buyer of raw materials and technology vendor at a competitive price. The increase in China's imports into the region was good news for the Latin American political and economic elites, who could receive these fresh incomes to continue maintaining the historic recipe of being suppliers of raw materials thanks to their endowment factors. However, in the last 5 years China has taken the initiative towards the establishment of a more complex cooperation based on the common good and complementary cooperation.

On the one hand, Chinese capital begins to diversify into sectors of infrastructure, energy and telecommunications, which include to a greater extent the transfer of technology. An example of this new approach is the participation of the Chinese company Baic Group in the bidding of the Chilean lithium, which was the only automotive company that proposed not only to extract the chemical, but also to manufacture the batteries and electric cars. Another element of this approach is related to the emergence of initiatives that go beyond commercial interests such as scientific, financial, political, etc., cooperation. This cooperation is translated into specific initiatives that involve joint work and greater links with the recipient countries. For example, China has worked on the creation of new instances of cooperation that allow to position Chile together with China as a regional platform for scientific and telecommunications development, specifically, through the creation of The South American Astronomic Research Center, Chinese-Chilean Big Data Center and Austral Fiber Optic project.

In this configuration, the rise of China in the international scheme cannot only be understood from economic growth, but also from the country's political relations and the utilized mechanisms of linkage. This period is marked by a more active China concerning foreign policy, using different tools to expands its influence and generate new types of cooperation which depend less on the international pre-established order (for example with the promotion of a new multilateral platform as the Belt and Road Initiative). The merit of China has been that in a short time it has understood that Latin America is not a homogeneous sociopolitical unit, for which the country has been articulating cooperation devices based on different profiles of nations. In this context, FTAs appear as an appropriate mechanism for small and medium-sized nations with free market economies in the region to operationalize their cooperation with China under parameters of economic complementarity, high degree of institutionalization and at the same time generate strategic alliances. In this line, it is observed that the coming years will strengthen this trend, since China is negotiating and establishing feasibility studies with three new countries in the region (Colombia, Panama and Uruguay).

In this sense, this study allows us to observe how after ten years, the Chinese FTA model is more ambitious, than the model implemented by the United States. The Chinese model has been more propitious for the Andean nation on the path of overcoming underdevelopment, since on the one hand China has become the first trading partner of Chile and on the other hand, both nations have developed initiatives in multiple sectors under the framework of the FTA, which include technology transfer, diversification of the productive matrix and optimization of infrastructure levels.

3.2 FTA as Alternative to Overcome Development Trap

The latest report about Chile by the OECD, *Production Transformation Policy Review of Chile*, indicates that although the Andean nation is stable, open and has an adequate macroeconomic management, it is not enough to sustain the development and the new demands of the society (OECD, 2018). The limited diversification and low productivity due to an overproduction without added value make the country's economy vulnerable to international changes. In this sense, the FTAs have two functions, which, by complementing each other, contribute to update the Chilean economy.

On the one hand, FTAs encourage the establishment of more competitive trade. Under this regime, small and medium economies have new markets to trade their products, but at the same time, local industries must update their parameters of competitiveness to have an effective penetration in global markets. This represents a great challenge, but in an increasingly interconnected world, it is imperative that industries move out of their comfort zone and achieve profits according to integral and changing parameters. In this same line, the FTAs accompanied by an adequate public policy of promotion and development of production can be a way to diversify the activities and companies that currently concentrate the economic opportunities of the country. Even though the advances in diversification are still lower, in 2016, Chile became the main fruit exporter in China, surpassing shipments from countries such as Thailand, Vietnam and the United States for the first time. This has allowed it to reduce its high dependence on copper exports. According to data from the Ministry of Foreign Affairs of Chile, since the entry into force of the FTA, shipments of fruit to China multiplied 18 times, from U.S. $ 65 million in 2007 to U.S. $ 1207 million in 2016 (Direcon, 2017).

On the other hand, the FTA encourages a comprehensive cooperation: as it can be seen in this study, the Chile-China FTA has 14 basic clauses, of which 5 promote an extra-commercial relationship (cooperation of small & medium enterprises, research & technology cooperation, telecommunication cooperation, cultural cooperation and financial cooperation). In this sense, FTAs can balance one of the four development traps identified by Paul Collier (2008): the natural resource trap. Chile is a country that highly depends on the extraction of natural resources. Its main exports are copper, fruits and fish under added value and, like most countries in the region, suffer from the volatility of the primary products market. In this sense, the abundance of a misused resource can generate an excessive concentration of production in primary tasks, limiting innovation and the level of industrialization (Collier, 2008). In this configuration, it can be seen that after 10 years of the Chile-China FTA there is progress on the road to development, since this instrument has not only served to encourage commercial exchange but has also become a complex cooperation mechanism which includes long-term initiatives focused on encouraging scientific research, the transfer of technologies and generating a culture that is more prone to innovation and the generation of added value. China works based on mutual stimulation in order to deepen the level of influence and cooperation with the associated country, transforming the agreement into a mechanism of wide-ranging and multi-layered cooperation.

4. Conclusions

In political science, the meaning of a concept is transitory and is subject to a constant critical review. This is what happens with the use of the concept of foreign influence or expanding the sphere of influence. In the Cold War era this concept brought to the scene a series of images related to interventionism and domination. Interventionism in the sense that foreign influence was a priority considered as a mechanism to manipulate the distribution of power and domination, alluding to arguments related to the threat to sovereignty. At present, a more positivist use is observed, addressing this concept to images related to participation and the search for mutual benefit. Participation, in the sense of the high level of adherence of the countries towards the role played by international institutions and the search for mutual benefit based on the logic of joint work and complementary towards a common goal.

This new approach does not mean that the historical view of this concept has disappeared and that there are no nations seeking to influence in an adversarial way (Little, 2007). But it indicates that a numerous flow of nations behaves in a more associative and complementary way, which implies at least a balance between both perspectives.

This is what has happened with the case of China and Chile, which through the signing of an FTA have been deepening the level of relations, from the mere economic exchange to the search for complex cooperation. China influences Chile to collaborate by taking advantage of the simultaneous dependence (economic complementarity), which has allowed them to work strategically and institutionally towards a common goal. In this context, the FTAs emerge as an alternative of cooperation that allows small economies such as Chile to advance on the road to development. Via using FTAs, the countries do not only pay attention to the transaction of primary products, but also to including long-term initiatives focused on encouraging scientific research, the transfer of technologies and generating a culture that is more prone to the generation of added value.

Although not all FTAs signed ten years ago at the international level show the same trend and level of results, it is worth noting that China has known how to use it to deepen the bilateral relation with other economies. On the one hand, it has understood that FTAs are convenient instruments not only for themselves, but also for small and medium open economies to operationalize their cooperation with major powers. In part, this explains why FTAs have a balance between security and flexibility, important elements for these nations to intensify their cooperation based on a high degree of standardization procedures (using the WTO framework and developing bilateral instances to evaluate and implement the agreements) and which at the same time allows them to advance in the generation of strategic cooperation (by means of supplementary or complementary agreements).

On the other hand, China has shown ability to extend its influence via FTAs with countries with an ideologically moderate profile and that historically have been close with the United States (Chile, Costa Rica and Peru). The merit of China has been that in a short time it has understood that Latin America is not a homogeneous sociopolitical unit, for which the country has been articulating cooperation devices based on different profiles of nations. In this line, it is observed that the coming years will strengthen this trend, since China is negotiating and establishing FTA feasibility studies with three new countries in the region (Colombia, Panama and Uruguay). This has marked a movement in the Latin American geopolitical puzzle where China not only manages to draw the attention of ideologically close countries such as Venezuela and Ecuador, but is also establishing different highly binding projects with more pragmatic countries. At a global level, this is also reflected, since China is currently negotiating 10 new FTAs, while carrying out feasibility studies of 10 other agreements. In this context, this trend is framed in how China is building new rules of global trade to adapt to the changing regional economic situation and allows developing countries to play a crucial role in influencing these rules.

Chapter 4
Mercosur and China: Partnerships, Challenges and Opportunities

Bruno Binetti

The Common Market of the South (Mercosur) was created in 1991 by Brazil, Argentina, Uruguay and Paraguay[①] in a global context very different from today's: the United States was the preeminent global power after winning the Cold War; regional institutions devoted to trade liberalization were being created all over the world; neoliberal economic policies were the norm in Latin America and elsewhere. More than 25 years later, it is a brave new world: the U.S. seems to be abandoning the institution-based world order which it helped build; China is a world power and one of Mercosur's strongest economic partners; the South American bloc is in look for a new integration pattern after years of stagnation.

As the massive and sometimes repetitive literature on China-Latin America ties points out, China's rise has had undoubtedly positive effects on economic and social development in Mercosur countries, but also posed significant challenges. On the one hand, China's economic rise in the early 2000s fueled a decade of sustained growth for these countries. As competitive producers of commodities, they had a lot to gain from China's growing appetite for soybeans, iron ore, oil, and other raw materials. In addition to trade, Chinese corporations launched ambitious investment plans, initially in the commodities and infrastructure sector but quickly making inroads in manufacturing and services as well. Chinese policy banks have also extended credit lines to finance much-needed infrastructure in Mercosur countries.

---

① This chapter will focus on China's relationship with the four founding members of Mercosur. Venezuela was suspended from the bloc in 2015, and Bolivia's ascension has been approved, but not finalized.

At the same time, members of Mercosur have been unable to diversify away from commodities and slow to embrace the potential of economic activities linked with services and innovation. These are necessary steps for achieving economic and social development, as China's own example shows. Further, China's slower growth rates in recent years has had a large impact in Mercosur countries, marking the end of the "commodity boom" and posing questions about the future viability of economic models based almost exclusively on the export of raw materials. Finally, China's growing exports of industrial goods has weakened Brazil's and Argentina's manufacturing sectors, encouraged Uruguay's ambition to leave Mercosur, and divested intra-regional trade.

The main theme of this volume is how China and Latin America can forge partnerships to overcome the middle-income trap (MIT). Within this framework, this chapter will analyze China's impact on relations among Mercosur members, and on their economic and social development. Despite more than fifteen years of growing ties with China, Mercosur has not been able to design a common strategy vis-a-vis the Asian giant. I will argue that if Brazil, Argentina, Uruguay and Paraguay are to take better advantage of the opportunity posed by China to break out of the MIT, strengthening cooperation through Mercosur will be essential.

This chapter is organized as follows. The rest of this introduction will provide a brief historical account of how Mercosur came into being and how it has evolved since 1991. Following this, section 2 will analyze China's rise as a partner for Mercosur countries starting in the early 2000s, and its consequences for the development of its member states. Section 3 will focus on the political economy of Mercosur-China relations, highlighting the reasons for the current stagnation of Mercosur and its lack of a unified policy vis-a-vis China. Following this, I will present a series of proposals Mercosur countries can implement to build a common position towards China, reform the bloc's institutions to strengthen its relevance, and turn Mercosur-China relations into a catalyst for better, fairer economic growth, to break from the MIT. Finally, a conclusion will summarize my findings and propose avenues for further research.

1. A Brief History of Mercosur

Two factors help explain the initial success of the integration process between Argentina and Brazil which started in the 1980s and eventually had way to Mercosur: First, on the political side, new but relatively weak democratic governments in Buenos Aires and Brasilia sought to promote geopolitical stability and economic growth by ending the historic rivalry between both countries. Second, from a more economic perspective, by the end of the 1980s and beginning of the 1990s Argentina and Brazil were experimenting with similar policies, based on the guidelines known as the Washington Consensus: privatization, trade liberalization, and deregulation. Coincidental macroeconomic policies in both South American nations facilitated discussions on the creation of an integration mechanism based on the principles of "open regionalism". Especially for Argentina under the presidency of Carlos Menem (1989–1999), Mercosur was seen as a platform from which to participate in larger trade blocs, including an eventual Free Trade Area of the Americas, an initiative first proposed by U.S. president George H W Bush.

When it became clear that Argentina and Brazil were serious in their intent of creating a free trade area, Uruguay and Paraguay jumped on board, leading to the signing of the Treaty of Asunción on March 26, 1991, which formally created Mercosur, the Common Market of the South. Through this document, members pledged to (1) create a common market with the elimination of all barriers to trade among members, (2) implement a customs union, with a common external tariff (CET) on non-Mercosur products, (3) coordinate key macroeconomic policies, and (4) harmonize regulations and laws to promote integration. Other protocols strengthened the bloc's institutions, including Ouro Preto (1994), which installed Mercosur as an international law entity and reinforced the CET, and Ushuaia (2002), which included a democratic clause that would be used twice to suspend countries' membership of the bloc: Paraguay in 2012 and Venezuela, from 2015 onwards.

Despite the initial enthusiasm, it quickly became clear that the promises of the Asunción Treaty were not going to be fulfilled in the timeline set by its signatories, if ever. Although Mercosur did reduce trade barriers, leading to a boom of intra-regional trade between 1991 and 1998, several obstacles remained. In particular, a series of macroeconomic crises in the late 1990s, which started with the Mexican crash of 1995 and deepened after the Asian financial crisis of 1997, strained macroeconomic cooperation between Argentina and Brazil. The unexpected Brazilian devaluation of 1999 effectively ended any chance of macroeconomic coordination between Brasilia and Buenos Aires, and contributed to Argentina's abandonment of its dollar-peso peg in 2002, amid a dramatic economic, political and social crisis. Paraguay and Uruguay, closely tied to their neighbors' economies, suffered similar economic setbacks in this period.

With neoliberal policies largely discredited after the crisis, Mercosur entered a "post-liberal" phase under Presidents Néstor Kirchner and Lula da Silva, who came into office in 2003 in Argentina and Brazil respectively. During the 2003–2014 period Mercosur took a more political role, while economic cooperation stalled. Despite rosy rhetoric, protectionist measures and the growing asymmetry between Mercosur's two largest members effectively paralyzed the bloc. With the end of the China-led commodity boom and the ascension of the pro-market governments of Mauricio Macri and Michel Temer in Argentina and Brazil, respectively, analysts expect the beginning of a new era for Mercosur, in which economic integration will be back at the center. Ongoing negotiations to finalize a Mercosur-European Union free trade agreement, if successful, would strengthen those views.

2. Mercosur, China and the Middle-income Trap

2.1 China's Growing Importance for Mercosur

As Mercosur was grappling with major social and economic crises in the late 1990s, the Chinese economy was expanding at a breakneck pace, thanks in large part to Deng Xiaoping's policy of "Opening up and Reform". Between 1978 and 1998, the Chinese economy grew by 9.8% each year on average, and trade as a percentage of GDP shot up from 7% to 37%. In the same period, China's GDP per capita rose from 156 to 828 dollars, and hundreds of millions of people were lifted out of poverty. When officials gathered in Beijing to approve the "Tenth Five-Year plan" (2001–2005), the first for the 21st century, China was already a main engine of the world economy.

If the first decades of the reform process were devoted to building a competitive industrial base with the assistance of foreign capital and technology, by the year 2000 China was ready to become a major player in the global economy on its own right. With that goal in mind, a new policy framework, known as the "Going Out" policy, was launched to encourage

Chinese corporations to invest abroad, with three main objectives: (1) Make Chinese large enterprises, most of them state-owned (SOEs), more efficient through competition in the global economy,(2) Gain new markets for China's growing manufacturing sector beyond Europe, the United States and Japan, and (3) Secure the raw materials (agricultural goods, oil, minerals) that the booming Chinese economy demanded.

As commodity producers with important domestic markets that were coming out of a serious crisis, Mercosur members were ideal partners for the "Going Out" policy. In order to deepen cooperation, Hu Jintao visited Brazil and Argentina in 2004[①] and announced a new era of Chinese economic and diplomatic engagement in the area.[②] Meanwhile, Mercosur leaders welcomed closer ties with China as a way to boost their economies, reduce their dependency on the United States and Europe, and obtain funds for infrastructure projects without the strict conditions of the International Monetary Fund (IMF), the World Bank and other multilateral institutions.

Hu Jintao's trip marked the beginning of a period of spectacular growth in the economic relationship between China and Mercosur, based on three dimensions: trade, investment and finance. Beginning with trade, from 2001 to 2016 Mercosur-China exchange grew by more than 20% each year on average, with total trade ballooning from less than 6 billion dollars in 2001 to more than 78 billion fifteen years later. Despite declining trade after 2012, China's remains Brazil's and Uruguay's top trade partner, and the second largest for Argentina and Paraguay after Brazil.

Secondly, starting in the mid 2000s, Chinese companies have gradually increased investments in Mercosur countries. In fact, Mercosur is by far the Latin American region that has most benefitted from Chinese investment inflows, with a total of more than 65 billion dollars since 2001. According to Dussell Peters and Ortiz Velazquez (2017), between 2001 and 2016 China has invested almost 55 billion dollars in Brazil, and 10 billion dollars in Argentina.

---

① Hashmi (2017) argues that the new era of China-Mercosur relations began in 2001, when Jiang Zemin visited Brazil and Argentina. Given Argentina's political and economic crisis in late 2001, and the beginning in 2003 of the Lula and Kirchner administrations in Brazil and Argentina, respectively, the auth or locate the beginning of this new stage with president Hu's visit.

② Paraguay does not have official diplomatic relations with China mainland.

Meanwhile, Chinese FDI in Uruguay is of a few hundred million dollars at best, and there is no record of Chinese FDI in Paraguay, likely due to the lack of formal diplomatic relations.

Finally, Chinese development banks have disbursed large sums in loans to Mercosur members, mainly for infrastructure and energy projects but also as direct financial assistance to Central Banks, with Argentina and Brazil being the main beneficiaries. According to Gallagher and Myers (2016), China has provided more than 32 billion dollars in loans to Brazil since 2004 (the second largest sum for a Latin American country after Venezuela), and 15 billion to Argentina (the third largest, topped by Ecuador). There is no recorded disbursement to Uruguay or Paraguay.

Naturally, not all Mercosur countries have benefited equally from closer ties with China. As the largest economy and most populated country in Latin America, an aspiring emerging power and a member of BRICS (Brazil, Russia, China, India, South Africa), Brazil has had a special relationship with Beijing since China launched the Going Out policy. All Mercosur countries are important regional partners for China within Latin America, but Brazil is one of China's few global partners.

Brazil's distinctiveness and size is reflected on the numbers. In 2016, for instance, China-Brazil trade represented 75% of all China-Mercosur trade, followed by Argentina with 19%, and Uruguay and Paraguay with less than 3% each. Meanwhile, Chinese investment in Brazil represents 84% of its FDI in Mercosur, with the rest going to Argentina. Finally, Brazil's predominance is also stark in terms of its attraction of Chinese loans and finance, since it represents 71% of all Chinese loans in Mercosur countries, with Argentina receiving the remaining 29%.

These figures show the dual asymmetries of Mercosur, which are a cause of tension among its members. On the one hand, Argentina distrusts Brazil for its global ambitions and ability to act alone on the world stage, including in relations with China. On the other hand, Uruguay and Paraguay frequently express their discomfort with being treated as "second-class" members of Mercosur. Decisions within the bloc (or the lack thereof) regarding China and other major issues are usually the result of direct negotiations between Brasilia and Buenos Aires, and tend to ignore Uruguayan and Paraguayan interests.

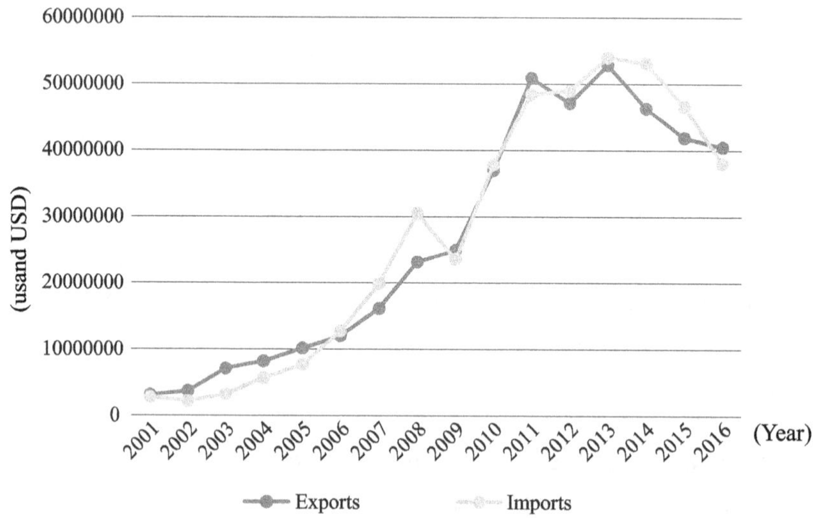

Figure 4.1 Mercosur: Trade with China (2001–2016)

Source: Trade Map.

2.2 The Development Impact of Trade with China

A rising China boosted Mercosur exports through two mechanisms: (1) direct purchases of the region's raw materials such as soybeans, oil, iron ore and others, and (2) rising global commodity prices due to China's demand.① In turn, this had positive effects for overall economic growth, as seen on Figure 4.2: Between 2002 and 2012, Brazil's GDP grew by 3.78% each year on average (versus 2.62% in 1992–2002), Argentina's by 4.19% (up from 1.71% during the previous decade), Uruguay's by 4% (up from 1.78%), and Paraguay's by 3.57% (up from 1.83% in 1992–2002).

Further, economic expansion and active government policies (especially in Argentina, Brazil and Uruguay) led to significant social improvements. For example, according to the World Bank, all four countries reduced their Gini index, an indicator of economic inequality where 100 is completely inequality and 0 complete equality, as relations with China boomed. The reduction of inequality is shown in Figure 4.3. Finding reliable information for poverty trends is harder, but according to one estimate based on national data (Rebossio,

① Paraguay, for instance, barely exports any soybeans (its main export product) to China, but has benefitted from rising global prices which are largely a result of Chinese growing demand.

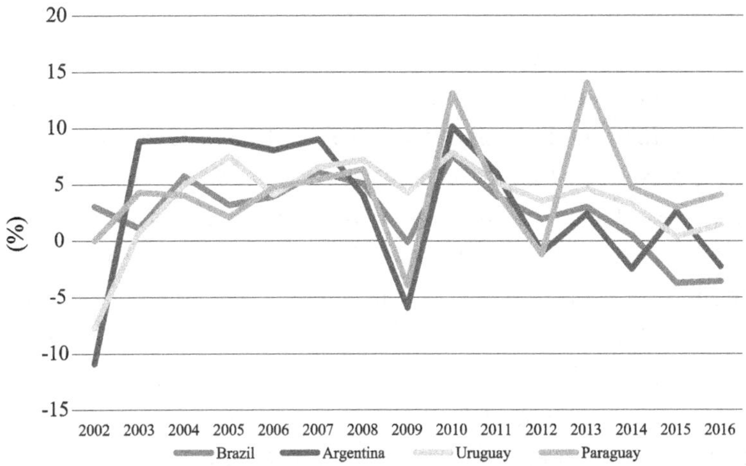

Figure 4.2 GDP growth in Mercosur countries

Source: World Bank.

2014), between 2005 and 2012—the strongest period of the China-led economic boom-Brazil's poverty rate dropped from 36.4% to 18.6%, Argentina's from 30.6% to 24.5%, Uruguay's from 18.8% to 5.9%, and Paraguay's from 56.9% to 49.6%. Mercosur countries, therefore, undoubtedly enjoyed a "China boom" in the early 2000s, more than other sub-regions of Latin America.

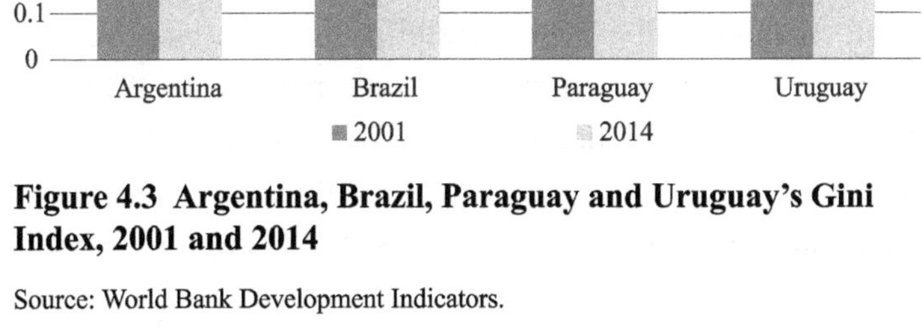

Figure 4.3 Argentina, Brazil, Paraguay and Uruguay's Gini Index, 2001 and 2014

Source: World Bank Development Indicators.

On the other hand, there is barely any intra-industrial trade between Mercosur and China, and trade patterns tend to follow a commodities-for-manufactures pattern more typical of North-South relations. The bulk of

Mercosur exports to China are concentrated on a few primary goods: iron ore (from Brazil), crude oil (from Brazil and Argentina) and soybeans (from Brazil, Argentina and Uruguay). In contrast, governments, labor unions and business organizations in Argentina and Brazil have raised the alarm about the growing presence of Chinese industrial goods, which are competing with local industries. Jenkins and Freitas Barbosa (2012), Bekerman, Dulcich and Moncaut (2014), and Paikin and Dulcich (2017), among others, have found empirical evidence of the way in which Chinese industrial imports are replacing intra-Mercosur industrial trade, and successfully competing with Argentinian and Brazilian industries in their domestic and regional markets. Further, with the exception of Brazil, all other Mercosur members have large trade deficits with China. This represents a problem for Uruguay, Paraguay and especially Argentina, since it aggravates these countries' current account problems.

Brazil and Argentina have adopted a defensive stance against the growing pressure of Chinese industrial exports: combined, both countries represent more than 16% of all anti-dumping measures against China presented at the World Trade Organization (WTO), only surpassed by the European Union. Argentina and Brazil have targeted Chinese imports in textiles, steel and other sectors. Not surprisingly, China has retaliated with trade counter-measures. For instance, in 2010 China suspended purchases of Argentinian soybean oil in response to Argentina's decision to impose anti-dumping measures to more than 20 Chinese products (El Cronista, 2010).

There are reasons to be optimistic regarding the diversification of trade ties between Mercosur and China. First, evidence shows that China is willing to accommodate some of Argentina's and Brazil's demands for more trade diversification whenever these countries present concrete plans, based on selected products, and with a clear possibility of supplying enough goods to make a difference in China's massive domestic market. In 2018, for example, and after years of diplomatic negotiations, China authorized imports of value-added beef cuts from Argentina (Beef Central, 2018).

Second, China's shift to a consumer-based economy, together with rising salaries for domestic workers, will increase demand for more sophisticated goods that Mercosur countries can provide, such as wine, processed meat, cooking oil, leather, and other agro-industrial products. In December 2017, for instance, China announced a tariff reduction for imports of value-added products Mercosur countries excel at, such as alcoholic and non-alcoholic drinks, pasta, shrimp, dairy, and jams. Diego Guelar, Argentina's ambassador to China, noted that "this is an opportunity we cannot waste" (Infocampo, 2017).

2.3 The Development Impact of Investment and Finance from China

Chinese corporations are investing heavily in Brazil and Argentina, especially in the energy and infrastructure sectors. This growing presence is in large part due to China's unique financing capabilities, mainly channeled through its two main policy banks: the China Development Bank (CDB) and the China Exim Bank. China's investments allow Argentina and Brazil to gradually close their massive infrastructure gaps, which limit competitiveness and growth, and provide Chinese corporations with new business opportunities in markets previously reserved for European and American corporations. The system is quite simple: Chinese corporations secure infrastructure contracts (usually avoiding public biddings) by offering financing conditions that cannot be matched by other countries, or by more traditional financers such as the World Bank and the Inter-American Development Bank.

For example, Chinese corporations are refitting one of Argentina's longest railroads, the *Belgrano Cargas*, which connects the port in Buenos Aires with northern provinces, and building to hydropower dams in Patagonia as well as a nuclear energy plant. In the case of Brazil, Chinese corporations already control a significant part of the country's energy grid, and are also building several hydropower dams. Chinese officials have also indicated their desire to build a trans-continental railroad between Brazil in the Atlantic and Peru in the Pacific, although the project has stalled amid environmental concerns.

Chinese corporations have also secured a large presence in Mercosur's oil sector. Chinese oil companies (especially Sinopec) have invested heavily in Brazil's *pre-salt* oil fields, and are shifting their presence in Argentina away from traditional oil extraction and towards shale gas and oil in *Vaca Muerta*. Further, financial assistance from Chinese sources has been critical for Argentina and Brazil in times of isolation from global financial markets. In the case of Argentina, the Chinese Central Bank extended multi-billion-dollar swap lines to boost the South American nation's depleted foreign currency reserves in the aftermath of a default in 2014. In Brazil, loans from Chinese banks supported oil giant Petrobras starting in 2015 after massive corruption scandals threatened the company's stability (Gallagher and Myers, 2016). Far from a "one-size-fit-all" approach, these cases show that Chinese loans are specifically targeted towards recipient countries' needs.

Together with the decision to pursue more sustainable growth rates of around 7% a year, Beijing has also indicated its goal of shifting the center of its development model away from heavy investment and exports, and towards domestic consumption. Further, China has also launched important initiatives to curb the environmental impact of its economic growth, including more investment in renewable energies both at home and abroad[①].

These new trends could have major repercussions for Mercosur countries, and Chinese investments are already shifting from commodities to manufactures and the service sector, a signal of Beijing's new emphasis on sustainable growth. Chinese manufacturing and service giants have specifically targeted Brazil, with the aim of supplying its major domestic market. Meanwhile, Chinese corporations have won biddings to build solar plants in Argentina and ICBC, China largest commercial bank, which is one of the most important in the country's financial sector. In addition, Chinese auto-manufacturers have gradually begun to set facilities in Uruguay, with the hope of entering the Brazilian and Argentine market from there.

Gallagher and Myers (2016) suggest that more is to come in terms of Chinese financing to Latin America, especially in funds designed to boost Chinese investment in critical areas. Beijing has created three funds for this purpose: A China-LAC Industrial Cooperation Investment Fund of 20 billion dollars, a Special Loan Program for China-LAC Infrastructure Project of 10 billion dollars, and a China-LAC Cooperation Fund of at least 10 billion dollars. While not all Chinese funds are active, China's decision to invite Argentina and Brazil to the launching of the Belt and Road initiative in Beijing in May 2017 suggests that Mercosur will continue to benefit from Chinese financing and investment in the infrastructure sector. Further, Brazil is a founding member of the China-lead Asian Infrastructure Investment Bank (AIIB), and Argentina applied for membership in 2017.

It will be up to Mercosur countries to also ensure more investment and financing to the manufacturing and service industries. So far the most succesful country has been Brazil, in large part because of the attractiveness of its large domestic market. Chinese manufacturing corporations have gradually began to open plants in Brazil to supply this market. That has not been the case in other

① For a detailed and excellent analysis of the potential of China's new development model for relations with Latin America see OECD/ECLAC/CAF (2015).

Mercosur countries. Further, between 2002 and 2012, Brazil and Argentina were Latin America's largest investors in China, with 424 and 131 million dollars, respectively. These figures pale in comparison to Chinese investments in Mercosur, but are a promising start. The relatively succesful experience of Brazilian airplane maker Embraer, which set factories and research facilities in China through joint ventures with local companies, should be studied and imitated by other Mercosur corporations (Inter-American Development Bank, 2014).

An integration mechanism born in a very different era, Mercosur has for years been a synonym for stagnation, internal bickering, and empty rhetoric. In order to seize this opportunity and move closer to overcoming the MIT, therefore, Mercosur will have to resolve its impending contradictions, and the differences among its members. That is the topic of the last section of this chapter.

3. Political Economy of China-Mercosur Ties

3.1 A Fragmented and Ineffective Bloc

In Mercosur's history the integration mechanism can be divided in two stages: a dynamic one (1991–1999) after the bloc's creation, and a stagnant one (1999–present). During the first stage, Mercosur countries took historic steps to reduce trade barriers among themselves, and Argentina and Brazil came to see each other as partners after centuries of rivalry and distrust. In contrast, the second stage, which followed the 1999 Brazilian devaluation and Argentina's economic, social and political collapse in 2001–2002, has been full of pro-integration rhetoric and photo-ops, but scarce of results.

In fact, more than 25 years after the creation of Mercosur, the bloc remains an imperfect customs union at best, since large and small members alike were granted a large number of exceptions to the CET system set in place by the Ouro Preto Protocol in 1994. The number of exceptions to the CET, in fact, has grown with time (Zelicovich, 2015). Without a functioning customs union and other policies (such as real freedom of circulation for people among member states), the creation of a common market is far from becoming a reality, despite Mercosur's name (Malamud, 2013).

In addition, Mercosur has been ineffective as a platform to negotiate trade deals with third parties. As of 2017, outside of Latin America (where members are allowed to negotiate individual deals), Mercosur has only signed FTAs with Israel (2007), Egypt (2010) and Palestine (2011), and preferential trade agreements with India (2004) and SACU, the South African Customs Union (2008) (Ministerio de Relaciones Exteriores de Paraguay, n.d.)[①].

More importantly for the topic of this book, relations with China are not an exception to Mercosur's paralysis. Despite the title of this chapter, there is no "Mercosur-China" relationship worth of that name, but a series of bilateral relations between China and each member state (with the aforementioned Paraguayan exception). Mercosur, for instance, gave no institutional response to China's policy papers on Latin America (issued in 2006 and 2012), in which Beijing highlighted its priorities and goals in relations with Latin America. Even more telling, member states could not agree on a response to China's then-premier Wen Jiabao to begin negotiations for a China-Mercosur FTA, made directly to presidents Cristina Kirchner of Argentina, José Mujica of Uruguay and Dilma Rousseff of Brazil during a video conference in 2012.[②] While Uruguay expressed immediate interest, Argentina's and Brazil's reaction was much more tepid (Niebieskikwiat, 2016).

There are at least four reasons for Mercosur's current state of dysfunctionality, which directly impact its ability to present a common strategy vis-à-vis China: (1) A weakening Brazil-Argentina axis, (2) Uruguay and Paraguay discomfort, (3) Empty institutionalization and (4) Excessive expectations.

3.2 A Weakening Brazil-Argentina Axis

In the past 15 years, relations between Argentina and Brazil have experienced setbacks, especially due to the growing asymmetry between both countries. Confident of its rising status during the 2003–2014 period, Brazil did not want to involve Buenos Aires in its growing relations with China, preferring a purely bilateral approach. This was particularly the case after 2006, when Brazil became a member of BRICS, a group of emerging powers, together with

---

① This situation could change if ongoing negotiations for an FTA between Mercosur and the European Union come to fruition. The parties have committed to close a preliminary deal by early 2018.

② The Paraguayan president did not participate in the meeting due to paraguay's lack of diplomatic relations with China mainland.

Russia, India and China (South Africa joined in 2010).

Trade patterns between both countries illustrate this divergence: Trade with Brazil represents 16% of Argentina's exports and 25% of its imports. In contrast, trade with Argentina is only 7.4% of Brazil's exports, and 6.7% of its imports. Argentina's growing trade deficit with Brazil raised alarms in Buenos Aires, leading to an increasing number of tariff and non-tariff measures, including non-automatic import licenses (Statford, 2017). Brazil also made use of protectionist measures to defend key-industries from Argentine competition. For example, the automobile industry has been kept out of Mercosur's free-trade provisions, leading to periodic and often tense negotiations between Argentina and Brazil (Castaño and Piñero, 2016).

Regarding trade with China, both Brazil and Argentina have expressed their desire to divest their exports and reduce dependency on commodities. This is an area in which both countries largely agree: Despite promises made during president Hu's visit in 2004, as of 2017 neither Brazil nor Argentina have recognized China as a market economy at the World Trade Organization. However, there is a key difference: Argentina has a growing trade deficit with China that reached 6 billion dollars in 2016, while Brazil has a trade surplus with the Asian giant. Argentina, therefore, is under more pressure than Brazil to find alternative trade opportunities with China.

There is also asymmetry regarding the importance each country places on Mercosur. While preserving Mercosur is an absolute priority for Argentina, Brazil's desire to conduct an independent foreign policy, carve a role as a regional leader and dilute Mercosur's importance is reflected on Brasilia's initiatives to create parallel regional institutions, the most important one being the Union of South American Nations (UNASUR, in Spanish), created in 2012. Buenos Aires largely saw this move as a Brazilian attempt to increase its regional clout at the expense of closer ties to Argentina (Russell and Tokatlian, 2016).

Some analysts argue that the roles have been somewhat reversed since Brazil entered an unprecedented political crisis and economic recession in 2014 and the pro-market Mauricio Macri became president of Argentina one year later (Mander, Pearson and Rathbone, 2016). President Macri's efforts to reform Argentina's economy have been praised by multilateral organizations and most world powers, including China, while Brazilian foreign policy under interim president Michel Temer, besieged by corruption allegations and political fragility, is a shadow of its former self.[①] Nevertheless, what remains is the discrepancy between Argentina and Brazil: One country's rise seems to correlate with the other's decline on the world stage.

3.3 Empty Institutionalization

In the beginning of Mercosur, presidential leadership ensured that integration moved forward despite resistances from some social and business circles. In Mercosur summits, Presidents solved differences through compromises that lower-ranking officials were unable to make for lack of political power. With time, however, the excessive concentration of decision-making power with presidents has become an obstacle to deepening integration, and has led to summit-fatigue (Malamud, 2013).

Despite lack of progress in economic integration, the second stage of Mercosur (which began in 1999) saw the creation of several institutions, albeit with limited powers and barely any activity. An attempt was made in 2003 to strengthen Mercosur's autonomy with the creation of the position of "President of the Permanent Representatives Commission of Mercosur", a way to give the bloc a more prominent individual voice beyond national governments. The experiment, however, was short-lived. After the tenure of two Argentinian politicians (Eduardo Duhalde in 2003–2005 and Carlos Álvarez from 2005 to 2009), countries were unable to decide on a suitable replacement, and the post was left vacant indefinitely. Thus, the top authority of Mercosur outside of the pro-tempore presidency (which rotates among member states) is now the Secretary of Mercosur, a bureaucratic entity whose mission is limited to administrative duties and record-keeping.

Following the debacle of Mercosur's "Presidency", two new institutions were created: The Parliament of Mercosur or Parlasur in 2007 and the Permanent Revision Tribunal in 2004. Regarding Parlasur, since Mercosur remains an inter-governmental body with no delegation of sovereignty from member states, there is little for this assembly to do besides issuing symbolic declarations and providing a comfortable retirement place for former politicians. Similarly, the Permanent Tribunal has barely performed any function in the

① For instance, President Macri was, together with Chilean president Michelle Bachelet, one of only two Latin American leaders to attend the Belt and Road forum in Beijing in May 2017, when he was also welcomed by Chinese president Xi Jinping in an official visit.

more than ten years since its creation: it has issued only 6 rulings, the last one in 2012, three of which had to do with a trade dispute between Argentina and Uruguay over the import of remolded tires (Tribunal Permanente del Mercosur, n.d.) Differences among Mercosur members, thus, continue to be resolved through bilateral negotiations, despite the existence of this permanent tribunal.

3.4 Uruguay's and Paraguay's Discomfort

A second source of tensions within Mercosur has been the growing number of grievances from its smaller members, Uruguay and Paraguay. Unlike Brazil and Argentina, these countries do not have large industrial sectors to protect, and its leaders have frequently expressed their desire to move further with trade liberalization. This is particularly the case with Uruguay, which for some time now has been attempting to reach trade deals individually with the world's largest economies, including the United States and China. Each time, however, Brazil and Argentina have blocked Uruguay's attempts, citing Mercosur regulations that demand full consensus from other Mercosur members to sign deals with non-Latin American economies.

Brazil and Argentina have refused to allow Uruguay to sign an individual FTA with China in order to protect their own industries from even more competition from Chinese manufactures. Brazilian and Argentinian officials fear that if Uruguay was to sign an individual deal with China, Chinese industries would flood their domestic markets using Uruguay as a beachhead inside Mercosur. Montevideo, in turn, complains of Brazil and Argentina's selfishness, for blocking Uruguay's attempts to sign FTAs on its own while doing nothing to reach deals on the Mercosur level. For example, in 2007 Chinese auto manufacturer Chery built a factory in Uruguay, only to close it in 2015 given Argentina's and Brazil's protectionist measures (Reuters, 2015). In response to this attitude, Uruguay has at times threatened to leave Mercosur, but the importance of the Brazilian and Argentinian markets for its exports have prevented any serious discussion of this "nuclear option".

A landlocked country with an economy closely interrelated to that of Brazil, Paraguay cannot credibly threat to leave Mercosur, but has also expressed its rejection of the "cartel" between Argentina and Brazil, which negotiates issues of bilateral importance ignoring Uruguayan and Paraguayan interests. Tensions reached its highest in 2012, when Mercosur suspended Paraguay as a member following the removal of president Fernando Lugo by the Paraguayan Congress, which Argentina, Brazil and Uruguay defined as "a coup".

Further, as the least developed member of Mercosur, with a GDP per capita that is roughly half of Brazil's and even less of Argentina's, Paraguay demands more solidarity from its powerful neighbors. Partially in response to these demands, in 2005 Mercosur launched its "Structural Convergence Funds" (FOCEC) of 100 million dollars, funded almost exclusively by Brazil and Argentina, of which 80% was devoted to infrastructure projects in Paraguay (Berrettoni, 2013). However, that small amount is insufficient to seriously reduce asymmetries among Mercosur members.

3.5 Excessive Expectations and Wrong Comparisons

Finally, Mercosur's current dysfunctionality could be a problem of perception, at least to a certain extent. The bloc has serious problems, which have been noted here, but in times the expectations placed upon it have been excessive (including in its founding treaties), and the acknowledgement of its accomplishments scarce. Andrés Malamud (2013), for instance, argues that at least part of Mercosur's current problems arose precisely because the bloc was successful in its original goals: building a peaceful and cooperative Brazil-Argentina relationship and providing a certain degree of economic integration between the two. If Mercosur has been unable to move forward since the 1990s, he argues, it is because there is simply not enough economic complementarity to achieve anything else.

Further, simplistic comparisons with the Pacific Alliance (PA), an integration mechanism created in 2010 by Chile, Colombia, Mexico and Peru, do not provide a viable model for Mercosur. Some analysts have urged Mercosur members to imitate PA countries, drastically reduce tariff and non-tariff trade barriers and fully liberalize trade among themselves. A simple political economy analysis, however, would highlight the difficulties of that approach. Among other things, PA countries differ from their Mercosur counterparts in their level of economic openness (which they had before launching their integration process), and the relatively low level of intra-PA trade, compared to trade among Mercosur countries. In other words, integration has been easier for the PA because there were less political and social costs to pay from the beginning. Argentina and Brazil, in contrast, have important but not competitive manufacturing sectors that depend on domestic and regional markets so survive and would suffer from further liberalization. Given that these industrial sectors (such as the aforementioned automobile industry) are highly unionized, and that those labor unions have close connections with key political actors [The Workers' Party (PT) in Brazil and Peronism in Argentina], economic integration is extremely sensitive for Mercosur countries, unlike their PA counterparts. Mercosur, therefore, will need to carve out a role of its own if it is to agree on a more assertive strategy towards China and other emerging powers.

4. An Agenda for a New Mercosur-China Partnership

How can Mercosur countries strengthen their integration process and build a common strategy vis-à-vis China? In the answer to this question lies the central discussion of this chapter: whether Mercosur countries can come together to deepen their diplomatic and economic relations with Beijing in a way that ensures economic and social development.

It has been frequently noted that in a globalized economy regional blocs such as Mercosur should promote the creation of regional value chains in order to compete. With this goal in mind, the author will propose five areas of reform Mercosur can tackle to build a more balanced relationship among its members, and to carve out a common policy towards China.

4.1 Dual-track Decision Making

All Mercosur countries are highly-centralized presidential systems and very protective of their national sovereignty. Delegating major powers to a supranational body such as Mercosur, therefore, is a non-starter. However, governments could retain full control over the most sensitive areas of integration (such as tariffs and trade policy), while delegating more technical but extremely important issues to a revamped Mercosur bureaucracy.

For instance, Mercosur countries have been negotiating trade facilitation measures for years, but progress has been painstakingly slow, since talks are held bilaterally and national parliaments take time in ratifying finished deals. A possible solution would be to strengthen Mercosur's secretariat with the financial and human resources it needs to play an active role in reducing bureaucratic hurdles, harmonizing rules and simplifying trade procedures between member states. With the necessary political backing, the secretariat could analyze the potential impact of trade facilitation measures, determine which regulations must be changed in each member state, and submit complete packages to each country, which they would send to their legislatures for approval.

With time, the bloc could experiment with supranationality on a limited number of issues. For instance, Mercosur's parliament could be given full authority to approve trade facilitation measures, simplifying the ratification process. In designing these reforms, of course, the secretariat would aim to reduce regulatory differences among Mercosur members and between them and their largest trading partners, including China.

4.2 Physical Integration and Solidarity

The poor quality of the infrastructure connecting its members is one of the main obstacles for the formation of Mercosur value chains. Ports, airports, railroads and roads remain highly deficient in all countries, and logistical bottlenecks dramatically increase costs for intra-Mercosur trade. Further, FOCEC is blatantly inadequate to address differences with Uruguay and Paraguay. Without incentives for governments to prioritize regional integration over politically-beneficial domestic infrastructure, these problems will persist.

Countries could devote a fixed percentage of what they collect from CET to a new Mercosur Infrastructure Fund, which would allocate money exclusively for infrastructure projects that facilitate connectivity between member states, based on the technical assessment of Mercosur's secretariat. China could be a key partner in this effort, and its development banks could extend credit lines to strengthen the role of the Fund, provided that Chinese corporations are hired to build part of the projects. Further, when negotiating infrastructure agreements with Beijing, national governments should prioritize projects that would boost regional integration, to facilitate the creation of regional value chains.

Several infrastructure projects that are key to Mercosur's development (such as more access to the Pacific through Chile and proper railroad connections between members) could be linked to China's Belt and Road Initiative, which seeks to boost infrastructure on a global scale. On January 2018, Chinese foreign minister Wang Yi officially invited Latin American nations to join this major infrastructure program of global scale (Cambero and Sherwood, 2018). However, Brazil and Argentina must accept their own responsibility in allocating resources for development projects in Uruguay and Paraguay in order to regain their trust. Rebuilding legitimacy for Mercosur is at least as important as boosting infrastructure connectivity among its members. This need will only become more acute when and if Bolivia becomes a full member of Mercosur.

4.3 A Common Industrial Policy

The slow progress of Brazil's and Argentina's efforts to diversify their trade with China away from a commodities-for-manufactures pattern shows the limits of bilateral negotiations. Mercosur-level strategies to integrate Chinese corporations into regional value chains could deliver more results. Instead of seeing Chinese competition as a threat to their own industrialization, Mercosur countries should see China as a partner for industrialization, making use of their large domestic markets of almost 250 million people combining of Brazil, Argentina, Uruguay and Paraguay.

A key area would be the automobile industry, which as previously stated is a priority for Argentina, Brazil and Uruguay. Through a joint strategy, Mercosur could ensure that Chinese corporations allocate their production facilities inside the bloc, generating value added and providing much needed capital and technology. Most automakers in Mercosur countries are already foreign (especially from the U.S. and Europe). Incorporating Chinese corporations to the industry would only provide more opportunities. A strengthened Mercosur secretariat could provide valuable sectoral analysis to inform regional industrial policy, and ensure that investment is allocated to all member states.

An important reason for Brazil's and Argentina's nationalistic view of their industrial policies has been the pressure of business associations and labor unions. Despite decades of integration, an Argentina-Brazil business council was only created in 2016, and merely as a defensive mechanism against Chinese competition. Countries and social actors need a less defensive and more assertive stance vis-à-vis China, one that sees the Asian giant as an indispensable partner and a potential source of investment in the industrial sector. Instead of resisting Chinese inroads in their manufacturing sectors, Mercosur countries could work to turn this interest into industrial investment and technology transfers. Further, by negotiating jointly with China, Mercosur countries could promote the allocation of research and development facilities from Chinese industries in their territories.

4.4 21st Century View of Trade and Integration

In many ways, Mercosur's governments have focused on the effect of

Chinese competition on their manufacturing sectors without addressing their own shortcomings. While the bloc has recently accelerated talks with the European Union towards a free trade agreement, more needs to be done to articulate an assertive external policy for Mercosur in the 21st century. Even if the United States is falling into a period of isolationism and protectionism, China and other countries remain steadfast committed to an open global economy, an opportunity Mercosur cannot let pass.

Having an innovative and competitive manufacturing sector is still a key element of a strategy to break out of the middle-income trap. However, it cannot to be the only one. Today's global economy is increasingly driven by the services industry, a sector which will gain in importance for China as it continues its new, more balanced approach to economic development. Mercosur countries can do much more to integrate their service industries and become larger providers of services for China, including tourism.

Further, as competitive producers of agricultural goods, Mercosur countries can be key players in increasing food security not only in China, but also in other emerging markets in Asia (especially India) and Sub-Saharan Africa. Diversification will not come merely from exporting more goods to traditional partners, but in opening new markets for Mercosur products, just like China did under the "Going Out" policy.

In order to take advantage of opportunities in services and open new markets for more traditional exports, Mercosur should strengthen its market intelligence capabilities, and its ability to negotiate jointly with third parties. Meanwhile, Brazil and Argentina should allow smaller members, especially Uruguay, to sign individual trade deals with third parties through a more flexible Mercosur, and apply strict rules of origin to prevent trade distortions.

5. Conclusions

This chapter has aimed to analyze the state of Mercosur's integration process through the lens of its partnership with China, towards the goal of overcoming the middle-income trap. The author have argued that China's rise has led to impressive economic growth for all Mercosur members, and new opportunities in trade, investment and finance. The author have also noted, however, that Mercosur countries will need a more assertive and joint strategy to ensure that China's rising role does not deepen their dependency on the exports of raw materials, which are not enough to break out of the MIT, as proven by Latin America's and China's history.

Most of Mercosur's problems have nothing to do with China. The bloc has been stagnant since at least 1999, years before China became a major trading partner. The emergence of the Asian giant, however, provided a significant challenge that some social, political and economic actors within Mercosur nations used as an excuse to protect their own particular interests and preserve the status quo.

Now more than ever, Mercosur members need to come together and design an integration mechanism for the 21st century, one that has the necessary institutional and technical tools to channel China's interest into industrial development, trade in services and innovation. China's political economy changes at a breakneck pace: what worked for Mercosur countries during the early years of the "Going Out" policy is not enough anymore. A more assertive Mercosur would address inequalities among its members, provide the expertise and technical analysis needed to boost integration, and actively pursue new markets and new opportunities.

China has given many signals of its willingness to diversify its relations with Mercosur countries away from a commodities-for-manufactures trade pattern. The inclusion of Argentina and Brazil within the Belt and Road Initiative, as well as China's multi-billion dollar funds for industrial innovation and technological improvement in Latin America are strong testaments to this.

Ultimately, taking advantage of this opportunity will depend on the political will of Mercosur governments. The good news is political elites in all Mercosur countries seem to agree on the importance of deepening relations with China: Brazil and Argentina, for instance, maintained their close partnership with Beijing despite government changes in 2014 and 2015, respectively. However, the Paraguayan exception remains an obstacle for Mercosur-China relations, one that should be resolved in order to facilitate negotiations.

As shown by China's own example, no country or region has set a path towards sustainable development from one day to another. Mercosur countries should slowly build the political and social consensus they need to deepen the quality of their integration and articulate a common policy towards China. Since China's successful reforms in the 1970s, Deng Xiaoping's reminder of "crossing the river by feeling the stones" has been used many times to argue for caution and gradualism. Its relevance, however, remains intact.

Chapter 5
China-Mexico FTA: Overcoming Trade Barriers to Escape the Middle-income Trap

Hua Zhou, Francisco J. Valderrey, Miguel A. Montoya

Trade and commerce are the pivotal basis of the prosperity reached in modern times. It will be difficult to dispute the benefits of exchanging goods and services across nations, but it is also hard to find the perfect system to carry out those activities. For a long time, multilateral agreements provided a framework for the promotion of trade and commerce, with a clear set of rules, mechanisms to solve disputes and physical venues where to solve issues. This trend became more robust once the World Trade Organization was established in 1995, replacing previous GATT agreements. The creation of the new organization benefited the advance of international commerce, but it did not provide solutions according to everyone's interest and desires. Therefore, countries have been permanently seeking some different alternative mechanisms, ranging from rudimentary bilateral deals to complex multilateral agreements. Sometimes, those deals include nations that could hardly have a meaningful interaction in the absence of those specific accords. In many cases, the countries are emerging markets with the drive to compete in foreign markets. Often, though, those nations obtain temporarily increasing levels of prosperity, before falling into the so-called "middle-income trap" (MIT) or the impossibility of sustaining those rates of growth that will allow their citizens to reach income levels similar to more developed economies.

In our research, we analyze the impact of trade between two of those nations, the People's Republic of China (PRC) and Mexico, under a possible free trade agreement (FTA). Historically, both countries have gone through a complicated relationship, often positioning themselves as commercial enemies. A few years ago, the thought of a closer collaboration between China and

Mexico would have sound unrealistic, due to the extreme dependency of the later upon the U.S. Recently, though, an unexpected event has turned the tables on the Latin American nation: the electoral victory of Donald Trump. In fact, his administration is looking with hostility at its southern neighbor, to the point of jeopardizing a long-standing friendship. As an example, the North America Free Trade Agreement (NAFTA), which also includes Canada and allows for a broad free exchange of goods and services among member countries, is under renegotiation. The renegotiation of NAFTA is no minor issue for Mexico, and regardless of the outcome, is already hurting long-standing business relationships among companies from either side of the border. Thus, Mexico is reluctantly searching for new partners, as the relationship with the Trump's administration shows constant signs of deterioration. Suddenly, the PRC is becoming a potential ally, due to the possibilities of developing commercial interchange at once, or of more permanent agreements, such as foreign direct investment (FDI).

Whether a FTA is feasible or not, opening the market to Chinese competitors is not a preferred choice for many local enterprises in Mexico. As most times happens in free trade, the impact of an FTA is not the same all across the board, with industries that may benefit and those that may suffer in other sectors of the economy. Therefore, it is crucial to include a sectoral view before opening the door to foreign competition. In the end, the government will receive many complaints from those companies absorbing the adverse effects. In the case of China, local enterprises do not find concern from facing Mexican competitors. After all, the PRC has already signed FTA agreements with other Latin American nations, with negligible negative impact for the Chinese companies. Assuming that most concerns will arise from specific sectors in both countries, coupled with criticism from the general population, we analyze the possibility of the hypothetical FTA under a sectoral approach and a welfare view. For that purpose, we compare the impact in both markets and industries, following the GTAP methodology, which has been used for many years to measure similar cases.

With the results from the Global Trade Analysis Project (GTAP) analysis, we intend to see whether or not both nations may benefit from mutual trade beyond current efforts. We evaluate the outcome from the perspective of the MIT to see if the two nations may benefit enough as to make the FTA a pivotal point for fostering sustained economic growth. Both countries, indeed, are going through promising times, with people reaching middle-income status, although living under the constant concern of never reaching the wealth and prosperity of advanced economies.

1. Under the Shadow of the TPP

The Trans-Pacific Partnership (TPP) has probably been the most appealing trade initiative during the last few years, promising to bring together the markets at both sides of the Pacific Rim. The projected figures, the aggregate size of the economies of member countries and their vital role in international commerce has been a point of debate for the nations involved, as well as a cause of concern for those countries left behind. Presently, though, the TPP is in no man's land. After Trump's withdraw in January of 2017, the agreement has gone through different stages, going from possible dissolution to the possibility of a reinvigorated treaty of eleven nations. The issue is far from being resolved, and unforeseen scenarios are gaining momentum.

1.1 Is the TPP Still Alive?

The TPP includes a heterogeneous group of nations, responding to a rather odd process of joining already established members. The initiative came from four countries, New Zealand, Chile, Singapore and Brunei, and was known as the Trans-Pacific Strategic Economic Partnership Agreement, signed in 2004. Judging by the geographical separation and irrelevant historical or business ties among some of those nations, the arrangement was more likely to yield opportunities for joyful travel and friendly reunions, rather than profitable commercial relations. However, with the addition of new member countries in 2010, the initiative gained strength. The momentum, though, was not so much the result of quantity, but of quality, since one of the newcomers was the United States. As of today, the countries requesting membership at the TPP, are as follows: Australia, Brunei, Canada, Chile, Japan, Malaysia, Mexico, New Zealand, Peru, Singapore and Vietnam. Many experts took for granted unanimous ratification until Donald Trump got elected to the White House and decided to leave the partnership. Anyhow, the possibility of the TPP becoming a reality is still raising concerns in many countries. This agreement may also have a robust geopolitical impact, due to the inclusion of Japan and its unexpected role as a promoter after the withdrawal of the U.S., and the recent interest from South Korea; their addition to this pact may have a profound impact in the Pacific Rim (Solís and Katada, 2015). In fact, there is a new label of the Comprehensive and Progressive Agreement for Trans-Pacific Partnership.

After the signing of the TPP in October 2015, the partnership immediately raised concern among citizens and enterprises of the member countries, even if their governments presented the agreement as a significant victory. Once the government reported the results of negotiations, criticism started to rise, especially among enterprises in neglected industries. Unfortunately, the political criticism left little room for reviewing the positive aspects of the proposed partnership. Indeed, numerous studies pointed out the economic benefits for all member countries, including the U.S. (Schott, 2016).

1.2 China and the TPP

Ever since the TPP built credibility and attracted global interest, the project raised concern in China. In fact, the impact of the TPP on China has been the focus of different studies, ranging from geopolitical analysis to detailed numerical simulations. A quantitative analysis of the potential effects of the TPP shows benefits for the member countries and minor adverse consequences for China (Li and Whalley, 2014). According to the same research study, a possible entrance to this country as a new member of the partnership will be beneficial for all the parties involved and even for worldwide trade. Other scholars advocate for convergence of essential nations in the Asia Pacific through multilateral agreements and cooperation (Petri, Plummer and Zhai, 2014).

Despite the American withdraw, the TPP poses a threat to the economic interest of China and its desire of playing a more critical role in the Asia Pacific. The implications for China from the TPP are many, considering the informal leadership of Japan and the interest from South Korea. Facing those nations on economic grounds is not the desire of the Chinese authorities, much less if joined by multilateral agreements with immediate neighbors that have sufficient muscle on their own. Furthermore, China has its own geoeconomics' plan through the Silk Road Economic Belt and the 21st Century Maritime Silk Road Initiative, which eventually may collide with the TPP.

1.3 Old Competitors May Become Best Friends

In the absence of realistic opportunities for bilateral agreements with the

U.S. or joining the TPP, an exciting alternative for the PRC could be a free trade agreement (FTA) with Mexico. As a member of the North American Free Trade Agreement (NAFTA), the Latin American country faces few restrictions for selling products and services or investing in Canada and the U.S. Even after the renegotiation of NAFTA, it still would be attractive for China to have a partner next to the U.S. Bilateral trade between China and Mexico is on the rise, even in the absence of a specific framework, such as an FTA or a similar instrument that will allow enterprises from both sides to increase exports, imports and investments. In this area, the Latin American country has considerable experience, with 12 FTAs already signed with 46 countries. The country has become proficient in using FTAs, with a broad range of similar instruments. Mexican trade treaties vary from concrete, sectoral oriented agreements, to treaties with the potential of going beyond commercial areas. Also, Mexico favors agreements either with large partners, such as the U.S., Canada, Japan and the European Union or with countries of much smaller economic scale or size, such as Israel or Singapore.

The nation may offer many lessons about the difficulties and the benefits of formalizing commercial ties with other countries under free trade treaties or similar schemes. For instance, we may consider both extremes: a limited bilateral agreement, the Mexico-Japan Economic Partnership Agreement and a broader scale commercial treaty, such as NAFTA. In the particular case of the partnership with Japan, a Mexican study shows that such agreement has not resulted in significant changes in the aggregate figures, although the country has benefited from the shift in product composition (Sánchez et al., 2016). Despite its detractors, mainly from the negatively affected American industries, NAFTA has yield positive results (Hills, 2014). In Mexico, those results have spread unevenly, with some geographical regions benefiting the most from convergence with global industrial chains (Díaz et al., 2015).

A possible FTA between China and Mexico may be perceived differently by both parties. For Mexico, such possibility might not be quite appealing years ago; however, after Trump became president, and he threatened Mexico to remove the U.S. from NAFTA and forced to renegotiate it, a new FTA with China represents an opportunity to diversify its markets. China, on the other hand, may have a desire to counterbalance the potential impact of future bilateral agreements of the United States. After the US's withdrew from the negotiations of the TPP, Japan, China's real competitor in the South-East Asia region, enjoys a leading role in the treaty; therefore, it has a lot more at stake.

1.4 Bilateral Economic Relations between Mexico and China

Economic relations between Mexico and China have been almost negligible until very recently. It is arguable that for many years, Mexico perceived China as a strong competitor in the American market and then in its domestic market. In any event, Mexico fiercely opposed the admission of the People's Republic of China into the World Trade Organization; it reluctantly agreed to accept China's entrance, but only after securing some trade privileges under a bilateral scheme of gradual decrease of tariffs for some products. Economic interests, coupled with a lack of mutual trust and the exclusion of the Chinese community residing in Mexico on issues of their concern, kept both countries at a distance (Hearn, 2015). Consequently, for many years, trade figures were not relevant. With the coming of the new century, bilateral exchange started to grow at a steady pace, while increasing significantly during our decade. The flow of trade can be easily identified, with a massive deficit for Mexico, while total bilateral commerce is on the rise, as shown in figure 5.1.

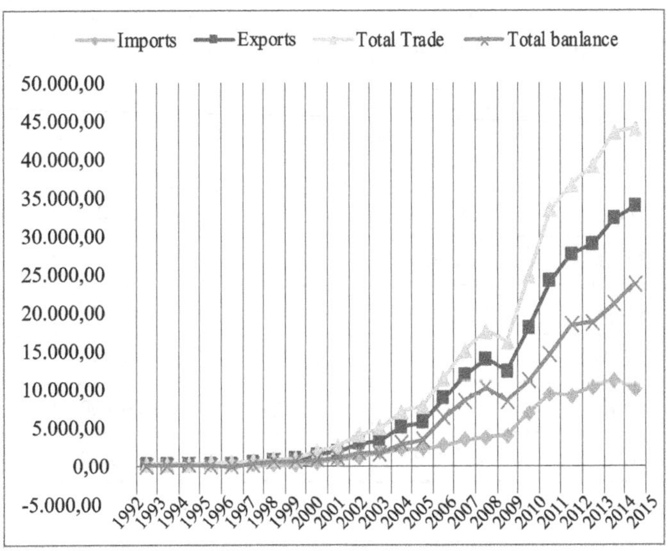

Figure 5.1 Total Trade between China and Mexico (Unit: Million USD)

Source: Author's projection with data from Comtrade Database.

For a long time, China maintained a competitive advantage over Mexico in the U.S. market thanks to its undervalued currency and competitive wages. Traditional Chinese advantages over the Mexican labor have been diminishing progressively to the point that ultimately there is no such a distinct advantage anymore or not enough for many American companies to justify establishing operations in a remote land. To those enterprises, physical distance and logistic costs are significantly lower when making products in Mexico. There are additional benefits, as well, such as serving American customers promptly and conducting business within manageable cultural boundaries. Rising labor costs and a stronger yuan, as compared to the Mexican peso, are setting up a new scenario, where almighty State-Owned Enterprises and large private enterprises from China, may move manufacturing operations to Mexico. From the Latin American nation, those companies could be in better position to reach the American consumer. In fact, China is becoming a significant investor in Mexico, especially since the year 2010. Nevertheless, figures are still very meager, as a percentage of both total FDI in Mexico and China's outflows (see Table 5.1).

Table 5.1 China's Share of Mexico's FDI Inflows and China's Outflows, 2008–2014 (in million USD)

Year	FDI from China to Mexico	Total FDI in Mexico	Percent of Mexico's Inflows(%)	China's FDI Abroad	Percent of China's Outflows(%)
2007	17.16	32,321.00	0.05%	26,510.00	0.06%
2008	5.63	28,610.00	0.02%	55,910.00	0.01%
2009	0.82	17,679.00	0.00%	56,530.00	0.00%
2010	26.73	26,083.00	0.10%	68,811.00	0.04%
2011	41.54	23,376.00	0.18%	74,654.00	0.06%
2012	100.42	18,951.00	0.53%	87,804.00	0.11%
2013	49.73	44,627.00	0.11%	101,000.00	0.05%
2014	140.57	22,795.00	0.62%	116,000.00	0.12%

Source: *China Statistical Yearbook* (various years) and UNCTAD database.

An agreement with Mexico could be beneficial for China's interest, but it is essential to measure the consequences for both countries, especially the overall impact on welfare. The evaluation also needs to address sectoral gains and losses, as well as the economic interest, measured in aggregate terms. The analysis is complicated, but it may be carried out using different methodologies. In our opinion, as explained ahead, the GTAP offers detailed analysis and is a proven instrument for this type of studies. The results of the analysis show that the FTA between China and Mexico will equilibrate the negative impact of the TPP on China. On the Mexican side, the agreement will bring additional benefits, beyond those obtained by signing only the TPP.

2. Model and Data

Defining the model that better suits the analysis of a China-Mexico free trade agreement presents some difficulties. EORA, EXIOBASE, WIOD, GTAP-MRIOT, GRAM or IDE-JETHRO'S AIIOTs have distinctive features and limitations, but none is a universal solution (Tukker and Dietzenbacher, 2013). A research study applying three widely computable general equilibrium models of trade to NAFTA shows a significant variability of results obtained from the different models (Fox, Shikher and Tsigas, 2015). After evaluating academic contributions from the usage of the different models, we found that GTAP best suits our needs. In fact, the model is relatively standard, widely used, and applies to the General Equilibrium Model (Domingues, Haddad, and Hewings, 2008).

GTAP is appropriate for measuring the economic impact derived from free trade treaties. In fact, the purpose of GTAP is to provide quantitative tools for analyzing policy issues on an international scale, while acquiring input information through experts, who collaboratively record and update trade data (Walmsley, Aguiar and Narayanan, 2012). Academics have applied the methodology to a broad spectrum of research projects and studies regarding economic effects of bilateral and multilateral trade agreements (Nakajima, 2002; Domingues, Haddad and Hewings, 2008; Solís and Katada, 2015). The GTAP model may also be useful to generate case scenarios that could advance specific proposals during the negotiation process. Additionally, identifying those industries that will bear the burden of adverse consequences of the FTA may serve to anticipate obstacles from enterprises in those areas, thus presenting specific proposals to compensate sectors involved before facing the opposition of affected companies or geographic regions. In particular, we followed the methodology applied to the analysis of the Australia-China FTA by Siriwardana and Yang, measuring the overall economic effects, with emphasis on welfare and sectoral aspects (Siriwardana and Yang, 2008).

2.1 Simulation Design

Our analysis was performed using the GTAP Model Analysis, aiming at presenting a broad view of economic impact and the consequences to selected industries. We used database version 9, which includes international business in 57 industries of 140 regions. Our analysis covers nine regions and ten sectors. The regions are: China, Mexico, USA, Canada, TPP (excluding Mexico and the U.S.), China Hong Kong and Taiwan, Latin America (excluding Mexico), European Union (with 28 members) and the rest of the world. The sectors included are: (1) Primary Agricultural Products, (2) Processed Food, (3) Mineral Resources, (4) Metals, (5) Textile and Wearing Apparel, (6) Wood, Paper, and Chemical, (7) Electrical Equipment, (8) Transportation, (9) Other Manufacturers and (10) Other Services. Appendix A shows more detailed information. We also used GTAP database version 9 to compare import tariffs as applied in their bilateral trade, as shown in Table 5.2. In both cases, there is a broad range of import tariffs enforced by both countries. In the case of Mexico, there are three categories of import products from China that pay high duties: Wearing Apparels (27.7%), Sugar (26.8%), and Beverages and tobacco (26.4%), while more than half of the categories carry double-digit tariffs. The highest tariffs imposed by China on Mexican products apply to Motor vehicles and parts (22.6%), Meat products (13.45%), Miscellaneous Manufacturing (12.2%), and Animal products (11.3%). Contrary to Mexico, China only imposes double-digit tariffs to one-fourth of the selected product categories.

Table 5.2 Existing Bilateral Tariffs of China-Mexico Merchandise Trade (%)

Sector	China*	Mexico**
1. Grains	0.06	1.00
2. Other crops	4.78	12.30
3. Animal products	11.28	5.69
4.Forestry and fishing	8.46	11.85
5. Mining and energy	0.06	10.58
6. Meat products	13.45	10.00
7.Other food products	8.18	19.69
8. Dairy	0.00	0.00

(Contd.)

Sector	China*	Mexico**
9.Sugar	0.00	26.80
10. Beverages and tobacco	4.15	26.41
11. Textiles	5.75	16.73
12. Wearing Apparels	7.19	27.71
13. Wood and paper products, publishing	1.58	12.65
14. Chemicals, rubber, and plastic	6.76	7.92
15. Ferrous metals	0.36	5.37
16. Metal products	10.23	10.31
17. Motor vehicles and parts	22.55	8.39
18. Machinery and equipment	2.38	3.32
19. Miscellaneous manufacturing	12.22	9.16
20. Services	0.00	0.00

* Chinese tariffs on imports from Mexico.
**Mexico's tariffs on imports from China.
Source: Purdue University (2011), GTAP database version 9.

Routinely, research based on GTAP analysis presents different scenarios. Although broadening the number of possible outcomes generates more extensive information, it may also deviate the analysis from the primary research objectives. Therefore, in our study we provided two different simulations: a) removal of all bilateral tariffs on goods and trade between TPP's countries; and b) removal of all bilateral tariffs on goods trade between TPP's countries, while at the same time, Mexico and China would sign the proposed FTA with zero-tariff, that we name as the China-Mexico Free Trade Agreement (CMFTA). In our analysis, we assumed the full liberalization of trade of goods. We used the year 2011 as a base for our calculations while holding all other factors constant. No more recent data was available at the time of this writing.

2.2 Simulation Results

Our GTAP simulation shows different results regarding macroeconomic and sectoral effects, as well as the impact on trade patterns. The outcome of the simulation is of great importance since these results provide the evidence needed to understand whether the China-Mexico FTA could bring trade creation or trade diversion. Additionally, these results present the estimated impact on trade flows in the international trade content, assuming that the FTA between both nations would be signed.

A first analysis shows the impact of the TPP alone (first scenario) and the addition of the CMFTA (second scenario) to real GDP, trade performance, and trade balance (see Table 5.3). Regarding real GDP, it is arguable that the CMFTA will bring benefits to both countries, with little impact on all other regions. Mexico will benefit under both scenarios, increasing real GDP from 0.04% to 0.12%, while China will experience changes ranging from -0.0007% to 0.008%. Therefore, the CMFTA will equilibrate the negative impact by the TPP that affects China regarding real GDP. From the Mexican side, the agreement will bring additional benefits beyond those of signing only the TPP. When taking into consideration the impact on trade performance, Mexico is a clear winner, with an export expansion rising from 0.32% to 0.77% and an import expansion increasing from 0.47% to 1.3%. In trade performance, China will see a smaller impact in both scenarios, with changes ranging from -0.01% to 0.1% and from-0.02% to 0.22%, respectively. Finally, regarding trade balance, the results will vary under both scenarios. In the first scenario, both nations will benefit in their current account position, but the second scenario shows a negative trade balance, with a broader deficit for Mexico and a trade surplus for China. In both situations, China will achieve minor improvements regarding trade, that range from -0.001% to 0.07%. In the case of Mexico, regarding trade, it will increase slightly from 0.06% to 0.1%.

An important aspect to consider when evaluating a possible FTA between China and Mexico is the overall impact on welfare. Following the methodology used by Siriwardana and Yang, we measure the net welfare gains using the equivalent variation (EV) and real consumption expenditure (RCE). EV is the indicator of the "amount of income that would have to be given or taken away from an economy before trade liberalization to leave the economy as well off as it would be after the policy has been changed" (Brow et al., 2005). In our study, thanks to trade creation, the TPP and the CMFTA show benefits both for Mexico and China in EV under both scenarios. However, in China, the positive effect on the first scenario is much smaller than with the CMFTA. The results are much different regarding RCE; with only the TPP, presumably, RCE will turn harmful for both nations, while the CMFTA will have a minor increase in RCE for both countries.

Table 5.3 Macroeconomic Effects of CMFTA under Two Scenarios

	Real GDP (%)	Export volume (%)	Import volume (%)	Terms of trade (%)	Trade balance (million USD)	Equivalent variation (EV) (million USD)	Real consumption expenditure (%)
Scenario 1: TPP							
China	0.00	-0.01	-0.02	-0.00	30.05	32.55	0.01
Mexico	0.04	0.32	0.47	0.06	-201.52	709.13	0.10
U.S.A	0.00	-0.02	-0.14	-0.06	2,125.58	-1,504.20	-0.05
Canada	0.03	0.11	0.42	0.22	-434.28	1,542.14	0.21
TPP	0.02	0.01	0.19	0.05	-2,416.28	2,648.54	0.11
China Hongkong and China Taiwan	0.00	-0.01	-0.01	0.00	19.87	5.60	-0.00
The rest of Latin America	0.00	0.01	-0.04	-0.02	247.17	-191.53	-0.04
EU28	0	0.00	-0.00	0.00	439.31	244.66	-0.01
The rest of world	0.00	0.01	-0.02	-0.02	190.10	-1,128.43	-0.03
Scenario 2: TPP & CMFTA							
China	0.01	0.10	0.22	0.07	-502.45	2,020.93	0.09
Mexico	0.12	0.77	1.30	0.10	-1,129.09	1,738.52	0.26
U.S.A	-0.00	-0.06	-0.27	-0.11	3,774.67	-2,960.59	-0.11
Canada	0.03	0.10	0.43	0.23	-461.79	1,582.96	0.20
TPP	0.02	0.01	0.17	0.04	-2,405.09	2,541.71	0.10
China Hongkong and China Taiwan	0.00	-0.01	-0.02	-0.00	16.36	-3.58	-0.01
The rest of Latin America	-0.00	0.00	-0.06	-0.03	248.90	-227.72	-0.05
EU28	0.00	-0.00	-0.01	0.00	367.36	70.08	-0.01
The rest of world	-0.00	0.00	-0.03	-0.02	91.11	-1,138.79	-0.03

Source: GTAP model simulation results.

Table 5.4 provides details about the decomposition of EV under both scenarios. The results show significant variations for both countries, according to the considered scheme. Mexico will obtain essential gains due to the allocative efficiency effect and change regarding trade; on the other hand, change in capital stock will affect negatively; nevertheless, the total remains positive. In the second scenario, Mexico will obtain even higher gains from the allocative efficiency effect and change regarding trade; moreover, even if the change in capital stock is small, it is favorable as well, resulting in a higher EV than in the first scenario. The outcome, as in the previous case, will be positive for the Latin American country, although in this last case, the increase will be more than double. The effects on China will not be that different: without the CMFTA, allocative efficiency effect and change regarding trade will be negative; however, the final variation of EV will be modest but on the positive side. If the CMFTA adds to the TPP, allocative efficiency effect, change regarding trade and change in capital stock will be positive, resulting in a remarkable increase in EV.

Table 5.4 Decomposition of Estimated Equivalent Variation on China/Mexico under Various Scenarios (million USD)

	Allocative efficiency effect	Change regarding trade	Change in capital stock	Total
China				
Scenario 1: TPP	-49.76	-25.15	107.46	32.55
Scenario 2: TPP & CMFTA	612.75	1,314.62	93.57	2,020.93
Mexico				
Scenario 1: TPP	502.55	208.21	-1.63	709.13
Scenario 2: TPP & CMFTA	1,391.71	329.26	17.56	1,738.52

Source: GTAP model simulation results.

2.3 Sectoral Effects

Our study gives proper importance to the sectoral implications of the TPP and the CMFTA, to account for their impact on the selected economic activities. As shown in Table 5.5, the effects of both trade agreements will vary widely across the different sectors. In Mexico, Transport, Processed Food, and Primary Agricultural Products show the most considerable improvement in the trade balance. In fact, Processed Food shows a more robust advance on both scenarios. Other Manufacturing and Other Services show negative results both with the TPP and the CMFTA. In China, the improvement in the Other Manufacturing sector is significant, followed by Electrical Equipment, Wood, Paper and Chemical, Metals, Textile, and Wearing Apparel will receive a negative impact just with the TPP. Primary Agricultural Products, Processed Food, and Transport also show adverse consequences in all scenarios, while Mineral resources, is only positive in the first scenario.

Table 5.5 Estimated Change in China/Mexico Trade Balance by Sector under Two Scenarios (million USD)

Scenario	*Scenario 1: TPP*	*Scenario 2: TPP & CMF*
China		
Primary Agricultural Products	-55.13	-227.12
Processed Food	-104.64	-698.34
Mineral Resources	6.66	-45.40
Metals	-96.45	557.43
Textile and Wearing Apparel	-152.86	293.81
Wood, Paper and Chemical	73.62	216.10
Electrical Equipment	82.14	506.42
Transport	-13.81	-483.12
Other Manufactured Products	163.05	-268.71
Other Services	127.46	-353.52
Mexico		
Primary Agricultural Products	22.42	48.12
Processed Food	717.42	672.58
Mineral Resources	-180.75	-205.68
Metals	50.81	-244.58
Textile and Wearing Apparel	-278.47	-463.86
Wood, Paper and Chemical	-186.88	-432.44
Electrical Equipment	-104.96	-388.53
Transport	72.25	843.58
Other Manufactured Products	-227.41	-680.68
Other Services	-85.96	-277.61

Source: GTAP model simulation results.

Table 5.6 shows the percentage changes in output under both scenarios. For both countries, the outcome is majorly adverse across the different categories. In Mexico, Transport is the most benefited sector, especially under the second scenario. Processed Food shows an even more significant effect on the first scenario; however, the effects are lower in the second scenario. Primary Agricultural Products shows adverse effects both with the TPP and the CMFTA, which is the opposite case for Other Services. In China, Primary Agricultural Products and Processed Foods show negative results in both scenarios. Wood, Paper and Chemical, Electric Equipment and Other Services show benefits in both scenarios.

Table 5.6 Estimated change (%) in output by sector in China and Mexico under two scenarios

Scenario	*Scenario 1: TPP*	*Scenario 2: TPP & CMFTA*
China		
Primary Agricultural Products	-0.01	-0.02
Processed Food	-0.03	-0.09
Mineral Resources	0.00	-0.01
Metals	-0.01	0.06
Textile and Wearing Apparel	-0.01	0.02
Wood, Paper and Chemical	0.01	0.00
Electrical Equipment	0.02	0.05
Transport	0.00	-0.10
Other Manufactured Products	0.01	-0.02
Other Services	0.00	0.01
Mexico		
Primary Agricultural Products	-0.06	-0.19
Processed Food	0.44	0.25
Mineral Resources	-1.03	-1.17
Metals	0.04	-0.43
Textile and Wearing Apparel	-0.42	-0.87
Wood, Paper and Chemical	-0.23	-0.62

(Contd.)

Scenario	*Scenario 1: TPP*	*Scenario 2: TPP & CMFTA*
Electrical Equipment	-0.31	-1.14
Transport	0.16	1.12
Other Manufactured Products	-0.11	-0.27
Other Services	0.03	0.10

Source: GTAP model simulation results.

2.4 Effects on Trade Patterns

Table 5.7 presents the effects on trade flows of the CMFTA. Under the first scenario, China will diminish its exports by US$-462.32 million, with an export reduction to all countries or regions, except for Hong Kong-Taiwan and the TPP. Under the second scenario, the situation reverts in aggregate terms, with an increase of exports of US$ 2,837.46 million. In this second scenario, the only gain is in Mexico, but it is of such a high magnitude that it will cancel out all the adverse effects of the TPP plus the CMFTA with all other countries and regions.

Table 5.7 Effects on trade flows of CMFTA (US$ million)

	Scenario 1: TPP	*Scenario 2: TPP & CMFTA*
China's exports to		
MEX	-309.00	9,747.06
USA	-12.88	-1,861.19
CAN	-33.71	-180.47
TPP	17.97	-992.41
Hong_Tai	39.95	-196.73
Rest of LatinA	-56.22	-366.16
EU_28	-49.50	-1,524.72
Rest of World	-58.94	-1,787.94
Total	-462.32	2,837.46
China's imports from		
MEX	-129.90	2042.3
USA	199.89	550.88

(Contd.)

	Scenario 1: TPP	*Scenario 2: TPP & CMFTA*
CAN	-442.68	-404.35
TPP	-568.13	-225.22
Hong_Tai	15.66	243.83
Rest of LatinA	-39.03	89.89
EU_28	94.39	25.69
Rest of World	450.81	1,098.13
Total	-418.99	3,421.14
Mexico's exports to	-129.90	9,747.06
CHN	-92.60	1,941.36
USA	-965.84	-1,000.81
CAN	-8.29	-115.47
TPP	2,660.55	2,572.07
Hong_Tai	-3.01	-3.34
Rest of LatinA	-64.90	-121.15
EU_28	-156.37	-219.55
Rest of World	-92.90	-139.41
Total	1,276.64	2,913.70
Mexico's imports from	-309.00	9,747.06
CHN	-323.47	10,363.82
USA	-2,103.92	-7,872.86
CAN	133.77	38.88
TPP	4,652.17	3,940.25
Hong_Tai	-49.23	-252.05
Rest of LatinA	-180.55	-353.22
EU_28	-395.63	-1,362.00
Rest of World	-253.45	-763.21
Total	1,479.69	3,739.61

Source: GTAP model simulation results.

When looking at China's imports under the TPP, the effects are detrimental for Mexico, U.S., Canada, TPP, Hong Kong-Taiwan and the rest of Latin America, with an aggregate adverse effect of US$ 419 million. However, the numbers are favorable for the U.S., Hong Kong-Taiwan, the European Union (with 28 countries) and Rest of the World. With the addition of the CMFTA, the picture changes drastically, and it turns positive on the aggregate, with US$ 3,421.14 million. In this second scenario, Canada and TPP will receive a negative impact, while the U.S., Hong Kong-Taiwan, Rest of Latin America and the European Union (with 28 members), will show a positive effect on Chinese imports. Mexico will be the most significant single beneficiary, with gains even more prominent than those for the rest of the world.

3. Is There a Way Out from the Middle-income Trap?

The results from the previous analysis favor an increase in bilateral trade between China and Mexico. There is a word of caveat, though, since we work with simulations of a model that incorporates some assumptions, such as perfect competition. In the following sections, we present a summary of the results, and we approach, as well, our fundamental question: is a China-Mexico FTA sufficient to raise significantly the possibility of either one of the two countries to escape from the MIT?

3.1 What GTAP Says

As shown by the GTAP analysis, the CMFTA may undoubtedly bring changes to China, Mexico and global trade. Regarding real GDP growth, the treaty will benefit both countries, with little impact on all other regions. Mexico will increase its real GDP under both scenarios, while China will equilibrate the negative consequences caused by the TPP. From the Mexican side, the agreement will add other benefits, beyond those of signing only the TPP, with higher trade performance. Both nations will benefit from changes in the trade balance, especially in their current account, although the terms of trade will bring a deterioration for both countries. The TPP and the CMFTA show positive results both for Mexico and China as a result of trade creation. However, the CMFTA magnifies the benefits. The effects of both trade agreements will vary widely across the different sectors, although the outcome is majorly adverse across the different categories for both countries.

For the majority of the economic sectors selected, there is a visible increase in the use of land, labor and capital; undoubtedly, both the TPP and the CMFTA will bring changes in all considered sectors. The monetary figures associated to the TPP show that China will diminish its exports by more than 400 million dollars, while the addition of the CMFTA will reverse the scenario to a gain of more than two billion dollars. What is noteworthy in this case, is the dramatic increase in exports to Mexico, which will offset the loss of exports to all other countries of the world, including the U.S. and other leading economies. The TPP will bring a detrimental effect to Chinese imports with an aggregate adverse effect of approximately 400 million dollars. If the CMFTA comes into effect, the numbers turn positive up to more than 3 billion dollars. Mexico could benefit the most by deviating exports to China from other countries, including leading economies.

The FTA may not necessarily be a full-scale treaty, but a workable agreement that could bring short-term benefits to enterprises in both countries. The proposal could also exclude those sectors more vulnerable to open trade between both countries while opening opportunities for direct investment. In this regard, it is important to point out the changing position of China as a net foreign investor since 2014. An evaluation of the top 10 sectors (Computer and Electronics, Utility and Energy, Automobile, Real Estate, Transportation, Oil and Gas, Mining, Healthcare and Leisure and Recreation) for global Chinese outbound investment in 2015 (KPMG, 2015) shows the potential for mutually beneficial projects in Mexico. This country, in fact, will welcome with open arms direct investments in any of those sectors.

3.2 Good Enough to Escape From the Trap?

The MIT is no novelty to economists. In fact, the concept attracted their attention from the time of its conceptual development in 2006, by Homi Kharas, an economist at the World Bank. In simple terms, the MIT states that some nations in the $ 8,000 to 18,000 per capita income will eventually moderate their rate of economic growth, barely sustaining the population within such range. The description of the phenomena as a trap comes from the idea that those economies overgrow for a period until reaching a point of permanent stability, far away from advanced economies. Therefore, the promise of convergence with the wealthiest countries will never materialize. The explanation comes from rising wages, and higher costs brought about by their moderate prosperity acquired before falling into the trap. Higher wages, coupled with little innovation and technological improvements, lead to lack of competitiveness in international markets. Once those nations fall into the trap, their export products become overpriced, with little value added. Whereas falling into the trap is relatively easy for many developing countries, the escape requires extraordinary measures and a clear strategy. In fact, avoiding the MIT means identifying strategies for introducing new processes and finding new markets to maintain export growth and boost domestic demand. After all, an increase in the purchasing power of the middle class may result in a quantitative and qualitative effect on the economy, either through the rise in total consumption or through the innovation processes that new demand for higher quality products may foster in the market. Naturally, such a leap will need massive resources allocated to infrastructure and education, building a high-quality education system that encourages creativity and supports innovations in science and technology.

Mexico and China are recently reaching middle-income status. Japan and South Korea are among the very few countries escaping from the MIT since most nations cataloged within that group have not entirely escaped the middle-income ground. Under a new conceptual revision, the MIT is evolving into the convergence trap, a concept "based on (i) unfavorable demographics, (ii) low level of economic diversification, (iii) inefficient financial market, (iv) insufficiently advanced infrastructure, (v) low level of innovation, (vi) weak institutions and (vii) inefficient labor market" (Pruchnik & Zowczak, 2017). Unfortunately, Mexico, as well as most Latin American economies, meets the requirements for remaining within the MIT. The only exception in the region is the first factor, since those countries enjoy a most favorable demographic situation, with a median population age well below OECD or even China. The Asian country, though, is in a much different situation, even with the capabilities to leave the MIT and guide Latin America. China, in fact, is presently moving from manufacturing to a service economy. In the process, is creating opportunities for companies in different countries in the Latin American region, for sustained growth, not based on commodity exports (Lin & Treichel, 2012). Therefore, China and Mexico should explore different mechanisms that will lead to their consolidation and growth of their economies.

There are different tools available to governments that will attempt to leave the MIT. In the case of Mexico, those are probably limited, although once considered in the aggregate, may gain more solid ground. Some areas where the country could use significant improvements are education, R & D, and infrastructure, especially if the private sector overtakes public projects.

4. Conclusions

The TPP may bring new dynamism to the Pacific Rim and create opportunities for growth, even without the U.S. Moreover, the agreement is extending beyond business opportunities. As previously stated, different countries in Asia are expecting to counterbalance the growing power of China in the region. Regarding China's interest, the TPP raises many doubts. On the one hand, there are many indications that such partnership, if approved, may have adverse consequences to exports, coupled with restrictions on its geo-economic projects. There is a possibility for trade diversion, as well; for instance, it is arguable that the TPP member countries could substitute the high-value Chinese exports to the Mexican market (Mendoza, 2016). On the positive side, China might benefit by joining the partnership.

The proposal of including China into a renovated TPP is appealing in its audacity and potential benefits to all interested parties, but it is nearly impossible to make it a reality, due to the political opposition that such a project will immediately generate. Therefore, we centered our analysis in a much more straightforward scenario, a possible bilateral treaty between China and Mexico, contained and limited to trade and commerce. Even if this situation is of lesser importance as compared to the inclusion of China into a renovated TPP, its impact should be revised in full detail, quantifying effects at national and sectoral level. Some advocate for China to "actively push its own FTAs," while cautiously considering joining the TPP (Song and Wen, 2012). In the end, the game may be much more complicated than it appears. A FTA between China and Mexico is by no means comparable to those initiatives, but it may also be the first step towards a more robust position of China in the Pacific Rim. Mexico is not equally motivated but surely will look positively at FDI, no matter from how far away the money is coming. China, on the other hand, may have to look beyond the economic benefits from the CMFTA and looks at gains in its geopolitical strategy. As shown through GTAP the possibility of enhancing the trade relation between China and Mexico may yield positive results for both sides. The results are not well balanced, though, since the Latin Americans nation will ripe most of the economic benefits, while the Asian nations' will see little impact on its trade results. Still, China may gain by placing a foot on the Americas.

Whether by signing an FTA either one of the nations will improve the odds for leaving the MIT, that might not be the case. The difference in the size of the economies leaves little room for changing the position of China in global trade and, except a few industries, with no significant improvement to welfare. Mexico does not have all the conditions to transform the benefits from the FTA into significant advances in its economy and population. Still, incremental trade may foster innovation and more suitable products for global markets, mainly when sustained over technological improvements. E-commerce, for instance, is paving the road for a digital extension of the Belt and Road Initiative throughout the region, bridging markets on both sides of the Pacific Rim (Nan, 2017). Furthermore, the growing presence of China in Latin America may eventually become the long-awaited game changer for those economies. After all, many decades of American leadership in the region have not been sufficient to bring Latin American nations into sustained prosperity. Within the regional framework, getting stuck in the MIT may not sound so poorly, at least in comparative terms to the neighbors.

Chapter 6
The Multimexicans in China

Mauricio Cervantes Zepeda
Andreas M. Hartmann

The history of multinational companies (MNEs) dates back to the colonial era (Wilkins, 2009) but really took up speed after the Second World War, when a large number of American, European and later Japanese companies endeavored to reach many countries in both rich and poor regions of the world. The international companies have been one of the central themes of research by International Business (IB) scholars, who have studied these companies explaining the reasons, advantages and strategies that have facilitated their success in most parts of the world.

Over the last decades, however, globalization has led to fundamental changes in international business and MNEs from the emerging economies have entered the arena, with some of them reaching world leadership positions. Among the leading MNEs from emerging economies, we just mention a few: baking company Bimbo and cement producer Cement from Mexico, banking corporation ICBC and e-commerce platform Alibaba from China, Brazilian protein producer JBS from Brazil, furniture board producer MASISA from Chile, among many others.

This chapter deals with the expansion of MNEs from an emerging economy to another country that is very distant, both physically and culturally, namely the activities of Mexican MNEs (multimexicans) in China. Our goal is to contrast both traditional and newer theories of the MNE to the reality of the firms in our sample. We will show that these theoretical approaches are only partially helpful for understanding real-world situations, which include a host of specific factors.

1. Models of Internationalization of the MNE

1.1 Traditional Models

The theory of the MNE was developed almost fifty years ago analyzing mainly U.S., European, and Japanese firms (Cantwell, 2009; Hennart, 2009). Dunning (1977) developed the Ownership, Location, and Internalization (OLI) model, which explains the existence of a multinational, as the result of the combination of three advantages: OLI. Kogut and Zander (1992) argue that knowledge is the key factor of internationalization because it enables the firm to obtain and manage all the other resources and capabilities. Another model is the FSA-CSA framework proposed by Rugman and Verbeke (1992). They discussed the existence of a multinational as the result of the combination of two types of advantages: firm specific advantages (FSAs), and country specific advantages (CSAs). One contribution of this model is to highlight the fact that some of the MNE's advantages are tied to a place and not transferable across countries. In contrast, other advantages are not location bound and support the ability of a company to become a multinational by transferring them across borders.

In a different avenue, from international marketing, other authors (Cavusgil, 1980; Czinkota, 1982) developed the Innovation Related Model referring to the idea of serving foreign markets as a way to achieve innovation or develop the innovation capabilities of the firm. They argue that once managers gain enough experience in serving domestic markets, they focus on foreign markets, transforming the firm to an active exporter. (For a more in-depth explanation of these models, see Cuervo-Cazurra and Ramos (2004).

Cuervo-Cazurra and Montoya (2018) explained that these traditional models are built on underlying assumptions derived from the study of MNEs from advanced economies. The models tend to implicitly assume that the home country is advanced and thus firms can develop the most innovative products and services to cater to the home market and later find other countries in which they can be sold most profitably. Thus, most of these models have not paid much attention to how the country of origin affects the behavior of companies, given that country of origin did not appear to influence the internationalization of companies or at most, it was a supportive influence.

1.2 New Models of the Multinational: Emerging Market Multinationals

Previous models expect emerging countries to be receptors of products, innovations and FDI by MNEs from developed countries. Following this logic and due to lower level of development, emerging countries should not be able to support internationally competitive firms. However, among the Forbes Global 2000, which lists the largest firms as a combination of revenue, profits, assets and market value, by 2016 we had 480 firms from emerging markets (*Forbes*, 2016).

Several authors have focused on this phenomenon (Aulakh, 2007; Cuervo-Cazurra, 2012; Cuervo-Cazurra & Ramamurti, 2014). Rugman (2010) suggests that these firms are internationalizing merely based on the comparative advantage of their home countries and economies of scale but lack home country sophisticated resources and capabilities that would support their competitive advantage. Additionally, he proposes that existing models of IB can explain emerging market multinational. However, other authors propose that new models or at least new versions of old models are needed because these companies are quite different (Guillén and Garcia-Canal, 2009; Ramamurti, 2012).

Cuervo-Cazurra and Montoya (2018) propose that there exist at the moment four main models of emerging market multinationals: the (Linkage, Leverage, and Learning) (LLL) model, the springboard model, the "new" model of the multinational, and the non-sequential internationalization model. The LLL model (Mathews, 2006) propose that emerging market multinationals internationalize due to a set of drivers different from those presented in the OLI model. Thus, they establish "linkages" to other companies to acquire advantages externally, have an outward orientation, and focus part of their foreign expansion on the access to strategic assets. Second, they "leverage" their connections with partners to obtain resource by using networks strategically. Finally, they "learn" and build their advantages via repetition and continuous improvement.

The second model for the internationalization of emerging market firms is the springboard model (Luo and Tung, 2007). These companies carry out aggressive, risk-taking acquisitions of critical assets of firms in advanced economies to compensate for their competitive weaknesses. They invest abroad to obtain strategic assets needed to compete more effectively against multinationals from advanced economies, and avoid home country institutional and market deficiencies.

A third model is so-called new model of the multinational (Guillén and Garcia-Canal, 2009), which is grounded in the fact that emerging market multinationals are internationalizing more quickly and widely than multinationals from advanced countries, despite limitations in their competitive advantage. They achieve this impressive international growth by using strong organizational and political capabilities as well as alliances and acquisitions.

Finally, there is the non-sequential internationalization model (Cuervo-Cazurra, 2011), which suggests that emerging market multinationals do not have to follow an incremental internationalization process in which they select countries that are similar to the home country first and countries that are more distant later, as advanced economy firms did. Instead, such firms have two paths to choose from. They can either enter countries that resemble their own home countries, such as other emerging countries, in which they can apply their knowledge more easily even if the size of the market is not very large. Or they can enter countries that provide better market opportunities, such as advanced countries, even if it is more difficult to use existing knowledge from home country operations.

One commonality in MNEs from emerging markets is that the relative underdevelopment of the home country affects the firms' development of resources and capabilities and subsequent internationalization. Their starting point is thus a set of less developed technological and managerial capabilities. Other handicaps include underdeveloped legal and intellectual property rights, a bad reputation of the home country in international markets of the home country, higher costs of capital, among others.

2. Minicases of Multimexicans

The majority of studies about MNEs from emerging countries has been devoted to analyzing firms from China, Russia, India and Brazil, maybe because of the popularity of the BRIC concept. However, among the world's 2000 biggest public companies in 2017, Mexico's number (15) almost matched Brazil's (20) (*Forbes*, 2017). A pioneering work on multimexicans is the book edited by Cuervo-Cazurra and Montoya (2018). They analyze the internationalization of multimexicans as a laboratory for identifying novel ways in which firms from smaller and mid-sized emerging countries raised their competitiveness to international levels and expanded globally. The majority of the multimexicans focus mainly on Latin America or the U.S. (specifically the large Hispanic market within U.S.) following the logic of the Uppsala model (Johanson & Vahlne, 1977), according to which firms' internationalization path is determined by high familiarity and low risk. Only a few of the multimexicans have ventured into China. These are cases of MNEs expanding from one emerging economy to another, although the high physical and cultural distance between them implies very special challenges. We pay special attention to how the context of operation of the firm affects these processes to present a comprehensive understanding of the issues that these firms faced when entering China.

China in the last decades has been the country that has received more FDI than any other nation. The size of its market and its growth rate has made it a mandatory target for the MNEs. The majority of *Fortune* 500 companies are already present in China. In addition to its huge market, China has made impressive progress in its infrastructure (ports, roads, airports, etc.), the quality of its workforce, and its world-class universities, which have been rapidly climbing in the worldwide rankings (3 in the top 50 of QS 2016), and its industrial and science parks. All these factors together have made China an ideal economic platform for many countries. In addition, the recent initiative of the Chinese president Xi Jiping of the Belt and Road (B & R), to be completed in the coming years, will give companies located in China the ideal platform to attack markets in the Middle East, Southeast Asia and Eastern Europe.

Despite the tremendous advantages that China offers, we must not forget the enormous difficulties from a Mexican point of view: First, the great physical distance requiring 14 hours of flight or 3 weeks by ship. Until 2006, there were no direct flights between Mexico and China (currently there are only three per week). Furthermore, the big differences in language and culture. In Mexico, a task that looks very difficult is said to be "in Chinese". However, a group of multimexicans has ventured into China and some have declared the country to be their platform for Asia.

We will analyze four companies in different industries to have a greater variety in the analysis: Bimbo (food, bakery), Softtek (services, IT), Nemak (aluminum vehicle components), and Interceramic (ceramic tiles).

Most of these companies thoroughly studied the Chinese market before going there; some went through acquisitions and learning from the market to incorporate new practices into the company. Others replicated their business model with minimal adaptation to maintain a homogenous corporate culture.

The main difficulties they faced and how they managed to overcome them are discussed in the remainder of this chapter. These multimexicans provide us examples of entrepreneurship, innovation and aggressive strategic moves. They also leave us lessons that can be applied by other multimexicans or even by small and medium enterprises.

2.1 Bimbo (Bakery)

Grupo Bimbo was founded in 1945 by Lorenzo Servitje, Jaime Jorba, Jose Mata, Jaime Sendra and Alfonso Velasco. Bimbo is the largest bakery company in the world with sales of USD $13,506 million and 130,913 employees worldwide in 2016. Grupo Bimbo produces, distributes and markets thousands of products, including a variety of fresh and frozen box bread, buns, cookies, pastries, English muffins, bagels, packaged products, tortillas, salted snacks and confectionery, among others. The company is active in 22 countries in America, Europe and Asia, operating 171 plants and distributing to 2.7 million points of sale. Since 1980, its shares have been listed on the Mexican Stock Exchange, and in the United States through ADRs.

Grupo Bimbo has made significant investments through the establishment of production plants, strategic partnerships and acquisitions of other baking companies in many countries, such as Pan Rico in Beijing, China, Pan Europa in Guatemala, Los Sorchantes in Uruguay, Lagos del Sur in Chile, Pastelerías El Globo and La Corona in Mexico, Lalo in Colombia, George Weston, and Sara Lee in the United States, Plus Vita in Brazil, among others.

These impressive achievements are due to the work culture, efficiency and productivity of the company, which has always focused on running its own distribution systems. Bimbo executives do not spend much time on strategy, focusing on increasing the efficiency of production and logistics. They seek the best practices throughout the world to incorporate them and increase productivity, says Daniel Servitje, Chairman of the Board and CEO of Bimbo (Guillén and Garcia-Canal, 2013).

The entry of Bimbo into the Asian market was cautious and required only a modest investment. Several market studies and focus groups with Chinese living in Mexico were conducted to understand the Chinese palate (Siegel, 2009). Bernardo Zermeño, Business Manager, points out that market research was an important factor in knowing what types of products could be regionalized (Suárez Ramírez, 2016). However, despite these studies, some products failed. This is the case of the famous Gansito (small cake with creamy filling and strawberry covered with chocolate). Gansito is the emblematic product of Bimbo and its top seller in many countries, but in China, it had to be withdrawn soon, since the Chinese public prefers stronger flavors. Hence, instead of conquering the market with its typical product, Bimbo had to innovate, looking for new ones like the meatloaf, the corn sandwich, a bread with pickled cucumbers and a muffin filled with sweet beans, which most Mexicans would find unacceptable (Kruger, 2014).

Bimbo decided to enter the Chinese market following the path of the acquisition of facilities and brands already known by the Chinese market. In March 2006, Grupo Bimbo bought the Beijing subsidiary of the Spanish company Panrico for 11.7 million dollars. Panrico had been operating in China since 1997, having at that time 775 workers, a plant on the outskirts of Beijing and distribution networks near Beijing and Tianjin. In this way, Bimbo acquired not only its product portfolio but also specific knowledge of this market. The operations consisted of a headquarters building, a manufacturing plant, five sales offices in Beijing and one sales office in Tianjin. In 2005, the Chinese company had sales of $11.1 million with an operating loss of $0.8 million (Siegel, 2009). Initially Bimbo expected higher growth rates than those they had in Latin America, said Jorge Zárate (Agencias en Beijing, 2006), CEO of Bimbo in Asia at the time. However, growth has not been as expected; the challenges have been many. The food taste is different, language is an important barrier, and so are ethical practices.

In 2007, Bimbo Beijing was officially established and launched with the well-known teddy bear logo. In 2009, to overcome the cultural differences in taste, Bimbo acquired the local brand Baiwanzhuangyuan, and later in 2010, Jinhongwei.

China's economic growth has generated cultural and nutritional changes. This has favored the spread of international food chains in the country. For instance, KFC opened 600 new restaurants across cities in China in 2016. Meanwhile, McDonald's aims to roll out 1,000 new outlets over five years. Starbucks is expecting that China will surpass the United States in terms of market size for the fast-coffee chain, and plans to double the number of its 2,300 outlets in China by 2021 (Ng, 2017). This taste for the West also has benefited the bakery business by opening a world of possibilities, as traditionally the Chinese did not consume bakery products.

The cultural differences and the adaptation to the Chinese palate have been a big challenge for Bimbo. For overcoming this situation, Bimbo Beijing has followed a process that they have called "Deep Consumer Understanding". The consumer has the last word, says César Cruz, director of operations at Bimbo Beijing (Zhang, 2011). In this way, the company has been adapting or creating new products. In a few years, Bimbo has launched more than one hundred varieties of products in the Chinese market. Its philosophy of adapting to the market has allowed double-digit growth rates every year.

On the other hand, China is the market that offers Bimbo the greatest learning opportunities, not only in terms of consumer habits, but also in terms of policy and regulations. Year after year, the challenges are changing. Currently Bimbo does not separately report the results of China, as they are included within Mexico financial statements. However, in 2016, they report 1,541 employees in China, which represents 1.2% of its 130,913 employees worldwide. "We cannot say that we are leaders in the Chinese market, but it is our great goal. China is too big and there is a lot of competition. We lack a lot, but we believe that we can become a national coverage brand. The Chinese consumer is very sensitive about the level of nutrition and food safety," adds Cruz.

Furthermore, Bimbo innovates in the retail distribution. Panrico did not sell in small or neighborhood stores since these are located in narrow and intricate streets. To solve this problem, Bimbo innovated using bicycle for delivery. In 2010, Bimbo attended more than 30,000 small stores with a fleet of 38 bicycles. However, the challenge has been difficult. Entry into the Chinese market has cost Bimbo triple the time it took in other countries. In China, distribution networks are more local than national. The infrastructure at the national level is still insufficient (Anderson, 2010).

"Without a doubt, the incursion into China was a great challenge. Among the key aspects are our long-term vision and openness to change. We are firm in remaining true to our values and philosophy, as well as flexible in adapting to a new culture from which we are constantly learning. Leadership and local talent have been essential for our development in that country, the mixture and interaction of the two cultures is a mutual learning that allows us to understand the market and speed up the resolution of problems," according to Daniel Servitje, CEO of Grupo Bimbo. In addition, Servitje stated that in terms of processes and methodology, Bimbo has followed the same scheme as in other locations, (such as IT, ERP, reports, key processes of methodology in the commercial, operational and administrative areas) but adapting and respecting the regulations and local laws (Latin Trade, 2014).

The plan is to keep growing in China, but there is still a long way to go as well as a recognition of the country's enormous potential. In April 2017, Bimbo announced its intention to expand its operations in China and venture into at least one other country in Asia and the Middle East (Milenio, 2017).

Bimbo in China works with a team of Mexican executives and Chinese employees, which help to adapt to the different market conditions. Bimbo maintains many of its global administrative, operation and control systems, but is making a great effort to adapt to cultural differences. Its main challenge is learning how to be a small competitor with around 2% of the market working in a small portion of China, whereas in Mexico and other Latin American countries, Bimbo is dominating the market or forms part of an oligopoly with large market shares and nationwide distribution systems.

2.2 Softtek (IT Services)

Softtek was founded in Monterrey, Mexico, in 1982 by a group of five former employees of Alfa Group. Blanca Treviño was appointed CEO in 2000 and has been holding this position ever since. The company has had rapid growth since its inception; by the year 1988, it already had 100 employees. In 1994, it became an international company by opening its first office in Brazil. Currently, Softtek is a global provider of services oriented towards IT processes with 12,000 employees in 30 offices in North America, Latin America, Europe and Asia. The company operates 15 Global Development Centers in the USA, Mexico, China, Brazil, Argentina, Costa Rica, Spain, Hungary and India. Softtek serves large companies in more than 20 countries. Through on-site, on-shore delivery service models and its Global Nearshore model, Softtek helps CIOs to increase alignment with their businesses (Softtek, 2017).

Softtek is a private firm that does not disclose financial or market information. However, Expansion magazine estimates the firm's sales in 2013 to be approximately \$505 million dollars (CNN Expansion, 2015a). This places Softtek as the 247th largest company in Mexico. Furthermore, according to the CNN Expansion ranking (2015b), Softtek is the second most internationally spread-out firm in the field of IT services based in Mexico and it is number 15 out of the top 100 global companies in Mexico. Throughout its 33 years of life, Softtek has been a preferred services provider for several Fortune 500 companies, and has been recognized by various organizations and industry analysts as one of the most important IT companies in Mexico and the world.

Softtek is playing an increasing role as a large organization that moves to a more diversified multi-sourcing model, and the company has seen a 35 percent annual growth rate during the past years, according to Beni Lopez, CEO of Softtek U.S. division. Softtek has operations and GDCs in Mexico, Brazil, the U.S., Argentina, Spain, China and India. Despite rising costs in India, Latin America still does not have a wage cost advantage over India or China. Latin America's primary advantage is geography: It lies in the same time zones as North America, making collaboration and communication with support staff easier, labeled as "nearshoring" advantage. Softtek's China operation may support projects in other countries. "There will always be work that can't be offshored easily and China wants more software," says Lopez (Mitchell, 2007).

One of the key advantages of Softtek's model is its operation management. Rather than a rigid pyramidal structure, with the CEO at the top making all the decisions, Softtek works like an umbrella of divisions. Softtek is a network of independent working units. This provides the flexibility of fast entry into new markets, new services, or new products. According to Romero, there was no strategy summit of the company on how they would go global. Softtek encourages its employee's initiatives and many projects flowed up from the bottom to the top of the company.

Softtek began attending U.S.-based MNEs in Mexico, but its first international office was opened in Brazil, at the initiative of one of its employees. At the beginning, Softtek sent Mexican employees to serve Brazilian companies and subsequently hired Brazilian employees. The entry into the Chinese market followed a similar path; it was the initiative of one of its partners. However, the foundation of the offices and GDCs in Spain and Argentina followed a different path: One of the important clients of Softtek opened facilities there and asked Softtek to support them on-site.

In August 2006, following the initiative of one of its partners to enter the Chinese market, Softtek acquired China's IT United, which in 2008 became Softtek Asia Company. This GDC has a cutting-edge access control and telecommunications infrastructure, including biometric identification devices, on-site 24/7 surveillance, triple redundant internet connections and isolated network segments per customer. In 2008, Softtek Asia operated in Beijing, Shanghai, Xiamen and Xi'an (Softtek, 2007c). "Since the union of these two teams (IT United and Softtek), we continue receiving great enthusiasm from our clients," says Cyrill Eltschinger, founder of IT United, who now serves as executive vice president of Softtek Asia and CEO of Softtek China (Softtek, 2008a).

In 2009, Softtek opened a second GDC in China, located in Wuxi, Jiangsu. Equipped with state-of-the-art access, computing and telecommunications control systems, this new center is designed to meet the needs of the company's global customers. It has the highest standards of security, telecommunications and process maturity. Softtek selected Wuxi not only for the high quality of its facilities, but also for its proximity to higher education centers, thus providing access to a large talent base (Softtek, 2009).

In 2013, the Softtek offices in Beijing transformed into an "Enterprise Mobility-specific Center of Excellence" dedicated to meeting the growing need for enterprise mobility solutions in Asia; from here, the company offers business solutions and interactive marketing for the Asian market on the major mobile platforms, including iOS and Android. According to the research study "Our Mobile Planet" (Our Mobile Planet, 2013) sponsored by Google, Asian countries are leaders in terms of market penetration and the use of smartphones. China, moreover, is the smartphone market with the fastest growth in the world (Softtek, 2013). Softtek plans to open facilities in India and keep growing in China to attend this increasingly important part of the world.

Softtek's devotion to its clients, i.e., MNEs that operate around the globe, pushed it to enter the Chinese market, initially through an acquisition and later through an additional greenfield investment. After the acquisition, Softtek maintained the original top management team with experience in the market, and made the founder of IT United, its vice president of Softtek Asia and CEO of Softtek China. Softtek's entry has been successful and smooth due to this factor.

2.3 NEMAK (Aluminum Vehicle Components)

Nemak, S. A. B. de C. V. has its headquarters in García, Nuevo León, Mexico, and acts as a holding company for operations in a total of sixteen countries. Armando Garza is its Chairman and Armando Tamez its CEO (Nemak, 2017).

Nemak started in 1979 as an 80%–20% joint venture between the diversified Monterrey-based conglomerate Grupo Alfa and US-based Ford Motor Co. from Dearborn, Michigan. Over the years, Ford Motor Co. reduced its equity participation to around 5%, while maintaining two seats on Nemak's board of directors (Nemak, 2017). Grupo Alfa, which in 2017 was also active in petrochemicals, refrigerated food, IT and telecommunications, and gas and oil exploration, kept a controlling interest of about 75% of Nemak's shares, while the other 20% were floated on the Mexican stock exchange BMV (Nemak, 2017), where Nemak has been listed independently from its parent company since 2015.

Different from many other Mexican multinationals, Nemak has used its internationalization to leave behind the ethnocentric staffing phase, including five Europeans among its top management team consisting of twelve members (Nemak, 2017). The following paragraphs will describe the company's path of development and its operations in China, which has been the world's largest auto market by number of units sold.

Nemak is the world's No.1 provider of aluminum foundry components for combustion engines, especially cylinder heads (52% or revenues) and engine blocks (34% of revenues) (Nemak, 2017). Additionally, Nemak produces aluminum structural components and transmission parts for the global auto industry. As of 2016, the company employed more than 21,000 people at 36 facilities, in 16 countries, and generated revenues of 4.3 billion USD (Nemak, 2017). The 2017 client list includes most major OEMs in the world, including BAIC, BMW, Fiat and affiliate brands (Alfa Romeo, Chrysler, Ferrari, Maserati), FAW, Ford, GM and affiliate brands (Holden), Hyundai, International Trucks, Isuzu, Iveco, Kia, PSA's Peugeot and Opel brands, Tata Motors' Jaguar and Land Rover brands, Mahindra & Mahindra's SsangYong, Mazda, Nissan, Renault, Toyota, Volkswagen and affiliate brands (Audi, Lamborghini, Porsche, Skoda), and Volvo Cars (Nemak, 2017a).

Because of its connection to Ford Motor Co., Nemak can be considered as an international company since its inception. From 1982 and 1996, Nemak bought in technological expertise from Italian-based Teksid (then owned by Fiat), which in 1988 even took a 20% interest in the Mexican firm that was repurchased in 1997 (Quesada, 2011). By 1990, the Mexican company started investing in its own technology through the creation of a proper R & D department (Valtierra Gallardo, 2013). This technological upgrading process and the accelerating growth of Mexican auto production due to NAFTA set the stage for Nemak's venturing into North America and Europe. For tier-one suppliers in the auto industry, a geographical proximity to client assembly plants is much preferred over import arrangements in order to integrate with JIT production systems. In 2000, Nemak thus acquired two aluminum casting plants from Ford

Motor Co. in Windsor, Canada (one plant was closed down in 2009). In 2005, Nemak acquired German-based Rautenbach-Guss with operations in three European countries. In 2006, Nemak took over its Mexican competitor Castech (partially owned by Norsk Hydro), fortifying its dominant position in its home market. In 2007, Nemak acquired part of the aluminum business of its former technology provider Teksid, including plants in Mexico, the USA, Brazil, China (Located in Nanjing), Poland and Argentina. Also in 2007, Nemak acquired Norsk Hydro's aluminum foundry business with plants Austria, Germany, Hungary, and Sweden (the latter one was closed shortly after). In 2012, Nemak bought US-based J. L. French Automotive Casting, which included three plants in the USA and one in Spain (Zapata and Hartmann, 2018). In 2016, Nemak acquired Turkish-based Cevher Döküm (Automotive World, 2016). Apart from these acquisition movements, Nemak also internationalized through greenfield investments: 2003 in the Czech Republic, 2012 in Chennai, India, 2014 in Chongqing, China, and 2015 in Ulyanovsk, Russia (Zapata and Hartmann, 2018).

Nemak's first and most important plant in China is located in the Jiangning Economic & Technical Development Zone in Nanjing, the capital of Jiangsu province. Originally created in 1997, the plant had been owned by the now defunct company TK Aluminum Ltd., which was in turn owned by Italian-based Teksid S.p.A. The location within China had been chosen close to the assembly plant of Nanjing Fiat Automobile, Inc., which was closed in 2006. In 2007, Nemak acquired parts of Teksid, including its Nanjing plant. It is thus Nemak's first plant in Asia and still its biggest in Asia, producing cylinder heads, bedplates and other high-tech aluminum auto components. The casting technologies applied in this plant are GSPM (gravity semi-permanent mold) and LPDC (low pressure aluminum die casting). The plant covers an area of 55,000 square meters and represents a total investment of USD 100 million. Nemak also established its Asia Product Development Center in Nanjing (Nemak Careers, 2014a).

Nemak's second plant in China was created as a greenfield investment in 2012: The rising city of Chongqing in central China is the location of a 120,000 square meter plant, which represents an investment of 120 million USD. Applying the modern HPDC (high pressure die casting) technology, Nemak Chongqing mainly provides engine blocks and transmission components (Nemak Careers, 2014). Employing around 600 workers (Automotive News China, 2013), its planned production capacity was 1 million units per year, mainly for

Changan Ford (IHS SupplierInsight, 2013), in which Nemak's minority partner holds a 50% participation.

Additionally to its production plants, Nemak established its Asian headquarters in Shanghai in 2011, for coordinating activities in India and China. The offices host regional functions such as purchasing, business development, sales, finance and human resources.

One of Nemak's main success factors has been that car manufacturers have been facing stricter standards which has led to replace iron with aluminum in parts of the engine, transmissions and bodies. Nemak has taken advantage of this trend thanks to its cutting-edge technology and its experience in aluminum smelting. This trend combined with Nemak's global presence allows it to serve its customers in all the countries where they manufacture, making its main success factor (Alfa, 2017).

The main challenge for Nemak in China is demand fluctuation. Tamez, Nemak′s CEO, declared in 2016 that at that point in time, the participation of Nemak in the Chinese market was not relevant, but that the growth potential was huge and that Nemak had to follow the pace of its clients. As Nemak's two Chinese plants reached 100% capacity utilization in 2016, Tamez was even considering opening a third operation (Sánchez, 2016), negotiating possible locations with its clients (Coronado, 2017). Another challenge, according to Tamez, was that the Chinese market was moving toward last generation engines that demand more value added.

Nemak's entry into the Chinese market was part of a packaged acquisition of a former partner and competitor, while the following stage was determined by an invitation by its minority stockholder, who is also a major client. Thus, Nemak's strategy for China is part of its worldwide positioning in the auto industry. As a B2B firm, Nemak's market entry decisions have been a function of its client networks, where local cultural and administrative conditions play a secondary role. Even though the car industry exhibits large fluctuations and uncertainty, and China is among the most competitive markets in this industry, Nemak's business in China has been so successful that the company is planning for a third manufacturing plant.

2.4 Interceramic (Ceramic Tiles)

Interceramic is a manufacturer of ceramic floor and wall tiles headquartered in Chihuahua, Northern Mexico. Interceramic is listed in the Mexican stock exchange and its CEOs have been members of the Almeida family, although in the early 2000s, Mexican billionaire Alfredo Harp Helú acquired a major interest in the company (Ramírez, 2004). Originally a brickworks, Interceramic was incorporated in 1979 and has experienced an impressive growth streak since the 1990s, punctuated only by the two economic crises of 1995 and 2009 (Interceramic, 2005, 2017). In 2016, its sales reached 444 million USD, of which 30% were realized abroad, namely in North and Central America, and in China, and had 4,874 employees worldwide. As of 2016, Interceramic operated three factories in Mexico and one in the USA, while production in China was handled by its JV partner. In 2017, Interceramic's CEO announced plans to double production within the following five years (El Economista, 2017), including a new plant in Guanajuato, central Mexico (Notimex, 2017). A large part of Interceramic's success can be attributed to its own distribution system, which includes over 300 franchised stores in Mexico, as well as outlets in Canada, the USA, Guatemala, Panama and China (Interceramic, 2017).

Mexico's ceramics industry has come under increasing pressure from Chinese imports. In 2014, Interceramic's domestic competitors Lamosa and Vitromex started an anti-dumping initiative for compensatory duties on Chinese imports (Ramírez, 2014), which were imposed in 2016 (Ramírez, 2016). In contrast, Interceramic's strategy has been to use China as a basis for outsourcing from 2002 onwards. Since 2006, Interceramic has operated a representative office in China (Díaz, 2016). In 2005, Interceramic had started working with the Chinese firm Guangdong Kito Ceramics, Ltd. The company was created in 2004 and its CEO is He Qian. It is located in Foshan, in southeast China, a city with a ceramics tradition dating back to the Ming era. In 2016, China was the source of 85% of all products imported by Interceramic, amounting to 5,000 containers worth of merchandise (Díaz, 2016).

In 2010, Interceramic entered into a joint venture agreement with Kito (EFE, 2010) for selling products under the ICC brand. While Interceramic oversees the design activities, Kito carries out the production. Over the first two years, Interceramic invested 10 million USD in its Chinese activities. The JV is targeting China's booming housing market and growing middle class, although ICC "will probably have to do a lot of education to let people in China know that Mexico is good at producing high-quality tiles", as marketing professor Qiaowei Shen stated (Knowledge@Wharton, 2013). With more than 90 ICC stores established by 2016 (Interceramic, 2017), this feat seems to have been accomplished.

Over the next five years, Interceramic is planning to double its sales (García, 2017), which will keep it in the top ten of the sector worldwide, announced the general director Víctor Almeida. In the coming years, they will invest in technology, modernization of existing facilities with the acquisition of new equipment, in which they will invest "several million dollars" in addition to the construction of the first phase of a new plant in the state of Guanajuato. The secret, Almeida said, is because the company focuses on competing globally and not just on being the best at the local level.

3. Discussion and Conclusions

Emerging countries, opposed to what traditional IB theory predicts, have been developing MNEs, and these MNEs not only has migrated to culturally similar countries and physically close ones but also have entered very physically and culturally distant countries like China. This chapter analyzes four multimexicans firms from different industries. Bimbo (bakery), Softtek (IT services), Nemak (aluminum vehicle components), and finally Interceramic (ceramic tiles).

Except the case of Nemak, which was founded as a joint venture by Alfa Group and Ford Motor Company, the other firms were family founded and are still family managed. Softtek remains private. Bimbo, Nemak and Interceramic have become public companies but with a strong percentage of shares belonging to the founders' families.

Table 6.1 Comparison of Multimexicans in China

	BIMBO (bakery)	**SOFTTEK (IT services)**	**NEMAK (aluminum vehicle components)**	**INTERCERAMIC (ceramic tiles)**
HISTORY	Founded by Lorenzo Servitje and others in 1945	Founded by Blanca Treviño and others in 1982	Founded by Alfa Group and Ford Motor Co. in 1979	Founded by the Almeida Family in 1978
TYPE OF OWNERSHIP	Family origins, public since 1980	Private	Public, Alfa 75%, Ford 5%, BMV 20%	Family origins, taken public

(Contd.)

	BIMBO (bakery)	**SOFTTEK (IT services)**	**NEMAK (aluminum vehicle components)**	**INTERCERAMIC (ceramic tiles)**
NUMBER OF COUNTRIES, 2016	22	20	16	6
EMPLOYEES WW., 2016	130,913	12,000	21,000	4,874
SALES WORLDWIDE, millions of USD, 2016	13,506	505	4.3	444
TIME, LOCATION, AND INVESTMENT FOR ENTRY INTO CHINA	2006, Beijing Plant, 11.7 million USD	(1) 2006 Beijing Center (2) 2009 Wuxi GDC	(1) 2007, Nanjing, 100 million USD (2) 2011, Shanghai Headquarters (3) 2012, Chongqing plant, 120 million USD	(1) Repo Shanghai (2) 2010, JV with KITO, 10 million USD
ENTRY MODE	Acquisition of plant and local brands, WFOE	(1) Acquisition, WFOE (2) Greenfield, WFOE	(1) Acquisition, WFOE (3) Greenfield, WFOE	(1) REPO (2) Joint Venture
MAIN CHALLENGES	Cultural difference in palate, lack of local distribution chain	Keeping up with technological pace	Demand fluctuation, keeping up with technological changes	Chinese ignored knowing that Mexico could produce high-quality tiles
SOLUTION	Deep consumer understanding, long-term vision and openness to change, flexibility in adapting to a new cultures, leadership and local talent	Offices in Beijing transformed into a "Enterprise Mobility-specific Center of Excellence" following the growing need for enterprise mobility solutions in Asia	Opening a third plant, increase value added to its products	Adapting design to Chinese tastes, developing sales points around China

(Contd.)

	BIMBO (bakery)	SOFTTEK (IT services)	NEMAK (aluminum vehicle components)	INTERCERAMIC (ceramic tiles)
SUCCESS FACTORS	Global experience, best international practices such as IT, ERP, reports, key processes of methodology in the commercial, operational and administrative areas	After the acquisition, maintaining the top management with experience in the market	Industry trend toward aluminum, excellent reputation with global clients	Distribution network, Chinese presence with JV for production
FUTURE PLANS	Scaling up the operation in China, developing China into platform for Asia	Keeping growth in China and India as platforms for Asia	Opening a third plant in China for products with more value added	Doubling sales in next five years, investing in technology, modernization of existing facilities with the acquisition of new equipment

Source: Authors

The least global firm in our sample is Interceramic with presence in six countries, while Bimbo and Softtek are each active in 20 or more countries. The variety of sizes is large, ranging from Interceramic's 4,870 employees to Bimbo's 130,913. Likewise, annual sales range from 444 million to 13.5 billion USD.

The period of entry into China begins in 2004 and is still ongoing. The initial entry modes include acquisitions (Bimbo, Nemak, Softtek) and joint ventures (Interceramic).

Both Nemak and Softtek used the experience gained through their initial acquisitions to try greenfield investments as next steps in their China strategies. Interceramic prefers to keep working with its JV partner. Conventional wisdom would suggest that B2B firms (Nemak, Softtek) with partially international clients suffer less from cultural distance, while B2C companies (Interceramic) would require a Chinese partner to be successful. The exception to this general rule is Bimbo, although it has to be remarked that their learning process has been slow and its products have not been distributed beyond the Beijing-Tianjin and the Shanghai areas.

The main challenges that multimexicans have faced are: fierce competition, cultural differences (even in palate), different regulatory systems, strong demand fluctuation; and furthermore a general ignorance of the Chinese regarding Mexico, its culture, and its products.

But the multimexicans in our small sample have not been intimidated by their liability of foreignness. Bimbo developed its policy of "deep consumer understanding", long-term vision and openness to change, flexibility in adapting to a new culture, leadership and local talent. Softtek transformed its offices in Beijing into an "Enterprise Mobility-specific Center of Excellence" following the growing need for enterprise mobility solutions in Asia. Nemak counterattacked the aggressive competitors of the car industry by opening a third plant, and adding increased value to its products. Finally, Interceramic formed a joint venture with a local company in order to combine Chinese production capacity with Mexican design and distribution knowledge.

Which were the success factors that allowed these multimexicans to thrive in this complex and extremely competitive market? Bimbo supports its operation in China with its global experience, best international practice such as IT, ERP, reports, key processes of methodology in the commercial, operational and administrative areas. Softtek after the acquisition kept the top management with experience in the market and made the founder of IT United its vice president of Softtek Asia and CEO of Softtek China. Nemak with its deep global vision took advantage of the industry trends toward aluminum. Interceramic, instead of complain about Chinese companies attacking the Mexican markets, partnered up with one of them and attacked the Chinese market establishing its own distribution network in China.

Any of these multimexicans has found ways to deal with the current situation in China. All are aware of the huge potential not only of China itself but of also its position as a gateway to East and Southeast Asia. Economists agree that Asia is the world region with the highest growth potential over the next years. Bimbo plans to scale up its operation in China, to be the platform for Asia. Softtek will keep growing in China and India. Nemak has plans for a third plant in China, for products with more value added. Interceramic's goal is to double sales over the next 5 years, investing in technology and by modernizing its facilities through the acquisition of new equipment.

All MNEs from emerging markets need clear strategies, agility to adapt to changing circumstances, and discipline in execution, more so in an extremely competitive market like China. The task is far from easy, but the four cases of multimexicans presented in this chapter show that it can be done. At this point, some in-depth studies would be most welcome to identify those elements that could be replicated by other firms as well as mistakes to be avoided.

Chapter 7
Strategies for the Construction and Internationalization of Chinese Brands Aimed to the Latin American Market

Otto Regalado-Pezúa
Gabriel A. Zapata
Miguel A. Montoya

Paus refers to the term "middle-income trap" as "a situation where a middle income country can no longer compete internationally in standardized, labor-intensive commodities because wages are relatively too high, but it can also not compete in higher value added activities on a broad enough scale because productivity is relatively too low" (Paus, 2017). It is known that one of the ways to generate more added value to an economy is the presence of its own big brands, "national champions" that enable it to penetrate international markets with greater strength and utilities.

In line with other works connecting China with Latin America (Cortes, 2018; Hase-Ueta et. al, 2018), in this chapter the strategic positioning in Latin America of six Chinese goods and services brands is analyzed. We found that, in the same way as their Western peers, the Chinese brands grow organically and inorganically. Chinese brands are progressively more present in the international markets. Companies have been following different strategies to position their brands in the markets they are directed to, these strategies differ according to the products and markets, as we shall see in this chapter.

The brand identifies the product's manufacturer, whether it is a good or a service. Therefore, it fulfills a strategic role in the development and growth of the firms, both locally and internationally.

Regarding the brand's strategic role, Wong and Merrilees (2007) pointed out that from it it is possible to design the development and expansion of the firm by aligning the internal capabilities and the external environment. Other authors like Urde states that the brand can be the starting point for the formulation of the firm's development strategy (Wong and Merrilees, 2007). In this sense, we agree with Urde in that a brand's brand strategy can constitute a competitive advantage in the markets in which it is present or wishes to develop.

The brands which evolve can be positioned and repositioned. A brand can have a position in the local market and look for another to enter the international market. This will depend on the brand's reputation and the strategy the firm decides to implement.

Specifically, on the Chinese brands, Fan (2006), in his article "The globalization of Chinese brands", identifies the year 1978 as the start of the evolution of marketing and branding in China and divides the process into the following stages:

The first stage, denominated production stage, was developed in the eighties. During that period, China was recovering from the problems that resulted from having adopted a centrally planned economy; there was a shortage of products and the internal market was dominated by the presence of international companies and joint ventures (joint ventures between Chinese and foreign companies). As an example of that, can be mentioned the alliance between Jialing and Honda for technology exchange in the manufacture of motorcycles and that of the Qingdao General Refrigerator Factory with Liebherr for the manufacture of refrigerators.

The second stage, known as sales and advertising, corresponds to the nineties. This stage was characterized by the oversupply of products, intensification of competition, and price war. The local companies, which began to be established, achieved a greater market share than the international companies. Advertising was considered a powerful weapon after the price variable; however, Chinese companies were confused about the concepts of advertising and branding in the belief, to some extent, that advertising expenditure would create great brands, which would generate sales automatically. In this second stage, companies invested large sums of money in trying to renew their corporate image, which caused the bankruptcy of many of them.

The third stage, known as brand creation and globalization, began at the turn of the century. Intense competition in the internal market, production overcapacity, declining profit margins as a result of price wars, among other factors, motivated the Chinese Government, in its eagerness to boost the country's economic development, to begin an internationalization policy (known as *Zou Chuqu*) to enable Chinese companies to seek business and investment opportunities in the external market (Armony and Strauss, 2012).

Among the Government's initiatives, it is also important to highlight the incorporation of China into the World Trade Organization (WTO) and the creation of the seal of quality, China Top Brand, awarded by the Chinese Brand Strategic Promotion Committee. The idea with this seal was to add value to Chinese brands in order to reduce their vulnerability in comparison with international brands, as well as protecting the internal market.

This stage produced rapid growth in the Chinese economy, but the brands simply served to identify a product or service; they were not perceived as an element through which a deep relationship with the client could be built. Companies were characterized by having bureaucratic organizations and centralizing decision making. During this stage, the average life cycle of a Chinese brand was seven and a half years, and the survival rate compared to the previous decade was 10% (Fan, 2006).

The consultancy firm Labbrand (2015) points out that between the years 2008 and 2012, a period that coincides with the third stage identified by Fan, the Beijing Olympic Games, and the economic crisis of the developed countries, China became part of the world scenario. The Chinese consumer formed part of the target audience for international companies, and sports brands such as Adidas and Nike carried out very intense branding campaigns aimed at obtaining a greater share of this market.

The country's economic growth and the development of its internal industry not only favored the modernization of large cities, like Beijing, Shanghai, Guangzhou, and Shenzhen, but also brought with it a series of changes in the lifestyle of the Chinese consumer, especially of a new middle class influenced by the West (Europe and America) and the East (Taiwan, Japan, and South Korea). Proof of that is the opening of stores dedicated to the commercialization of Hollywood movies in DVD, as well as the rise of bakeries, fast food, and coffee chains (Labbrand, 2015).

Regarding this stage, it is important to refer to the studies of Aaker (Hollis, 2013), who states that Chinese companies have not developed brand management tools or systems, nor have they bothered to attract the best talents to manage these tools effectively. Their unwillingness —he states— arises from senior management, due to the vision of their executives, whose mentality, purely functional and commercial, does not help in understanding what is needed to build a strong brand. Aaker also explains that the lack of motivation to build a brand lies in the fact that companies in China owe their success to State support.

1. Perception about Chinese Brands and Presence in Latin America

Studies regarding the perception of Chinese brands in Latin America have not been found. Nevertheless, through a survey done to 1,100 consumers in the United States in 2016, Blue Focus, a Chinese company dedicated to marketing and brand management consulting, found out that Chinese brands are less reliable than the brands of other countries to the consumers. Most of the respondents perceived Chinese brands as lacking in transparency and sustainability. It was also discovered that over half of the American consumers (57%) believed that Chinese brands were not doing enough to assure their transparency. Factors like information spreading, intellectual property rights, honesty, and sustainability (contamination and work and safety conditions) limit the brands' transparency.

The survey also indicates that Chinese brands failed to build an emotional connection with the customer. Although being emotionally reserved and humble is a prominent trait of character in Chinese culture, it may become an obstacle for Chinese brands expressing their personality.

Chinese brands lack visibility. The exposure to the brand is a critical factor in purchase decisions; consumers who are more frequently exposed to announcements of Chinese brands will show a greater tendency to choose Chinese products. 7% of the respondents of this survey knew about Chinese brands through the social media and the results of search engines, while 18% of the respondents found it difficult to obtain information on Chinese brands and their products.

The same survey pointed out that, while these findings correspond to the United States, these problems also arise in regions like Africa and Latin America, emerging markets where Chinese brands have had greater acceptance as an alternative to Western and local brands (BlueFocus, 2016).

As pointed out by Fan (2006), the third stage of the evolution of Chinese marketing and branding marked the beginning of the globalization of the Chinese companies. For Fetscherin and Sardy (2008), in their article "Chinese brands: the build or buy considerations", there are two strategic reasons producing said globalization: the need to sell because the domestic market is saturated and the supply of raw materials.

The first motive refers to the termination of manufacturing contracts between Chinese Original Equipment Manufacturer (OEM, is the name given to the company whose products are bought and sold under the brand name of a buying company) companies and foreign companies. The situation was made worse with the entry to the local market of foreign brands and the appearance of other local competitors, causing a price war with very low profit margins. This overcapacity of production (or oversupply of products) had to be confronted with the search for new foreign markets.

The second motive refers to obtaining sources of energy supply, raw material, and other inputs. China has important investments in Africa, Asia, Latin America, and the South Pacific, which are driven and financed by its government (Fornes and Butt-Philip, 2014). Access to these resources allows boosting the growth of Chinese industry and the development of new markets for the commercialization of its products (Fetscherin and Sardy, 2008).

A clear example of the new markets' development is represented with the Chinese automobile industry. In recent years, South America has become the third export destination for Chinese automobiles, after the Middle East and Africa. The growth of the Latin American economy is the main cause of the great potential in the region's automobile market. According to data from the Chinese Council for the Promotion of International Trade, between the year 2008 and the first quarter of 2013, the percentage of commercial automobiles increased from 14.71% to 20.62%, Chile, Peru, and Venezuela being the main export destination for said vehicles (Xiaofei, 2014).

Since the Latin American market is attractive for the commercialization of Chinese vehicles, brands like Foton, JAC, Lifan, among others, they tried to establish their assembly plants in Brazil, Colombia, Mexico, and Paraguay, in order to better understand the market and to introduce their products to other countries in the region.

It is true that those vehicles have a low-level brand positioning, so the perception of many consumers regarding the quality does not make them their first option. Despite this, the low Price and the technology incorporated play a key role in the purchase.

2. Brand Building Strategies or Brand Internationalization Strategies?

Initially, the studies from Gao, Woetzel and Wu (2003) and, later on, those of Fetscherin and Sardy (2008) and Armony and Strauss (2012), pointed out that Chinese companies have focused on two forms of brand building: organic growth and the purchase of overseas assets by means of mergers and acquisitions (inorganic growth).

2.1 Organic Growth

This strategy, also known as Greenfield, refers to gradual brand building. In this case, the company's objective is to position the sale of its products and services in the local market (China); once it has achieved this positioning, it takes advantage of the experience acquired and the resources generated to seek its globalization based on its incursion into emerging markets (or developing markets) and, subsequently, into developed markets.

The most attainable emerging or developing markets are, mainly, the countries of Southeast Asia. These markets do not present barriers to entry, both because of the presence of Chinese immigrants in the area and due to the similarities in language, customs, and beliefs. Other developing markets are Africa, the Middle East, Central Asia, and Latin America (Gao, Woetzel and Wu, 2003).

This strategy is characterized, above all, by generating slow growth and requiring a smaller initial investment, which make it an attractive option for a small or medium company wishing to expand its operations.

The disadvantages, however, lie in the lack of brand recognition outside of the local market and the lack of technology that allows a competitive product to be offered abroad (He, 2012). Some examples of companies which followed this strategy are presented below:

2.1.1 Jialing

China Jialing Group, founded in 1875, was dedicated to the manufacture of motorcycles for military use. In 1979, it ventured into the development and production of motorcycles for civilian use and positioned itself as the founder and leader of the industry. In 1981, Jialing and the Japanese company Honda formed an association for the manufacturing of motorcycles. In the nineties, the two companies created a joint venture and began the distribution of their products in Colombia, Brazil, United States, Indonesia, and Vietnam, where they established assembly plants and representative offices. Currently, their products are exported to more than ninety countries and regions around the world.

Jialing motorcycles are commercialized in: Venezuela, Argentina, Uruguay, Ecuador, Costa Rica, Peru, Mexico, Chile, and Nicaragua. It is evident that

Latin America represents an important market. The users look for low-cost vehicles that allow them to reduce their travel time due to the high vehicular traffic and low-quality public transportation services (Rodríguez, Santana and Pardo, 2015).

In the Colombian market, their positioning strategy was based on the implementation of distribution channels in the country's main cities, with the support of a network of distributors, authorized workshops, and the sale of spare parts, thus offering true brand support (Jialing, 2014). One of the core ideas for achieving said positioning was training in each one of the areas and the constant search for improvement of the products' quality, with the ISO 9001–2000, ISO 14001, certifications, and United Kingdom Royal Crown Recognition, among others.

For Tun (2017), Jialing's entry method to new markets corresponds to that of Greenfield investment (see Table 7.1). The presence of Jialing in Colombia dates back to 1995 with the installation of a motorcycle assembly plant in Cali, in order to attend the need for low-cost transport. Subsequently, with the experience acquired in that market, they began the commercialization of their products in other markets of Latin America, with Colombia as the region's center of operations.

2.1.2 UnionPay

China UnionPay was founded in the year 2002 by the principal banks of China (The Industrial and Commercial Bank of China, ICBC; Agricultural Bank of China, ABC; Bank of China, BOC; and China Construction Bank, CCB) as an alternative to Visa and MasterCard. The bank's card is well known: only in Asia, there are more than 3,500 million UnionPay cards, more than Visa and MasterCard in the entire world (Morris, 2016).

In 2012, the company established as one of its objectives to become a global brand and enter countries throughout the world: Asia, Europe, America, Oceania, and Africa. Today, UnionPay cards are accepted in 162 countries, including Latin American countries such as Mexico, Brazil, Argentina, and Peru (People daily, 2016). Its strategy has enabled it to position itself among the world's principal payment networks, above Visa and MasterCard.

Outside of Chinese territory, the UnionPay market is made up of Chinese tourists who travel to different countries for work or pleasure. These tourists increase the demand for cross-border payments and want their credit cards to be accepted. UnionPay has taken advantage of the trend of cross-border travel and of the commercial opening of China with various countries to sign agreements with various financial institutions (Morris, 2016). In this way, it seeks to position itself as a comfortable and secure payment service, offering a variety of discounts in shopping centers, air tickets, hotel accommodations, among others.

Cuba was the first country in Latin America and the Caribbean to establish a diplomatic relationship with China. The political, economic, and cultural ties between countries made it possible that since 2013 ATMs started accepting UnionPay cards. Thanks to this, many Chinese travelers could make use of cash. Afterwards, UnionPay's services expanded to all the stores in Cuba, helping improve the level of electronic payment services in Cuba, according to UnionPay International (Cubadebate, 2016).

The objectives of UnionPay are to achieve the global acceptance of its cards and to compete with global brands like Visa and MasterCard. In this regard, they are seeking agreements with banks so that their clients can also have access to the UnionPay card. Electronic commerce (E-commerce) is another strategy that allows the company to offer various technological solutions for payment through mobile phone or tablet (Morris, 2016).

2.2 Inorganic Growth (M & A)

This brand building strategy consists of acquiring foreign companies located in developed countries to use brands already positioned in those markets to offer their products. A clear example is Lenovo, manufacturer of laptops and cell phones, which has acquired the PC Division of IBM and Motorola (including assets, like brand rights) to enter and position itself in the North American market.

The developed markets are characterized by being very competitive, complex, and presenting high barriers to entry (Gao, Woetzel and Wu, 2003). The use of this strategy allows the company to have rapid growth in new markets. However, it requires a major investment, financial incentives, and government policies.

In a recent study of fifty Chinese manufacturing companies, Tan (2017), in his article "Generic internationalization strategies of emerging market multinationals: The case of Chinese firms", points out that the presence of Chinese companies is greater in developed countries than in emerging countries. The developed markets are the United States and the countries of Western Europe, like Germany, France, and Holland. The markets corresponding to emerging countries are South America, Eastern Europe, and Asia.

The study also points out that most Chinese manufacturing companies open overseas subsidiaries, in order to obtain access to the market, brands, or technologies, while another group of companies is dedicated to product diversification or resource extraction.

Access to technology and marketing knowledge is exploited to cover any gap or disadvantage that the company may have vis-a-vis the competition. However, these companies would not opt to relocate their production abroad, since in China they can manufacture large quantities at low cost. Tan (2017) classifies the brand building strategies described previously as modes of entry, as Table 7.1 shows. These modes of entry form part from the generic strategies of internationalization.

Table 7.1 General Internationalization Strategies

Chinese EMMNC	No. of EMMNC	Destination	Chain value movement	Brand	Entry method	Brand's internationalization strategy
Coship, l, Geely, Jialing, Lifan	6	South-South	Mid-end and low-end market	OBM	Greenfield	Local optimizer
Sailun, Himile, Zhongding, BYD Electronic, Great Wall	22	South-North	High-end	OEM	Greenfield and M & A	Low cost provider
Hikvision	8	South-North	High-end.	OBM	Greenfield and M & A	Advanced markets' seeker
Lenovo, ZTE, TCL Communication	5	South-North and South-South	Mid-end and low-end market	OBM	Greenfield and M & A	Global consolidator
TCL Multimedia, Hisense	9	South-North and South-South	Mid-end and low-end market	OEM y OBM	Greenfield and M & A	Dual Strategy

* EMMNC: emerging market multinational corporation. OEM: original equipment manufacturer. OBM: original Brand manufacturer.
Source: Kun Tan (2017).

Let us look at some examples of companies which have followed the strategy of inorganic growth:

2.2.1 Haier

Haier was created in 1984 as a result of the alliance between Qingdao General Refrigerator Factory and the Liebherr Group of Germany. Since its creation, the company has been managed by its CEO, Ruimin Zhang, who has always had a very clear objective: to manufacture reliable, high quality products.

During the decade of the nineties, Haier made a series of acquisitions trying to diversify its product portfolio (washing machines, air conditioning systems, televisions, computers, among others) to obtain a secure and profitable position in China. Then, it embarked on brand internationalization and building.

Haier focused on the areas of research and development (R&D) and manufacture and marketing. The adaptations of its products to the consumers' needs in local markets are carried out in the R&D centers located in Germany, China, Japan, Korea, and the United States, and manufacture in its plants located in Europe, Asia, Middle East, Africa, and the United States (IPMark, 2013). The company has the greatest share in the global appliance market—around 10%, with a global turnover exceeding 28,860 million euros.

Haier intends to increase its global presence, in the USA, and in other regional markets. After acquiring General Electric's (GE) home appliances division, Haier also got participation from Mabe, Mexican firm dedicated to the home appliances' manufacturing. This acquisition allowed Haier to use GE's brand "Made in America", as well as to enter the competition in the premium sector of home appliances, becoming a key player in the industry. The experience and recognition that it acquired from the developed markets allowed it to enter the Latin American market (Kithany, 2016).

The building of the Haier brand is based both on traditional marketing as well as digital marketing. Among the traditional marketing activities, television advertising, point of purchase advertising (POP), participation in events and fairs, and the sponsoring of cultural and sporting activities stand out. The company also forms part of social responsibility and care for the environment programs, initiatives which have contributed to creating a positive influence of the brand in the consumer market.

Within the activities of digital marketing, Haier has a Facebook page, a channel in YouTube, a 3D online resource room, and a renewed website (www.haier.com). In addition, it makes investments in Search Engines Marketing, Search Engine Optimization, and blogs (Egido, 2013).

2.2.2 BYD

BYD (Build Your Dreams) Company was founded in 1995 and was initially dedicated to the manufacture of rechargeable batteries for mobile phones. In 2003, the company acquired the Qinchuan Vehicle Factory and ventured into the manufacture of battery-powered automobiles, resulting in the formation of BYD Autos. The idea of its founder, Wang Chuanfu, is to manufacture electric vehicles (EV), 100% environmentally friendly, at a reasonable price (eclass, 2010).

BYD Autos not only manufactures electric vehicles, but also gasoline vehicles and hybrids. The company stands out for its development of technological innovations, as well as the manufacture and supply of airbags, ABS systems, and other electronic components for other automotive companies in China. BYD has 20 factories, 14 of which are in China and 6 in Russia, Syria, Egypt, Sudan, the United States, and Brazil (Massiero, Ogasavara, Jussani and Risso, 2016). Regarding internationalization, BYD made two acquisitions and established joint ventures with other companies in order to increase its resources (Jianhui, 2013).

BYD manufactures both public transport vehicles (buses, taxis) and private vehicles (automobiles, pickup trucks, and SUVs). Although China is an important automotive market, the company has made inroads into Europe, the United States, and Latin America with electric vehicles like the E6, the ebus or K9 (a bus 12 meters long with a maximum speed of 70 km/hr. and a fuel range of more than 250 km.), plug-in hybrids like the F3DM, and the Qin (BYD Autos, 2017).

In Latin America, the Chinese firms' participation has increased in the last years because their vehicles present commodities from the high-end cars at a significantly more affordable price for the general public (Xinhua, 2016). BYD is a brand characterized for offering vehicles with innovative technology, safe, and not polluting, complemented with a comfortable, pleasant drive for an accessible price (TODOAutos, 2017).

BYD's strategy to enter new markets consists in establishing agreements with government and municipal entities, providing electric vehicles for the public transport (taxis and buses) for a similar price to that of gas vehicles. The brand's image is created once the users realize that these vehicles work correctly, are comfortable, and environment friendly (Aldama, 2014).

The advertising of BYD does not stand out much in comparison with other battery-powered vehicles like Tesla Motor, Nissan Leaf, or Chevrolet Volt.

For BYD, the development of electric vehicles is a way to satisfy the global trend towards the better use of renewable energies. Its principal challenge is to position itself in the Western market and compete consistently with brands like Chevrolet, Nissan, or Tesla (Barredo, 2016).

2.3 Born Global

The born global, also known as global start-up, are characterized by venturing into the international market from the moment they start operations, or within a period very close to it; that is, they present a process of accelerated internationalization.

These companies, composed of small and medium enterprises, are led by young entrepreneurs with prior knowledge and experience in the sector in which they compete. This attribute, which is essential in the constitution process of this type of company, is accompanied by the following characteristics (Leiva and Darder, 2008; Nardali, 2017):

- Commercialization of a small variety of products or services attractive for different markets.
- Access to foreign markets through networks or alliances (coworking and cooperation).
- Use of information technologies (Internet, e-mail, E-commerce, and social media) for the promotion and commercialization of products.
- Simple and flexible organizational structures.
- Scarcity of financial, human, and productive resources, because they place special emphasis on controlling assets instead of owning them.
- Limitations for collecting and interpreting information related to the market. To compensate for this lack, they resort to the information that may be provided by the networks.

As a result of being small companies with scarce resources, they have a low production capacity. Therefore, they have to focus on a previously identified segment or small niches of the market.

2.3.1 OnePlus

OnePlus, one of the principal smartphone manufacturers from China, was founded in the city of Shenzhen in 2013. In 2014, it launched for sale the OnePlus One, a smartphone of similar technical characteristics to those of the Samsung Galaxy S5, but at half the price. By the start of 2016, it had sold more than a million telephones in thirty-three countries, its revenue exceeded three hundred million dollars, it had more than six hundred employees, and was a well-known brand in the world (Romero, Rodríguez Escudero, Rodríguez Pinto and Temprano García, 2017).

OnePlus is a type of company denominated as born global; if its products are observed or its web page visited, it could not be identified as a Chinese company.

According to Romero et al. (2017), the factors which contributed to boosting sales were the following:

(1) *Customizable operating system.* OnePlus One was sold with Cyanogen, an operating system based on Android which, due to its performance and price, was comparable to the best telephones of Samsung and HTC.

(2) *Direct distribution through the web.* Distribution was carried out between Shenzhen and Hong Kong, with the support of logistical bases located in California and London. Given the huge demand for OnePlus One, express messenger and customer assistance services had to be contracted.

(3) *Creative campaigns and Internet community.* The company opted for creative and economic campaigns. One of them requested users to register in the web and record and send a video showing themselves destroying their smartphones. The first hundred people to do so would receive, for one euro, a OnePlus One. Within a few days, more than a thousand videos in YouTube showed how telephones of other brands were being destroyed.

(4) *Sale system by invitation.* The acquisition of a OnePlus One was made by invitation. This was received after participation in the contests created in the forum or by means of an invitation from another person who had already acquired it. This method contributed to reinforcing the idea of the exclusivity of the product and controlling the inventory more efficiently.

Thanks to the forum and the sales system by invitation, OnePlus created a group of brand advocates, who came to its defense in the social media in the event of any problem. The cost of this strategy was only the equivalent of the price of some T-shirts that were given to the most active members. From the forum, it was also promoted that users should spread the news of the activities organized by OnePlus, such as contests or raffles.

Starting in 2016, OnePlus was going to be introduced into the Colombian market through the operator Trigo. The firm had no expansion plan to the Latin

American market, since it preferred to focus on the American and European markets (Collado, 2016).

Nonetheless, despite OnePlus did not commercialize its devices officially in the Latin American market, various products can be found at the market's disposition through sites like Mercadolibre, Linio, and OLX in countries like Peru, Colombia, Venezuela, Argentina, Brazil, Chile, among others.

2.3.2 Xiaomi

Xiaomi, a company dedicated to the design, development, and sale of smartphones and other electronic devices, was born as a small company in Peking in 2010. In the following year, it announced an association with the second operator of mobile telephony "China Unicom" and, in 2012, the company decided to enter the European market (Nardali, 2017).

Its business model consists of producing cellphones at low cost, but with specifications corresponding to high-end equipment (BBC Mundo, 2014), for which it has suppliers like Sharp supplying the liquid crystal (LCD) touch screens, Qualcomm providing the processors, and Taiwan's Foxconn (manufacturer of iPhone) assembling the Xiaomi telephones. Unlike the competition, Xiaomi does not spend money on traditional advertising, nor does it have a network of own stores. Xiaomi sells its telephones directly to the consumers through e-commerce distribution channels.

The company has a total estimated value of US$ 4 million and is the largest seller of mobile phones in China, the world's largest market. Xiaomi is also present in the markets of Asia and Latin America and occupies the position of the world's third manufacturer of smartphones, behind Samsung and Apple (Glowik, 2016).

When Xiaomi ventured into Latin America, it changed its brand to "mi". For non-Chinese speakers, "mi" is easier to pronounce and remember. Its flagship model mobile phone, the "hongmi," was renamed "redmi" to help the consumers understand and remember the name of the product (BlueFocus, 2016).

Xiaomi started operations in Brazil during 2016. Initially, it offered its products through virtual stores. It then had to change its strategy, since the sales volume was less than expected. Its new strategy consisted on complementing the sales by email through retail (Cuartas, 2017).

Xiaomi then entered the Mexican market commercializing its models Redmi Note 4 and Redmi 4X. It also launched an app through Google Play, so the brands' fans could access the information of the firm, have access to events, promotions, and discounts, and new launches (Cuartas, 2017). This brand is famous for offering discounts for its products for certain amount of time (flash sales), tactic that allowed it to grow in recent years.

Other markets where Xiaomi phones are commercialized are Uruguay, Paraguay, Bolivia, Colombia, and Chile through official distributors (Segura Martín, 2017). The Company has a variety of products, among which are activity wristbands, external batteries, televisions, earphones, speakers, and tablets (Xiaomi, 2017).

3. Conclusions

In the Table 7.2, a summary of the six analyzed cases in the chapter is presented. In each case, the most relevant characteristics are indicated: establishment year, product or service category offered, market entry strategies, and brand building (if they are part of the top 30 Chinese brand builders, according to the consultancy Brandz 2017), along with more information.

It is evident that the firms have followed different development strategies. All of them stand out for the use of technology, presence in the Latin American market, and intensive use of social media to position the brands in the target markets.

Figure 7.1 shows graphically, through a timeline, the facts we considered relevant for each of the analyzed brands. In every case, can be appreciated the establishment year, the years for joint ventures, and key mergers and acquisitions, the entrance in stock markets, as well as the expansion to international markets. In general, it can be seen that starting in the nineties, there is a greater presence of the brands internationally, an offer diversification, and a usage of diverse entry and development strategies for new markets.

It can also be observed that the growth and expansion speed varies between firms. For example, OnePlus and Xiaomi have little time in the market and have positioned themselves faster than other firms like Jialing or Haier, with a longer time in the international market, mainly due to the usage of social media.

Throughout this research, it has been appreciated that the Chinese industry is capable of offering high-quality products and services, adapted to the needs of the local consumers. Haier is a clear example of that. Chinese companies have the capacity to acquire existing brands in order to enter and compete in developed markets. This implies that they have limited capacity for building brands from the start in these markets, like the United States and Europe.

Table 7.2 Summary of Brand Strategies

	Jialing	UnionPay	Haier	BYD	OnePlus	Xiaomi
Founded in	1875	2002	1984	2003	2013	2010
Category	Motorcycles	Financing Services	Home Appliances	Automobiles	Purchase Electronics	Purchase Electronics
Segment	Middle class young people	Tourists and businesspeople from China	Middle class young people	Middle class young people	Middle class young people	Middle class young people
Strategy	• Joint Venture with the market's leader • Innovation and certification in product quality • Training about the brand and products to workshops and distributers	• Alliances with banks and payment agencies • Offering a customers' benefits program	• Competitor in advanced markets. • Acquiring other firms • Disruptive innovation • Commitment to the environment (RSE)	• Low cost supplier • Competitor in B2B market, then B2C	• Low cost supplier • Low cost, creative marketing • Promotion through massive events. • Purchase system through invitations	• Low cost supplier • Promotion through massive events. • Campaigns or sales
Position within the top 30 China's global Brand builders (Brandz 2017)	—	—	7	—	12	5
Brand's Power (Brandz 2017)	—	—	572	—	454	716

(Contd.)

	Jialing	UnionPay	Haier	BYD	OnePlus	Xiaomi
Countries where it commercializes products/ services:	Colombia, Brazil, Venezuela, Argentina, Uruguay, Ecuador, Costa Rica, Peru, Mexico, Chile, Nicaragua	Argentina, Bahamas, Brazil, Canada, Colombia, Costa Rica, Cuba, Ecuador, Greenland, Martinique, Mexico, Peru, Puerto Rico, Surinam, Virgin Islands, The USA, Venezuela	USA, Colombia, Mexico, Chile, Peru, Venezuela, Cuba	Costa Rica, Curacao, Colombia, Chile, Aruba, Argentina, Guatemala, Chile, Panama, Uruguay, Bolivia, Paraguay, Peru, Dominican Republic, Nicaragua, Ecuador, Venezuela	Peru, Colombia, Venezuela, Argentina, Brazil, Chile, among others without official representation	Mexico, Brazil, Chile, Colombia, Peru, Bolivia, Uruguay, Costa Rica, Paraguay
Social media presence	• Facebook • Twitter • YouTube	• Weibo • Facebook • Twitter	• Facebook • Twitter • Pinterest • Google Plus • LinkedIn • Instagram • YouTube	• Facebook • Twitter • Google Plus • LinkedIn • YouTube	• Facebook • Instagram • Twitter • LinkedIn • YouTube	• Facebook • Twitter • Google Plus • YouTube • Instagram • Weibo

Source: Made by authors.

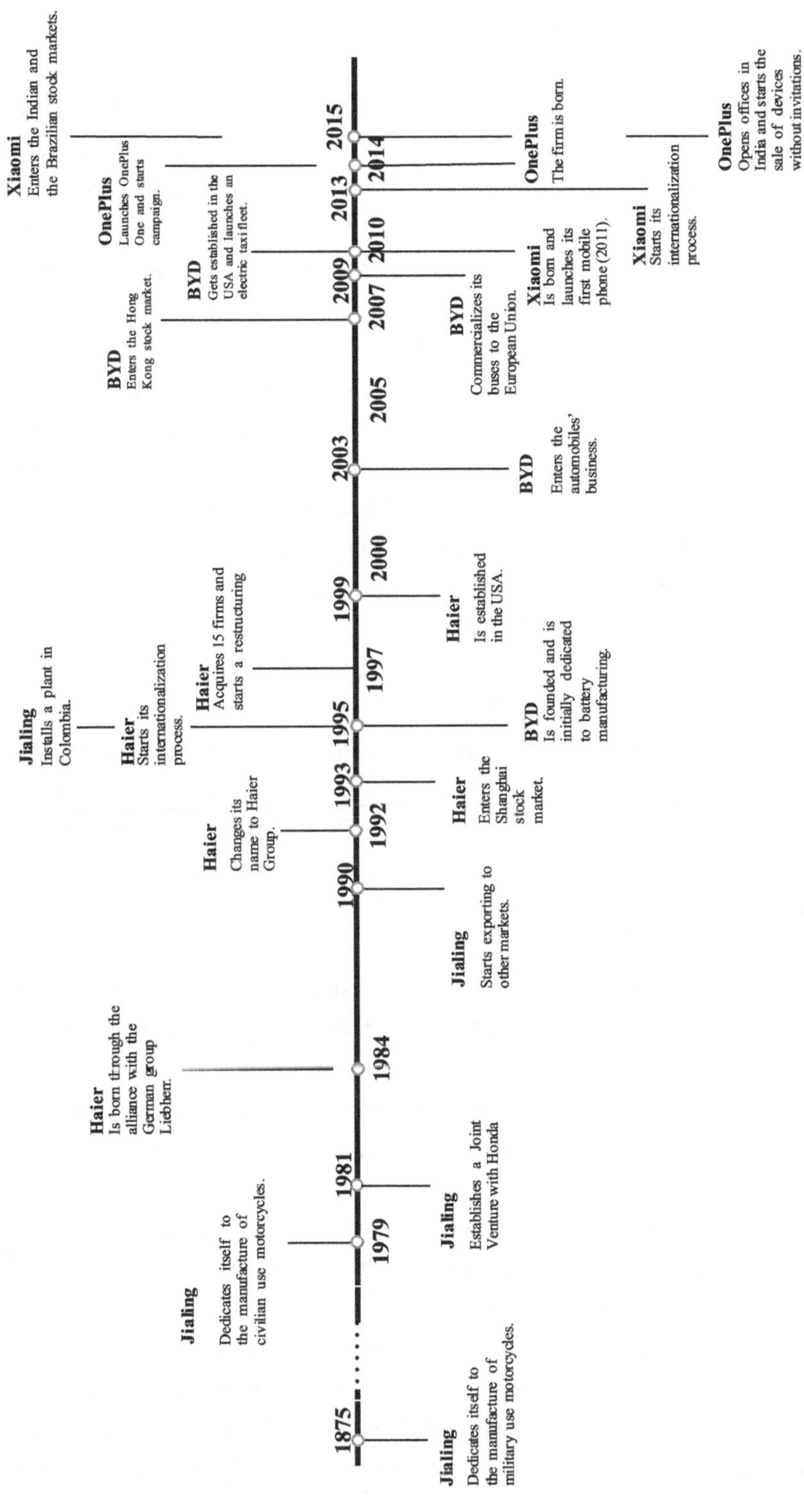

Figure 7.1 Timeline of Chinese Companies' Activities in Latin America

Source: Made by authors

In emerging markets, the strategy is based on the building of an own brand. The advantages of competing in an emerging market are the few barriers to entry, the scarce number of competitors, and the favorable conditions for innovation. One disadvantage is their limited flexibility to respond rapidly and appropriately to problems, which may affect the brand. OnePlus received many complaints from consumers regarding failures in the functioning of the operating system of their smartphone, therefore it had to subcontract a company to attend to the clients' complaints.

Chinese companies have based themselves both on organic and accelerated growth, in order to build brands on an international level. However, the perception of the consumers regarding the quality of the products and services which are offered through these brands, the influence of the western brands in the different markets, and the short-term focus of obtaining higher income at the expense of investing in long term brand creation activities—such as public relations, advertising, and commercialization—make companies reconsider their brand building strategies in the following ways:

1. Seek associations and acquisitions at a local level.

Chinese companies need to associate with local companies through joint ventures, mergers, or acquisitions, since the right association can boost the brand.

The hiring of local talent in the markets where they operate is also important, so that they can take better advantage of technological, regulatory, and marketing knowledge.

2. Reorganization.

Many Chinese companies centralize the decision making of their overseas operations. This can cause distortion of information, given the number of people involved in the process of generation and transmission of reports, as well as delays in decision making regarding the strategies to be followed and demotivation of the personnel not participating in the decisions related to brand building.

Organizational structures must understand the political, economic, cultural, and technological factors of the markets in which they operate. To this end, the coordination between the headquarters and the overseas offices must be improved, so that the latter are empowered and can make decisions related to brand strategies in the local market. The feedback of the local operations and market research, instead of the typical directives of vertical organizations (centralized decision making), help incorporate the local culture into the brand, at the same time establishing stronger emotional ties with the local consumers.

3. Rebuild the brand from the inside out.

Branding has been a poorly understood term, being associated with the use of the logo, advertising, or packaging in the products commercialized by Chinese companies. However, branding goes beyond redesigning the logo or the change of name. Chinese companies must offer innovative products and services, of high value and good quality.

Chinese companies know that, in order to build a global brand, they are required to have a presence in different digital media, like Facebook, YouTube, Twitter, among others. Digital technology has provided new channels for brands to communicate with their clients. The focus of the brand has changed drastically; it has passed from "boosting sales" to creating discussion forums on relationships with customers: how to build them and maintain them.

To gain a wider audience, Chinese companies must start to create stories in which the consumers' emotions are appealed to, in order to connect them to the brand. For that, it is important to identify the emotional needs a brand can satisfy in people's lives and respond to them through the building of the brand and in those activities or events that are related to the brand.

Another communication strategy that has been employed with great success is using opinion influencers or leaders to show the operation and the advantages of the product or launch promotional campaigns in the social media.

It is also important to be clear that the marketing and communication strategies must have an impact in the short, medium, and long term. This will permit Chinese companies to free themselves from the negative perceptions of poor quality and build a brand that connects with clients around the world.

It is also recommended that the companies take initiatives to reduce the negative impact on the environment and contribute in questions of a social and economic nature, in order to improve the perception of the Chinese brands.

Finally, we can point out that the Chinese brands' globalization is marked by the different growth strategies each of them is following. In the shown cases, we can notice that some of them decided to build their brand and others opted to internationalize to get to the Latin American market. In this path, many of them are positioning themselves in the global market and others are disappearing in the process.

Chapter 8
Chinese Creative Cities as a Path to Escape of the Middle-income Trap

Juan González García.
Daniel Lemus Delgado

One of the most critical challenges of Latin American governments is to find and to implement a formula to escape from the middle-income trap. Notwithstanding significate cycles of economic growth in different periods of their contemporary history, many countries of Latin America as Brazil, Argentina, Colombia and Mexico, are caught in the middle-income trap. When we observe the successful economic growth and development of East Asian nations, the contrast is more evident. The consequences of the process of industrialization were very divergent in both regions (Gereffi, 1990). Currently, the fact is that Latin American economies evidence a slowing productivity growth since decades ago (CEPAL, 2008). As a result, nowadays it is improbable that Latin American countries will become equal to the top global economies in the immediate period.

Taylor evidences how Latin America countries are losing competitiveness with poor economies on manufactured exports. At the same times, these nations are also incapable of competing with flusher economies in high-skill innovation. In consequence, these countries are "stuck" in the middle-income category (Taylor, 2017). On the other hand, since 2010, China passed Japan in the second quarter to become the world's second-largest economy behind the United States, after three decades of enormous growth (Barboza, 2010). However, this is not enough. Nowadays, China is facing the challenge of determining how to move smoothly beyond the middle-income stage of economic development (Cai, 2012). Thus, from different paths, China and Latin America have reached the same crossroads: how to ensure an inclusive economic growth that allows overcoming the middle-income trap. In other words, how to implement an effective route to transform itself in developing countries.

According to the World Bank (2013), among the 101 middle-income economies in 1960, only 13 had become high-income economies by 2008, and the remaining 88 either lingered at the middle-income level or downgraded to a low-income level. Although multiple factors determine that a country can escape the middle-income trap, it is a fact that the States must maintain an average national income growth rate of 5% during 50 years or more to make the transition from a middle-income level to a high-income level (Yao, 2015).

In this regard, a key to achieving this stage of development is the possibility to maintain high and constant rates of economic growth. The problem is that many risks on the horizon can prevent accomplishment this goal. Despite the recovery of the financial and economic crisis of 2008, some factors can avert constant economic growth. The principal elements are the financial market stress, the impact of a renewed sharp slide in oil prices on oil exporters, the increased protectionism, the trade retaliation, the slowdown in potential output growth, and different geopolitical risks (World Bank, 2017).

In this context, we suggest that the creative economy can be a path to development. The creative economy has the potential to generate income and jobs while promoting social inclusion, cultural diversity and human development (UNCTAD, 2008). In fact, creativity, knowledge, and major access to information are powerful engines of economic growth and privileged way to the promotion of development in a globalized world. Therefore, the creative economy contributes to entrepreneurship, feeds innovation, improves productivity and promotes economic growth (AEA, 2017).

One of the most positive effects of the creative economy is the development of trade not only in the local context but also internationally. Besides, business in innovative products and services experienced unprecedented growth compared to the more traditional services and manufacturing industries. Probably, the rapid expansion in this sector will continue in the coming years. In this context, the creative industries are a catalyst for the benefits of trade and open up new opportunities for many developing countries (Santos-Duisenberg, 2008). At a national level, it is indispensable to inspire the development of the regional network and push policies to support a local economy and the relationships between public and private sectors to strengthen creative and cultural industries (Bocella and Salerno, 2016).

In sum, in the era of enormous globalization, creativity and knowledge have become an essential element to achieve the economic growth and social development. Many facts indicate that the creative economy is positive for developing countries. Indeed, while the traditional branches of the economy always have many problems to access international markets, this situation is different in the case of products and services derived from creative activities. Hence, creative economy can be an option for growth and even reduction of poverty for developing countries (UNCTAD / UNDP, 2010).

On the other hand, economic activities related to creativity do not grow in a vacuum. On the contrary, these events need appropriate territory to emerge and consolidate. This space is mainly cities. The creative economy is typically highly concentrated in a geographic area, yet their market reach often extends to the far corners of the world (Scott, 2008). Therefore, the creative city embraces the development of all aspects of the economy and the society and goes through the contents of different sectors in the urban development. However, "the cultural strength is playing a leading role in the expansion of a modern city, and its combination with a creative city will result in the development of all aspects of the city" (Zhou, 2014). The case of China shows how the promotion of creative activities in cities can be an essential element for growth and development.

This chapter analyzes the creative economy in China from the perspective of creative cities. The goal is to explain how the Chinese experience can be an example that inspires found new opportunities to achieve the economic growth in Latin American countries. With this purpose, the chapter has four sections. In the first segment, we discuss the concept of creative economy and creative cities. Afterwards, we analyze how the creative economy could be a strategy for development. In the next section, we explain the creative economy and creative Cities in China. Finally, we conclude with some ideas about the Chinese experience can be useful to Latin America cities.

1. The Creative Economy and the Creative Cities

Creativity has become one of the most important elements of regional economic theory. As well as technology and innovation were drivers of economic growth in the last century, nowadays creativity plays a similar role in shaping the economic trajectories and dynamics of the regions around the world (Florida, 2011).

Obviously, there are many definitions of creative economy because this concept is still under construction (UNCTAD, 2008: 15). In addition, there is not a singular list of elements of the creative economy. However, all classifications about this topic share a series of common characteristics such as the reinforcement of creativity, innovation, cultural development and the pursuit of economic development. The cultural and creative industries, not only recognized for their economic value, but also for the role that they play in the production of new technologies and creative ideas and their non-monetized social benefits (UNESCO, 2013). Thus, the "creative economy" could be understood as an evolving concept based on creative assets potentially generating economic growth and development. These elements are characteristics of this type of economy: It can foster income-generation, job creation, and export earnings. It embraces economic, cultural and social aspects interacting with technology, intellectual property, and tourism goals. It is a set of knowledge-based economic activities with a development dimension and cross-cutting linkages at macro and micro levels to the overall economy. It is a feasible development option calling for innovative, multidisciplinary policy responses and interministerial action. Above all, at the heart of the creative economy are the creative industries.

The central input of the creative economy is the creative elements. The creation process or creative phase signifies the essential contribution of the value chain, in which finally an idea with cultural value is created (Piedras, 2010). According to Hartley (2005) the creative economy includes sectors and processes whose input is creativity, especially culture. The goal is to generate at the local level and distribute globally goods and services with symbolic value and economic, provoking and incorporating to profound social, organizational, political, educational and economic changes. The creative economy is not only creating new ideas but also seeking to combine all the possible elements such as culture, society, technology, economy, politics, among others, in order to create a value that remains engraved in people. As something innovative and with avant-garde characteristics is based on the potential of creative goods to generate economic growth and development. The concept includes economic, cultural and social aspects, technology, intellectual property, and tourism. Composed of the so-called creative industries, defined in four categories: heritage, arts, media and functional creations (Oliveira, 2014). According to Murphy (2012: 179), cultural and creative industries "are those concerned with the development amd dissemination of goods and services that are cultural in nature: works of art, crafts, music and architecture; television programs, theater productions and movies; toys and video games; published materials; advertisements; cultural tourism sites and more".

The creative industries have been classified into four groups. First, there are "core" or "key" industries that produce and distribute works subject to copyright protection and additional rights such as movies and the video industry, music, performing arts, publishers, computer programs, and databases. Data, television and radio, advertising, and visual and graphic arts, including photography.

The second group is made up of the so-called "interdependent" industries, which include those that produce, manufacture and sell the equipment necessary for the creation or use of works or other protected products. In the field of interdependent industries, activities such as the production of television sets, compact disc players and DVDs, equipment for electronic games, computers, musical instruments, paper, photocopies, and photographic and cinematographic instruments, among others, are included.

The third group, called the "partial" industries, includes those where a portion of the activities is related to jobs and other protected materials. This group includes clothing, architecture, sports footwear, interior designers, furniture, glass, porcelain, jewelry, handicrafts, wallpaper, carpets, toys and museums industries.

Finally, the fourth group is that of "non-dedicated" industries, in which part of the activities are linked with the communication, transmission, diffusion or sales of products/services and whose activities are not contemplated in the "central" or "key" industries (UNCTAD, 2008). As shown in Table 8.1, due to the wide variety of creative industries in the world, WIPO and UNESCO have classified creative industries differently.

Table 8.1 Classification of creative industries

Classification according to WIPO	Classification according to UNCTAD
Core industries:	**Traditional cultural expressions**
Advertising	Handicrafts
Video society	Festival celebrations
Film and video	**Performance arts**
Music	Live music
Performing arts	Theater
Editorial	Dance
Software	Opera
Television and radio	Circus
Visula and graphic art	Puppets

(Contd.)

Classification according to WIPO	Classification according to UNCTAD
Industries	**Audiovisual**
Electronics material	Cinema
Electronics instruments	TV
Paper	Radio
Photocopiers	Other
Partial industries	**New media**
Architecture	Software
Clothes	Video game
Footwear	Digital creative content
Design	**Creative services**
Fashion	Architecture
Household goods	Advertising
Toys	RD creatives
	Cultural
	Recreational
	Design
	Interior
	Graphic
	Fashion
	Jewelry
	Toys
	Editorial and print media
	Books
	Press
	Other publications
	Visual arts
	Paintings
	Sculptures
	Photographs
	Antiques
	Cultural sites
	Archaeological
	Museums
	Libraries
	Exhibitions
	Google Translate for Business:Translator ToolkitWebsite Translator

Soruce: UNESCO 2013

A creative economy must integrate economic opportunities and social inclusion to succeed for reasons of social and economic justice for the creative economy to become a creative society. We need to see people as more than gears in the economy, see people simultaneously as workers and citizens and develop an approach that recognizes both (Grams and Warr, 2003).

The economic activities related to creativity and culture happen mainly in cities with particular characteristics. In this regard, Landry (2000) claims that cities have the single most important reserve: its people. Creativity replacements locality, natural resources and access to the market, become the crucial factor of the dynamic growth of the city. Landry argues that now numerous cities in the world are going through evolution eras, which often are evoked by renewed vitality of globalization. These changes fluctuate from region to region. In areas such as East Asia, cities raise, and elsewhere, such as Europe, the old industries are decreasing and cities added value does not depend on what is produced, but rather on the intellectual capital, that is used for products, processes and services (Landry, 2006).

The concept of a creative city refers a city where varied cultural activities are an essential element of the city's economic and social activities. "These cities are often created on a strong social and cultural infrastructure; they have relatively high level of employment in the creative sectors and try to be attractive to inward investment due to its good cultural infrastructure" (Levickaitė, 2011). Another important factor is the cooperation among different actors in a precise atmosphere. Therefore, to improve a city as a creative, the enhancement in the business environment and effective cooperation among enterprises, governmental, research and development institutions is important (Navickas and Malakauskaitė, 2008). Finally, the basis concept of a creative city is: "to stimulate the innovation of the individuals and institutes inside the city, to excavate their potentials, and to create the values" (Zhou, 2014).

However, creative cities employ their creative potential in diverse ways. Some play as hubs, offering cultural experiences for visitors and inhabitants of the city, showing their cultural heritage, or cultural activities through performing and visual arts (Levickaitė, 2010). Therefore, a few cities such as Beirut, Edinburgh or Salzburg are building their identity through festivals while others cities attend of larger cultural and media industries, which provide employment and income. In other cases, the important role of culture in the creative city is associated with arts and the ability of culture to promote the city's well-being, social relationships and cultural identity (UNCTAD, 2008).

In this context, creativity plays a key role in the development of the cities and their residents. The cities contribute to spreading the economy and creating jobs while also enhancing the quality of life of citizens by contributing to a city's social fabric and cultural diversity, and serving to define common identities (UNESCO, 2016). In addition, "by boosting cultural participation and by generating or reviving public living spaces, creativity also becomes a driver of inclusion and well-being. Cities are at the heart of these development processes based on the potential of culture and creativity. Cities are vital spaces for growth, innovation and inter-cultural dialogue" (UNESCO, 2016).

2. The Creative Economy as a Gear for Development

As world economies become increasingly competitive and productive, the key to success in the international market lies in the ingenuity and individual skills of their creators, and the support that they can obtain from governmental or private sources to reach the global market. The creative and cultural industries have become prominent agendas in recent years, not only governments have identified the growing consumer potential for the creative/cultural economy in the local markets. They have also seen the agenda of the creative economy as a center for the growth of external markets. This programme includes creativity, innovation, the growth of small businesses and access to global markets. (O'Connor, 2009). The creative industries are setting fundamental precedents, as opposed to less agile and dynamic sectors of the economy: they interpret and apply knowledge in innovative ways, they adopt cutting-edge technologies and new business and cooperation models with ease, they think according to international plans, and they use technology to get closer to their customers (Araujo, 2015).

One reason why the idea of the creative industries has been widely spread is that it joins two contemporary policy clues. On the one hand, it promotes elements of high-growth production of ICT and R & D in the new economy. On the other, it impulses forms of consumption based on cultural identity and social empowerment (Cunningham, 2007). Thus, the creative economy has become a topical issue of the international economic and development agenda during this decade.

Governments fast accepted the prescription that the creative economy can help to a rapid economic growth as well to add value. In addition, states recognize that this economy is essential for economic development and the assumption that creative people need unique environments to be successful. Finally, the creative economy has been linked to an apparently transformational aspiration: creativity as a means of "modernization", that is, to change the mentality and the industrial structure (European Institute for Comparative Cultural Research, 2008).

In developed countries, the creative economy is overgrowing. In fact states that belong to the Organization for Economic Cooperation and Development (OECD), the creative economy grows at twice the speed of the service sector and four times as compared to manufacturing (Rosas, 2012).

Consumption drives the post-industrial economies more and more, and their nature is changing. Increasingly consumer activity around the media and culture is the "do it yourself ", meaning content generated by the user. For some years now there has been more user-generated content on the Internet than those produced and produced professionally (Cunningham, 2007).

An idea of the creative economy in the developing world focuses on creative capital, rich cultural resources existing in all cultures. While exploiting these resources, creative industries allow countries to know their heritage, define unique cultural identity, also provide the source of economic growth, opportunities to establish new workpaces, react to globalized global challenges. The creative economy fosters social participation, cultural variety and the social evolution of humanity. (Levickaitė, 2012)

Undoubtedly, the trend towards digital is currently the highest. The use of digital technology has evolved with cultural development, both for consumers and for businesses. Not only has our way of working changed, but it has also driven the creation of wholly new business models, concerning production, distribution, and consumption, which integrate valuable content with technology.

As an engine of development, creativity and culture are recognized by the economic value that the cultural and creative industries generate regarding job creation, and by how they stimulate the appearance of new technologies or innovative ideas. More importantly, the non-monetized benefits of culture also drive development and can lead to transformative change. (UNESCO, 2013). On the other hand, the creative economy can generate economic growth, jobs, and profits for export and at the same time promote social inclusion, cultural diversity, and human development (UNCTAD, 2008).

As mentioned by UNESCO there is a firm belief that the promotion of local industries should be further developed to improve living conditions in poor regions (UNESCO, 2013). Policymakers need a higher capacity to understand how individual creative workers and small cultural enterprises operate, and closer links between them and creative workers are required.

In this context, China's international trade is characterized as being "cheap", so they usually face trade difficulties with other countries. With a low cost of labor as a comparative advantage, China has concentrated on developing a processing industry oriented to labor-intensive and resource-intensive exports, which has a characteristic of high energy expenditure, high pollution and high dependence on raw materials, which is why in China the faster foreign trade grows, more natural resources are demanded; the more it is exported, the more deterioration is caused to the environment and, at the same time, the less dynamic there is to adjust the sectoral structure (Trápaga, 2012).

The initial objective of the creative economies may be to seek the development of the economy, but nowadays many countries have ended up changing their purpose for their economic interests, that is, the states have decided to produce goods in mass, that even if they are considered creative products and they do not worry about the welfare of their society, bringing with them child exploitation, long working hours, and lack of benefits.

Currently, the destructive economy is determined by the interest of companies and governments to obtain only economic benefits, which prevent the objectives of the application of the creative industry in an economy from being adequately carried out, since its use avoids the permanence of culture as one of the foundations for development.

3. Creative Economy and Creative Cities in China

The "creative economy" sector has outperformed many other traditional growth sectors during the last world economic recession, boosting economic performance and offering employment opportunities during a period of slow global economic growth (BID, 2014). China is moving and goes beyond just ensuring essential supplies. It is acquiring shares of African companies with productive potential. By buying 70% of the shares of Zimbabwe's only electric power generation plant in Hwange and Kariba, in addition to shares of the national railroad, the Chinese entered areas where other developing nations are afraid to tread. In addition, at the micro level, Chinese entrepreneurs are quickly replacing small retailers and local manufacturers on the streets of Harare (Ramanathan, 2008). Another example of the expansion of Chinese economy beyond the traditional role as a manufacturing country drive to export is the Belt and Road Initiative. This initiative, as a whole, is part of China's development strategy, in its quest to deepen its economic ties with countries in Asia, Europe, and Africa. In its national states and connect more than four billion people (Valderrey and Lemus, 2017).

From this perspective, the governmental support to the creative economy in China is part of a more broad vision: consolidate the welfare of the Chinese population. About that, the China President Xi Jinping, in a discourse to UNESCO in 2014, explained that: "the Chinese dream will be realized through balanced development and mutual reinforcement of material and cultural progress." (Thiruchelvam, 2014). Therefore, creativity and culture are a binomial that is strengthening the economic activity in China.

According to Keane (2010) this gradual change from the cultural to the creative is structured around the shift from "made in China" to "created in China", a change from repetitive and copied products to original products, and from industrial products to postindustrial, which demands and provokes a mobilization of creativity, and all this under the heading of the "new great leap forward". The development of creative industries in China has taken many forms. In this country, creative industries are relatively new, and their development, similar to that of other industries and services, depended in the first stage of foreign support (Fung, 2016).

In 2009, with the publication of the Cultural Industry Promotion Plan by the State Council the Chinese government provided a comprehensive and systematic road to Chinese cultural reform and development, with the goal of building a Socialist culturally strong nation. So, cultural industries were elevated to the level of national strategy (Xiang, 2014). Now, China is trying to move away from the label of being a manufacturer of only low-cost products. Politicians want Chinese companies to do things that not only help boost demand for their exports but also create better-paying jobs. One of the reasons has been the economic slowdown of its primary export markets, such as the United States and the eurozone, which has hurt the demand for their goods (Patience, 2014).

It will also develop the cultural industry until the sector becomes a pillar of its economy by 2020 through the creation of large cultural groups, the opening of theaters, leisure complexes or bookstores and other measures to boost demand. This is reflected in a government plan published by the official Xinhua agency, which aims to place cultural business groups as world leaders in a matter of a few years (El Informador, 2017).

Worldwide there are currently 116 cities considered "Creative Cities" by UNESCO (2010). UNESCO's Creative Cities Network was created in 2004 to promote cooperation to and between cities that identify creativity as a strategic factor for sustainable urban development. These cities work towards a common goal: to position creativity and cultural industries at the center of their local development plan and to cooperate internationally on the subject. In the UNESCO Creative Cities Network, China has eight cities on the list.

The UNESCO Creative Cities Network, established in 2004, reflects the changing perception of culture and its role in society (UNESCO 2010). This Network was based on the idea that even though many cities in the world realize that the creative industries play an increasingly important role in their local economic and social development plans, they obviously do not see how they could use this potential or recruit suitable staff for this development.

Table 8.2 Creativies Cities in East Asia

Country	City	Type
China	Beijing	Design
	Changsha	Media Arts
	Chengdu	Gastronomy
	Hangzhou	Crafts and Folk Arts
	Jingdezhen	Crafts and Folk Arts
	Macao	Gastronomy
	Qingdao	Film
	Shenzhen	Design
	Shanghai	Design
	Shunde	Gastronomy
	Suzhou	Crafts and Folk Arts
	Wuhan	Design
Japan	Kanazawa	Crafts and Folk Arts
	Kobe	Design
	Hamamatsu	Music
	Nagoya	Design
	Sapporo	Media Arts
	Sasayama	Crafts and Folk Arts
	Tsuruoka	Gastronomy

(Contd.)

Country	City	Type
Republic of Korea	Bucheon	Literature
	Busan	Film
	Daegu	Music
	Gwangju	Media Arts
	Jeonju	Gastronomy
	Icheon	Crafts and Folk Arts
	Seoul	Design
	Tongyeong	Music

Source: UNESCO, 2017.

The main goal of this Network is to facilitate the development of cultural groups around the world—to exchange technical knowledge, experience, examples of successful activities and promote local economic and social development through creative industries. To achieve better development results, the cultural industries must be divided into separate subsectors so the Creative City Network has been divided into seven thematic networks. Cities can choose one area, in which to focus their efforts.

Cities with the recognized creative products of literature, film, music, folk music, design, information technology (new media) and gastronomy can connect to the network. Cities are encouraged to focus on those areas that have the greatest economic and social development potential.

The Creative Cities Network was initiated and developed on the basics of arts and main cultural industries such as literature, music and folklore. An economic evaluation problem has appeared and later solutions have led to the network model, which is based on more innovative and market orientated attitude rather than on elite arts and their advantages.

Table 8.3 The Creative Cities in China

Creative Field	City	Year to joint to network creative city
Gastronomy	Chengdu	2010
	Shunde	2014
	Macao	2017

(Contd.)

Creative Field	City	Year to joint to network creative city
Design	Shenzhen	2008
	Shanghai	2010
	Beijing	2012
	Wuhan	2017
Crafts and Folk Arts	Hangzhou	2012
	Jingdezhen	2014
	Suzhou	2014
Media Arts	Changsha	2017
Films	Qingdao	2017

Source: UNESCO, 2017.

In the Chinese case, some dominant cities have begun to focus on their cultural alignment in urban construction, wholly exploit their cultural details and civilization with the aim of contour their urban landscapes and form innovative enterprise culture, thus to strengthen their reputation in the world (Zhou, 2014). For instance, Guangzhou, Guangdong Province, projected to construct the city into a modern cultural central city. Wuhan, Hubei Province, planned that the innovation of urban environment should be showcased to the world, and the city should display its characters, highlight its cultural details, create the new bright spots, and transform into "Cultural Wuhan". Hangzhou, Zhejiang Province, proposed the cultural concept of urban development, namely, Learning in Hangzhou, Living in Hangzhou, Business in Hangzhou. Ningbo, Zhejiang Province, proposed the construction of cultural amenities such as Culture Corridor along the Three Rivers, which demonstrates its cultural meaning and modern atmosphere (Zhou, 2014).

According to Florida (2011) Shanghai, Beijing and Tianjin are the top creative cities in China. Shanghai is located on the east coast of China near the Yangtze River Delta. Shanghai is considered internationally for its combination of Western and Eastern cultures (UNESCO, 2016). The city is the largest commercial and financial hub in China, with a surface area of 6,340.5 square kilometers and a population of 24.15 million inhabitants (National Bureau of

Statistic of China, 2017). Shanghai was the first city in China to have creative industry units such as the first design, film and music studios (UNESCO, 2016). In fact, although the beginnings of the film industry in China dates back to 1905 when for the first time a studio in Beijing filmed famous actors of the Chinese opera, the establishment of the film industry originated in the city of Shanghai in the decade of 1920 (Zhong, Zhang and Zhang, 1997). In 2010, Shanghai joined the UNESCO Creative Cities Network as City of Design. In 2013, the creative industries in Shanghai reached an added value of 255.5 billion Yuan, an increase of 11.8% from the previous year (UNESCO, 2016). The added value of industrial design increased by 10.3% to attain 63.6 billion Yuan meanwhile the added value of architecture design increased by 10.8%, to reach 128.5 billion yuan RMB (UNESCO, 2016). By the end of 2013, Shanghai was home to 87 Creative Clusters, over 4,000 innovative design-related agencies and institutions, 283 art institutions, 239 art and cultural community centres, 100 museums, 25 libraries and 743 archive institutions (UNESCO, 2016).

On the other hand, Beijing has an enormous and vibrant past. The city was an ancient historical capital and political center of China during the Yuan and Qing dynasty and capital of People's Republic of China since the triumph of the communism in 1949 (Haw, 2007). Undoubtedly, the city is the country's cultural center. Beijing has 47 public libraries, including the National Library of China, more than 170 museums and more than 300 theatres, including the National Centre for the Performing Arts, giving more than 12,000 performances every year (UNESCO, 2016). Also, the city has 119 design colleges and more than 30,000 students (UNESCO, 2016). At the same time, Beijing excels in its animated design sector. The design sector is one of Beijing's pillar industries, employs nearly 250,000 people and has a total value estimated at over 160 billion yuan RMB (UNESCO, 2016). Also, the capital of China holds worldwide events in this sector as the Beijing Design Week, the China Red Star Design Award, Beijing Fashion Week, the Beijing International Film Festival, the Beijing International Cultural & Creative Industry Expo and the Beijing Science and Technology Exposition (UNESCO, 2016). Beijing has more than 30 Creative Cluster Areas and provides approximately 270 design and creativity workshops to enhance women's employment (UNESCO, 2016). Finally, the city is home to some of the world's most renowned architectural designs, such as the National Centre for the Performing Arts, the Galaxy SOHO designed and Terminal 3 of Beijing Capital Airport as a consequence of developers and government officials to promote Beijing as a new global city (Ren, 2008).

Shenzhen is a significant design hub and one of the leading design cities in China. The city, which used to be an ordinary border town neighboring Hong Kong, was chosen as one of China's first special economic zones in 1980 (Lemus, 2011). As the frontline leading China's reform and opening-up policy, the city has been regarded as the model for the country's economic success over the past three decades (UNESCO, 2016). Increasingly, Shenzhen established the concept of modern Chinese design. Thus, it has gradually become a part of the city and its inhabitants. Shenzhen has more than 6,000 design firms accounting for 100,000 employees, creating a yearly output of around 11 billion yuan (USD1.54 billion) (UNESCO, 2016). Designers in Shenzhen cover various design fields such as graphic design, industrial design, interior and architectural design, fashion design, toy design, jewelry design, crafts design, and others (UNESCO, 2016). Also, in the evolution from national production toward globally oriented economy China's textiles and apparel industry have been experiencing considerable changes concerning the establishment of regional clusters, a process that Shenzhen has not been exempt (Zhang and To, 2004). The city has become China's largest production base for women's clothing. More than 30,000 designers work for more than 800 Chinese fashion brands (UNESCO, 2016). The ability for innovation is robust in Shenzhen. Nowadays the city is one of the vast Chinese bases for high-tech industries and an important center for the development of intellectual property rights (UNESCO, 2016). Annually, Shenzhen's enterprises promote about 40,000 patents, half of which are concerned with innovative designs (UNESCO, 2016).

The last example of how the creative industries is a lever to economic growth is the transformation of the city of Hangzhou. After hosting the World Leisure Expo 2006 and the China Creative Expo 2007, Hangzhou has development a creative cluster to boost the development (Wuwei, 2011). This city was one of the ancient capitals of the Chinese empire during the Southern Song dynasty, from 1127 to 1276. In this period, Hangzhou had become "the largest and richest city in the world" (Mungello, 1994: 14). In the last years, Hangzhou has taken a route for the economic transformation of the secondary and tertiary industries through the development of its cultural and creative industries. Hangzhou's vast history and culture have proven to be most vital in this progress, notably regarding craft industries (UNESCO, 2016). The city is famous for numerous handicraft traditions including silk and tea production and porcelain and bronze sculptures: "Having long been the historic design, production and trade center of Chinese silk, Hangzhou has been able to preserve this traditional craft heritage" (UNESCO, 2016). In addition, Hangzhou is famous for being China's Tea Capital. The city has always been one of the country's most famous tea production regions, principally concerning the production of the West Lake Longjing Green Tea. Additionally, the stone carvings by the Xiling Seal Engraver's Society are particularly notable as a witness of the city's long-lasting crafts and folk arts tradition. The Chinese Government has recognized the city as a "National Cultural and Creative Centre". In 2014, the creative industries made up 17.5% of the city's GDP, with more than 336,000 people employed in the sector (UNESCO, 2016).

4. Conclusions

Although there is no specific definition of what a creative economy is because it is a new concept that is still in development, it is possible to affirm that this thought encloses a powerful idea: how to improve the life of the residents of the city through creativity. In this sense "Creativity is a lot like innovation, it comes with high risk, uncertainty, transaction costs, network externalities, spillovers and public good effects that imply that markets alone will not be sufficient to create an adequate resource base" (Barrowclough, D. and Kozul-Wright, Z., 2008: 5). The sudden emergence in the last decade of the creative industries as a sector for initiatives and businesses, whether governmental or private, nationally or internationally, demonstrates that the creative economy seeks to improve the conditions in which the population finds itself, thus taking advantage of the resources with cultural value that are characteristic of each society, region, country.

In the era of globalization everyday something "new" will be introduced to the market. This fact means that daily there are new creations, products, and services that can be integrated or supported by activities linked to the creative industries. We have reached an era in which boosting the creative industries has given solutions to the internal problems of different economies, which is why more and more countries seek to be part of the list of "creative cities". The Chinese show the importance of public policy that supports the transformation of the traditional economic activities in creative economic activities.

Due to the benefits that the economies have obtained through the implementation of creative industries, not only at the local level but also for the development of the trade they generate with other nations, developing and even marginalized countries have begun to boost their creative industries to generate the development of the country. Owing to the creative economy suggesting a concern for the socio-economic inclusion of marginalized areas or classes, the emphasis on the results of the concept fell on the aggregate statistics of economic impact, especially its contribution to GDP and the growth rate of the economy. The bet is then to take full advantage of this economic potential for growth and development derived from the comparative and competitive advantages of our economic-cultural activity.

The Chinese experience of creative industries offers some clues about how those activities could be implemented to obtain benefits in countries that are in the process to develop. First, history matters. The creative industries are linked, in one way or another, with the cultural richness product of a solid past. It is not only to have a history but also to re-create, spread and be proud of it. In this way, the past, recreated in new ways, can be an essential input to inspiration to elaborate cultural products. Second, the creative does not bloom in a material vacuum. Creativity needs a unique space. In this sense, the cities are the best place to attract talent and create innovative space. The towns can transform in cultural hubs with an appropriate public policy that encourages the cultural activities, the adequate spaces to art exhibitions with a robust and modern infrastructure. Finally. The changes are no immediate. Adopting a medium and long-term approach is necessary. This approach needs to combine the interest of the government a local, regional and national level with the entrepreneurs and businessman. The Chinese case demonstrates that it is possible to set long-term goals and work for them every day until you reach them.

Chapter 9
The China's International Cooperation, a Pathway to Escape the Middle-income Trap in Latin America?

Roberto Hernández Hernández

In recent years, China has significantly increased aid and cooperation to investment in countries of all continents through various cooperation mechanisms, both novel and customary. This has preoccupied traditional donor countries, as well as government and business entities with historical ties of aid and cooperation investments around the world; especially worried are the United States and Europe, which have seen how China's influence extends in Asia, Africa, and Latin America.

The Chinese government upholds that international cooperation is an important element to alleviate the consequences of underdevelopment, such as poverty, malnutrition, lack of infrastructure, administrative inefficiency, and low levels of education; but it emphasizes that external cooperation *per se* will not bring the development of the recipient countries. This task is the responsibility of each country, and its fulfillment has to be in accordance with its own socioeconomic and political conditions.

Beijing carries out its strategy of international cooperation with the objective of reinserting China in the global economy with geopolitical implications. By delivering loans, increasing FDI, and building stronger trade ties, China is ensuring market access for its companies' export sector and opening new markets for sectors with excess capacity, such as infrastructure. Maintaining strong economic growth is also important for China's social and political stability (Avendano, Melguizo and Miner 2017; Delfsma, Wilfred and Duyters Greert, 2009).

China's international cooperation policy is based on the idea of the UN's

International Cooperation for Development (ICD)[1] rather than on the Official Development Assistance (ODA) of the OECD. Since China has gone away from a recipient country to a donor aid, and evaluated how ODA is running and applying, Beijing defined its own international cooperation, but without facing OECD approaches.

Chinese government sustains that through foreign aid "it promotes development and international cooperation" within the South-South context, providing assistance and support to other countries for reducing poverty and improving living standards in the least developed countries (State Council Information Office, 2014). On the other hand, in the context of general concept of cooperation, China has established the Belt and Road Initiative (formerly known as One Belt One Road program), and established financial institutions such as the Asian Infrastructure Investment Bank (AIIB), the BRICS Bank, and other investment funds to support cooperation with Asian, European, African and Latin American countries, competing with the resources provided by Western countries or international organizations. This article aims to contribute to the improving of the understanding of international cooperation, the way China uses it, and which are the implications for Latin American region.

1. Some Basic Concepts of International Cooperation for Development (ICD)

To improve the understanding of China's support to foreign countries it is necessary to define international cooperation concepts and foreign aid, and the sense in which China understands and uses these ideas. In this respect, it is necessary to start from the fact that there are deep differences between Chinese and Western discourses on development cooperation and foreign aid (Zhang, Gu and Chen, 2015).

According with Alonso and Glennie (2015), in one sense, the term development cooperation remains almost synonymous with financial aid or, even more narrowly, with ODA. And on the other hand, development cooperation may be defined very broadly, to include, for instance, market flows (i.e. remittances or foreign direct investments). However, exist grey areas in this field. In particular, the real intention of an intervention is whether to favor

① See some basic definitions in the next section.

a particular developing country or to promote the interests of the international partner (whether a country of private organization).

Traditionally, International Cooperation for Development (ICD) has been conceived as an instrument to provide goods and services to solve poverty-related problems in developing countries. In this sense cooperation is related to aid and assistance to attend the poor countries low standards of life; that basically means that resources flow from industrialized countries to developing ones (North-South cooperation). This is known as Official Development Assistance (ODA), a concept defined by the Development Assistance Committee (DAC) of the Organization for Economic Cooperation and Development (OECD).

In this way, ODA is defined as government aid designed to promote the economic development and welfare of developing countries (loans and credits for military purposes are excluded). Aid may be provided bilaterally, from donor to recipient, or channelled through a multilateral development agency such as the United Nations or the World Bank (OECD, 2018).[①]

Another vision of international cooperation, which concerns the implementation of a wide range of mechanisms for cooperation, refers to the provision of public goods, such as the ozone hole, climate change, HIV-AIDS, drug trafficking and financial volatility. These latter themes are not directly related to poverty but are an important matter for the international system (Kaul, Inge, Grunberg and Stern, 1999).

A broader conception of ICD is the one promoted by the United Nations (UN), which is to tackle global poverty, to which issues related to international public goods have recently been added. Thus, in September 2015, the UN General Assembly adopted the "2030 Agenda for Sustainable Development". The UN resolution approving the 2030 Agenda, recognizes that the greatest challenge in the world today is the eradication of poverty and affirms that its elimination is necessary to achieve sustainable development. The topics covered in the 17 objectives, broken down into 169 targets, are poverty, hunger, food security, nutrition, sustainable agriculture, healthy living, well-being, education,

---

① ODA includes grants, "soft" loans (where the grant element is at least 25% of the total) and the provision of technical assistance. The OECD maintains a list of developing countries and territories; only aid to these countries counts as ODA. The list is periodically updated and currently contains over 150 countries or territories with per capita incomes below USD 12 276 in 2010. A long-standing United Nations target is that developed countries should devote 0.7% of their gross national income to ODA. This indicator is measured as a percentage of gross national income and million USD constant prices, using 2015 as the base year. (OECD, 2018).

gender equality, water availability, affordable energy, economic growth, infrastructure, industrialization, reduction of inequality between countries, adequate urbanization, supply of sustainable products, climate change, conservation of the oceans and ecosystems, access to justice, and sustainable development (ONU, 2016).

The immediate precedent of 2030 Agenda is the Millennium Development Goals (MDGs) adopted in 2000. The MDGs, which should have been achieved by 2015, were: (1) to eradicate extreme poverty and hunger; (2) to achieve universal primary education; (3) to promote gender equality and empower women; (4) to reduce child mortality; (5) to improve maternal health; (6) to combat HIV/AIDS, malaria, and other diseases; (7) to ensure environmental sustainability; and (8) to develop a global partnership for development. Obviously, these objectives are far from being achieved, such as halving extreme poverty worldwide. But now, the UN proposes a new agenda with objectives extended by another period of 15 years.

In order to systematize international cooperation actions, several countries, including developed and developing countries, have organized their own development cooperation units. There are also international and multilateral organizations, as well as non-governmental organizations that carry out actions of this type. At the international level, 43 countries have a development aid agency; China, for example, has the Ministry of Commerce's Foreign Assistance Department (MOFCOM), although as it will be seen in the following section, China's international cooperation is carried out through several national institutions.

On the other hand, there are several ways of framing international cooperation. The most common are North-South (vertical), South-South (horizontal), multilateral, regional, bilateral, decentralized, triangular, etcetera, which often overlap with each other. Specifically, North-South and South-South cooperation have a great ideological connotation: the first, refers to that traditionally granted by developed countries to developing ones, and the second is that which excludes rich countries. However, even among the "south" nations, there are degrees of development, which makes the relationship between the countries of the "south" a deal between unequal, such as China, Brazil, India or Australia, which provide funds with a South-South connotation. Even among the emerging countries the South-South contributions are very marked (Table 9.1).

Table 9.1 Donation from Selected Emerging Countries, 2009–2013

(Unit: Millions dollar)

COUNTRY	2009	2010	2011	2012	2013
China	1,803.90	1,857.40	2,469.90	2,644.20	3,136.90
Brazil	362.2	499.7	NA	NA	NA
India	488	576.9	730.7	605	NA
South Africa	121.2	118.2	160.5	151.9	156.7

Source: OECD (2013) statistics on resource flows to developing countries.

China, like the other international agents—states and agencies, interacting in an anarchic international system, proceeds accordingly to its self-interest. In the last three decades, we have witnessed a radical change in China's identity. This country, while fundamentally defending the international status quo, tries to modify it and operate it according to its interests. China, like any other great power, has several nuances in its foreign policy, which it socializes, depending on the field where it is operating. In addition, without violating the standards, it interprets and exerts them in line with its national objectives. This idea is fully applicable to the field of International Cooperation.

2. China's International Cooperation

Consistent with the objective of turning China into a global power, the Chinese leadership has been implementing various schemes of international cooperation. In this way, China has been participating in the cooperation mechanism explained above, but also has defined two schemes of international cooperation.

The first is that of foreign aid, conceived and implemented as an instrument to assist poorer countries in the context of South-South cooperation. The second is cooperation in the broad sense of the term, which includes mutual support to deal with problems of public goods, such as climate change, science and technology enhancing, education development, face pollution, combating terrorism and lack of governance, etcetera. On these aspects, China accepts the two-way assistance, and the modalities of bilateral, trilateral or multilateral cooperation.

2.1 Foreign Aid

China's foreign aid materializes in the strategy and actions in one direction, that is, from China to the less developed countries, especially in Africa and Asia, and to a lesser extent in Latin America and Europe. In this way, the Chinese government, through various government agencies, provides external assistance to several countries—which could be classified as "for development"—in the form of infrastructure projects and grants, concessional loans for project funding, disaster relief, scholarships to students, etcetera. Nevertheless, China's official aid program is poorly transparent and therefore insufficiently understood (Brautigam, 2011).

China's international aid, from a Western perspective, is related to the concepts of "rising" or "growing power". However, the position of the Chinese government differs from that approach; in this way, international aid for development and the concepts of "ascending" and "growing power" are rarely correlated in official discourse.

Most of China's current official aid to foreign countries, of financial nature, does not meet the parameters of the ODA's IADC. Specifically, export credits, unsubsidized state loans, or investment promotion support do not fall under the category of ODA. In this sense, the very different perspectives that China and the West hold on these issues stand out.

From a Western perspective, China's separation of international cooperation for development and foreign aid may seem contradictory, given China's experience in this field. That is, since the end of the 1970s, China was one of the largest recipients of development aid through the ODA, but recently it has become a very important player as a donor country in the field of international development. Apart from the concept of "international cooperation for development", "aid for development" and "aid", commonly accepted, it interprets and implements essentially two concepts: "aid to the outside", which is framed in the speech of Chinese leaders within a clear foreign policy strategy (Zhang, Gu and Chen, 2015).

The rapid expansion in recent years of China's participation in the support of developing countries has awakened the international interest and concern of developed countries. Critics in general, see the Chinese program of country support as enormous and focused mainly on underpinning out-of-state regimes or pave the way for Chinese companies to gain access to external resources. They are concerned that Chinese practices will challenge the reforms achieved with great difficulty in the area of official aid and financing. Others believe (echoing Beijing's official speech) that China places emphasis on mutual benefit and South-South cooperation, and argue that China is not a donor, but an equal partner. Admirers say China's financial leverage is an important counterpoint to official development assistance to the DAC Donor Committee, which allows countries to build infrastructure and invest in productive activities, areas neglected by OECD development cooperation in recent years (Bräutigam, 2011).

According to the Chinese leadership, the fundamental expressions about the CID are forceful:

> *China must continue to foster international cooperation, in order to maintain its current pace of development (...) in an increasingly globalized world, isolation brings nothing but ruin to countries. In order to achieve better development, it must be opened up. The drive for development and cooperation with the outside world will remain China's central policy in the coming decades. Whatever China does must be in line with this policy (People's Daily, 2011).*

2.2 China's Information on Foreign Aid

The institutional setting of foreign aid is somewhat complicated. Under the Chinese State Council there are three ministries and two financial institutions involved. Among the Ministry of Finance, the Ministry of Foreign Affairs and the Ministry of Commerce there is an "inter-agency coordination mechanism" (Government of China, 2011). The Ministry of Commerce, with its Department of Foreign Aid, is the leading coordinator. In total, there are estimated 15 to 23 agencies involved in implementing development aid (Stallings, 2017).

Government information is described in the white papers on foreign aid for 2011 and 2014. The first document provides a historical overview of China's foreign aid, with some basic figures on China's regional aid distribution. It explained that by the end of 2009, China had assisted 161 countries and more than 30 international and regional organizations, including 123 developing countries receiving regular Chinese aid (State Council Information Office, 2011; Zhang, Gu and Chen 2015).

The White Paper also provides a breakdown at the continental level of resources earmarked for China's foreign aid program, including 30 in Asia (which received 32.8 percent of China's foreign aid funds), 51 in Africa (45.7 percent), 18 in Latin America and the Caribbean (12.7 percent), 12 in Oceania (4 percent) and 12 in Eastern Europe (0.3 percent).

It is also noted that the poorest people live in Asia and Africa, and China accounts for 80% of that of external aid (State Council Information Office, 2011; Zhang, Gu and Chen, 2015). These figures show a slight change during the 2010–2012, as mentioned in the white paper "China Aid Abroad 2014" (State Council Information Office, 2014). In this sense, it is stated that Chinese aid covers 121 countries: 19 in Latin America and the Caribbean and 9 in Oceania.

According to the White Paper of 2014, from 2010–2012, China allocated $14.41 billion for foreign assistance through grants, interest-free, loans and preferential loans. During these three years, China provided 4,657.3 million dollars (36.2%) in grants, most of which was allocated for the creation of small or medium-sized welfare projects for recipient countries. The grants were also awarded to finance technical cooperation and human resources development, material assistance and emergency humanitarian aid in host nations.

During the same period, China offered 1466.2 million dollars (8.1%) of interest-free loans, which were used mainly to help the recipient countries build public facilities and launch projects to improve the people's living conditions. The largest amount of 7.17 billion dollars (55.7%) was earmarked for loans for large and medium-scale manufacturing projects and infrastructures, as well as to supply complete equipment, machinery and electronic products (Xinhua, 2014).

According to the same document, China spent most of its assistance funds on low-income developing nations, mainly those in Asia and Africa, in order to promote the realization of the Millennium Development Goals. In the same period, China provided assistance to a total of 121 countries, including 30 in Asia, 51 in Africa, 9 in Oceania, 19 in Latin America and the Caribbean and 12 in Europe (Xinhua, 2014).

The 2014 White Paper emphasizes China's cooperation through regional institutional structures such as the FOCAC (Forum on China Africa Cooperation) and ASEAN (Zhang, Gu and Chen, 2015; Sun, 2014). In the case of Latin America, China has taken as a regional reference the Community of Latin American and Caribbean States (CELAC). At the China-CELAC meeting in early 2015, the goal was to "build a community of shared future with the countries of Latin America and the Caribbean and a new example of South-South cooperation" (OIC, 2015).[①]

In both white papers, the main thematic priorities are identified, and these are agriculture, industry, economic infrastructure, public facilities, education,

① For more details on aid and cooperation for each Latin American countries, see Stallings (2017).

medical and health care, and climate change issues. The figures provided refer to the amounts of the projects that were completed, rather than the funds disbursed; these figures are rarely broken down by country or region.

Another characteristic of Chinese aid is the separation of the political and the strictly economic issues. From the official perspective, it is stated that when China offers foreign assistance, it adheres to the principles of not imposing any political condition (neutrality), not intervening in the internal affairs of the receiving nations (non-interference) and fully respecting their right to choose independently for its own path and development model (Xinhua, 2014).

Recently AidData (2017) published a detailed report on the official information of financial resources abroad in support of various projects title "China's Global Development Footprint. The clearest look yet at Chinese official finance worldwide". Taken from this database, in the following table are listed the main countries receiving foreign aid from China. ①

Table 9.2 Top 10 Recipients of Official Chinese Development Aid, 2000–2014

Country	Billion USD
Cuba	6.7
Cote d'Ivoire	4.0
Ethiopia	3.7
Zimbabwe	3.6
Cameroon	3.4
Nigeria	3.1
Tanzania	3.0
Cambodia	3.0
Sri Lanka	2.8
Ghana	2.5

Source: http://aiddata.org/china

2.3 China's International Cooperation from a Wide-Ranging Perspective

This type of cooperation refers to international supports focusing more

① See the database Chinese Global Official Finance Dataset, which captures the known universe of Chinese financed projects in 5 regions of the world from 2000–2014. It includes concessional and non-concessional sources of funding government institutions: Retrieved from http://aiddata.org/data/chinese-global-official-finance-dataset.

on public goods for economic development, instead of projects for alleviating poverty and its consequences, mentioned before in external aid. A paradigmatic case of this type of cooperation is the bilateral agreement Horizon 2020 WP 2018–2020 signed between European Union and China which include "24 new topics with a total budget of over 100 million euro will promote research and innovation cooperation", the "new package of flagship initiatives targeting the areas of Food, Agriculture and Biotechnologies, Environment and Sustainable Urbanization, Surface Transport, Safer and Greener aviation, and Biotechnologies for Environment and Human Health" (European Commission, 2017).

China's international cooperation, like that of the vast majority of countries, especially the developed ones, is an essential component of countries foreign policy, and respond fundamentally, to their national interests. In the specific case of China, the expansion and strengthening of foreign direct investment and international trade strategies is also related to its objectives of internal development and improvement in the standard of living of the population.

Other interpretations of China's international cooperation, range from the geopolitical perspectives to those centered on the general balance of classical economics and Marxism itself. That is, a country with excess capital and technology needs to address the international market to avoid the indigestion of available resources.

As Avandano, Melguizo and Miner (2017) state:

> *Chinese companies are also racing to get some of their cash out the door. China's economy has slowed from double-digit growth rates to around 6.6% (OECD estimate for 2017), and many large Chinese firms are overly reliant on the domestic market for their revenue streams. In addition, and despite the economy's impressive performance and unprecedented poverty reduction (nearly 700 million have been lifted out of poverty since 1980), economic imbalances have arisen. At the same time, while China's growth has long been driven by investment, supported by high savings rates, the growth model has obvious financial risks, as well as excess capacity in heavy industry and real estate (Avandano, Melguizo and Miner, 2017).*

According to Buckley, et al (2007), the general theory of FDI, applied to China's circumstance pointed out that the three primary motivations for exporting capital are: "Foreign market seeking, efficiency (cost reduction) seeking, and resource seeking (including a subset that is known as strategic-asset seeking)". Analyzing more specifically the case of China FDI, the authors describe more accurately the following factors: (1) Capital market imperfections, (2) Ownership advantages of Chinese MNEs, and (3) Institutional factors influencing Chinese outward direct investment (ODI).

Finally, it is worth mentioning another critical perspective related to the Dependency Theory, widely developed since the mid-1950s by several reformers and Marxists. Applying Dependence approach to the case of China, it can be seen that this country has demanded raw materials and offered industrialized products, as developed countries have done for several decades. If this is the fundamental cause of underdevelopment, stagnation or reprimarization, is a fault that can hardly be attributed to a country that seeks its development, in many respects with great costs.

2.4 The Belt and Road Initiative

In the context of a wide-ranging international cooperation China is developing the Belt and Road Initiative. This strategy responds to the President Xi Jinping policy of increasing and reinforcing China's influence globally. To this end, it has placed a special emphasis on strengthening cooperation with the outside using any means at its disposal. In this sense, the Chinese regime has increased and strengthened regional free trade treaties, created new financial institutions and increased their influence on traditional ones, such as the International Monetary Fund and the World Bank.

The BRI is an important platform for deeping economic integration (Elek, 2015). It includes more than 68 countries and international organizations that have already signed an agreement with China. Many routes have been defined, departing from China, passing through Central Asia and reaching Africa and Europe. According to the Chinese government, the BRI cooperation mechanism is open for any region of the world. The BRI's global reach is well illustrated by the below map.

China has also recently signed memorandums with Brazil and Peru to begin studies of the railway construction project that would communicate the Atlantic and Pacific Oceans.

Although the mass media have put more emphasis on the construction of major infrastructure works as ports, railways, and highways, and the provision of financial resources by the Chinese authorities, (Elek, 2015; Zhang, 2015; Zhang Feng, 2015; Chanda, 2015), the BRI's general proposal embraces five areas of opportunity: policy co-ordination, facilities connectivity, unimpeded trade, financial integration, and people-to-people bonds (HKTDC, 2016). The projects that have been proposed in this context are of great importance for China, not only because of its geographic reach but also because of its emphasis on economic cooperation and its political and national security considerations.

The mechanisms of international cooperation have a clear Sinocentric perspective. From this viewpoint, supply chains linking China to the rest of the world need to be reorganized to allow the transfer of labor-intensive goods to other countries, which are no longer profitable in China. Beijing has indicated that it is willing to make the huge investments needed in infrastructure, providing the necessary human resources and carrying out the institutional modernization necessary to implement them. Capacity-building cooperation is vital to achieving a positive sum game that can be applied immediately, without the need for long and tortuous international treaties (Elek, 2015).

In order to put the BRI into operation, considered as a global reach initiative, the Chinese government is using all mechanisms of cooperation available to it at the bilateral, regional and multilateral levels (CNDR, 2015).

Financing options for the Silk Road Economic Belt and the 21st Century Maritime Silk Road include the already announced $40 billion Silk Road Fund, the China-ASEAN Interbank Association, the Shanghai Cooperation Organization Interbank Association, the China-Eurasia Economic Cooperation Fund, and—the most important—the AIIB, with an initial capital of 100 billion dollars raised among the initial 57 members.

Other multilateral development banks, such as the World Bank and the Asian Development Bank, have not only declared their willingness to support AIIB's success but also expressed their propensity to seek ways to accelerate their own lines of financing for Infrastructure development (Elek, 2015).

By mid-2016, the projects proposed by the Chinese government are the following:

- The New Eurasia Land Bridge Economic Corridor
- The China-Mongolia-Russia Economic Corridor
- China-Central Asia-West Asia Economic Corridor
- China-Indochina Peninsula Economic Corridor
- China-Pakistan Economic Corridor
- Bangladesh-China-India-Myanmar Economic Corridor[①]

---

① For more details about these projects, see HKTDC Research (2016), "The Belt and Road Initiative", https://beltandroad.hktdc.com/sites/default/files/ imported/beltandroadbasics/hktdc_1X0K715S_en.pdf.

Speaking at the Belt and Road Forum opening ceremony (Beijing, May 15 2017), Chinese President Xi Jinping announced an additional $124 billion in funding for the Belt and Road Initiative, including loans, grants and $8.7 billion in assistance to developing countries. Also, some $1 trillion has already been invested in BRI, with another several trillion due to being invested over the next decade (Griffiths, 2017; Perlez, and Huang: 2017).

2.5 The Belt and Road Forum Beijing

The Belt and Road Forum (BARF), took place in Beijing in mid-May 2017. 28 heads of state, 100 lower-level government officials, dozens of major international organizations and 1,200 delegates from various countries, attended the meeting. At this summit, international cooperation was the central concept in the dialogue and analysis of the participants. Only in the joint *communique* of leaders round table, this idea was mentioned 44 times in its various meanings, such as:

- Development and cooperation;
- Multilateral, Bilateral, North-South, South-South, and Triangular cooperation;
- Connectivity cooperation;
- Economic, industrial and financial cooperation;
- Besides deepening, promoting, strengthening cooperation.

2.6 BRI Ongoing Projects

1. A 260-mile railway to connect eight Asia Countries: 6 billion dollars project.

2. Building power plants in Pakistan to address chronic electricity shortages: $46 billion worth of investment.

- Gwandar Port in Pakistan.
- Kasakhstan's joint cross-border free trade zone.
- Hambantota deep sea port.
- Colombo Financial City.
- Chinese planners are mapping out train lines from Budapest to Belgrade, Serbia, providing another artery for Chinese goods flowing into Europe through a Chinese-owned port in Greece.

It should be noted that in respect of these projects, and in general on the BRI proposal, there are opinions that doubt the authenticity of the investments, the feasibility of some of these projects, and the insurmountable political problems in the schemes proposed by the Chinese government. The most obvious difficulties of Chinese investments in Latin America are in the mining sector in South America. Other projects have had to be canceled, such as the interoceanic canal in Nicaragua, the cancellation of the construction of the Dragon Mart in the Cancun area and the high-speed train between Mexico City and Querétaro. The opposite opinions to the BRI arise mainly, in some sectors of the USA, Europe, and India (Shepard, 2017).

The Chinese government recognizes the difficulties mentioned by the detractors of the BRI but carries out on a daily basis great diplomatic and administrative efforts to solve them. Faced with a geopolitical and geostrategic approach of global scope such as this Initiative, it is natural that there are voices in favor of and against it. In addition, an important element of China's international "cooperation" concerns the sale of arms and advice on their use.

3. China-Latin America Cooperation

Considering that China's aid to Latin America is very small (just 8.4%), it is more accurate referring to cooperation domain, where the experience and perspectives are much broader. Thus, since the perspective of this article, Chinese cooperation to Latin America (including aid), responds to the following criteria: ① economic, demanding raw materials and market for its industrialized products; ② political, participating in global geopolitics, by occupying spaces that the U.S. and other developed countries of Europe have neglected, and coping with the centre American Countries which did not have official diplomatic relation with China Mainland.

Regarding China's trade with Latin America and the Caribbean, cooperation is a way to expand it. Keep in mind that in recent years the trade between both parties has stalled. In 2000, the commercial volume was 12.5 billion dollars, for 2012 the figure exceeded 260 million, that is, an increase of more than 2000 percent in 12 years. From 2012 to the present, the figure has decreased slightly given the reduction in China's trade growth with Latin America, especially due to the decline in China's imports. But despite the impressive rise in the PRC's trade with Latin America, it accounted for only 6.7% of China's total trade in 2012. Trade exchanges have been generally asymmetrical. In addition, the composition of transactions has been defined, first, by China's huge demand for natural resources such as ferrous steel, copper, oil and soybeans, and second, by the push of manufactures into the Latin American market. (Mussacchio, 2015).

The cultural aspect is also part of China's push towards Latin America. In this sense, China's foreign policy toward Latin America (as to the rest of the world) takes into account smart power, defined as "the capacity of an actor to combine elements of hard power and soft power in ways that are mutually reinforcing that the actor's purposes are effective and efficient" (Wilson, 2008: 110).

China's cooperation with Latin America and the Caribbean has manifested in various changes in the economy, trade, politics, technological development, education, and so on. International cooperation in all its aspects is undoubtedly one of the fundamental issues that give meaning to the paper China's Policy Paper on Latin America and the Caribbean (Xinhua, 2016). This document analyses a wide range of areas and concepts, which define the Beijing perspective on cooperation with Latin America and the Caribbean (ALC). According with this official document:

> *Since 2014 the China-ALC relations have entered a new stage of comprehensive cooperation thanks that China-CELAC Forum has provided a new platform for cooperation between the two sides, setting the course for simultaneous and complementary development guided by the China-Latin American and Caribbean Countries Cooperation Plan (2015-2019), utilizing trade, investment and financial cooperation as driving forces, and identifying energy and resources, infrastructure construction, agriculture, manufacturing, scientific and technological innovation and information technology as cooperation priorities Latin America, enabling healthy interactions among the enterprises, society and government, and expanding the three financing channels of funds, credit loans and insurance, and speeding up quality improvement and upgrading of the cooperation promoting international cooperation, equity and justice.*

The document describes in detail all types of cooperation (both conceptual and political-strategic regional and global) that could be possible to carry out between China and Latin America and the Caribbean. The document is plenty of wishful thinking, that serves as a framework for any meeting at the bilateral, regional and multilateral levels.

Specifically, the Paper examines the following cooperation concepts: Win-win, South-South, Collective, among local governments, trade end services, e-commerce, industrial investment, financial (including monetary and with national, regional and international financial institutions), energy and resources, infrastructure, agriculture, scientific and technological innovation, civil aviation, civil nuclear energy, space, maritime, customs, social governance, social development, environment protection, poverty reduction, narrowing the gap between the rich and the poor, industrial investment, disease control, cultural, sports, mass media, tourism, consular, international political affairs, 2030 Agenda for Sustainable Development, cyber security, military exchanges and trilateral cooperation with relevant countries outside the region and international organizations.

In respect of Global Economic Governance the Paper strengthens coordination and cooperation in international economic and financial organizations and mechanisms such as the Group of 20, APEC, IMF, World Bank, Bank for International Settlements, Financial Stability Board and Basel Committee on Banking Supervision, advances multilateral trade negotiation processes with the WTO as the core, promotes the establishment of a balanced, win-win and inclusive multilateral trading system, and promotes economic integration in the Asia-Pacific region (Xinhua, 2016).

3.1 BRI and Latin America

In the face of BRI Chinese project, what could be the options for regions that are not specifically mentioned in this proposal, as is the case in Latin America? In this respect, it should be noted that the BRI is not a fixed plan, but an open and flexible initiative (as had mentioned before in this text) from which it can be interpreted that projects in any region or country would be able to anchor with the resources available in the Chinese financial institutions. For instance, Chinese media refers that BRI projects are included a railroad construction in South America.

More recently, the Asian Infrastructure Investment Bank (AIIB), announced its approval to the incorporation of Chile and Bolivia as members of this institution, which, with the integration of Bahrain, Cyprus, Greece, Romania and Samoa, brought the total number of AIIB members up to 77. In addition to Brazil, which as a founding member of the BRICS group is a partner of the BRI, Argentina, Venezuela and Mexico have been invited to be part of it.

3.2 The Belt and Road Initiative and Latin America Middle-income Trap

The BRI is a good option for Latin American countries to have additional options for financing and technical cooperation on behalf of the execution of important infrastructure works (railroads, superhighways, dams, energy production centers) and technology in digital and satellite communication, as well as for the exploitation of natural resources. These amounts could be taking advantage of China's international cooperation in its broad sense (not just external aid). In this sense, the BRI is another tool for Latin American countries to escape the middle-income trap (MIT). However, a fundamental aspect to achieve this objective is to make domestic efficient use of available resources at China, the United States, Europe and international organizations.

The mechanisms of international cooperation are various, including trade and foreign investment, The countries also need to abide by the international regimes of trade and finance shaped by capitalism in the post-war period, but adjusting them to their conditions just as other economies have managed to escape from such a trap, such as the "Asian Tigers" (South Korea, China Hong Kong, Singapore and China Taiwan) and how China is doing at this time. The formula to get out of this trap is "simple"; the difficult thing is to put it into practice[①].

Several experts, including economist, have long recognized the problem of the middle-income trap. The authors argue that countries in the MIT face two major institutional and political challenges. "First, the policies necessary to upgrade productivity—as in human capital and innovation—require enormous investment in institutional capacity. Second, these institutional challenges come at a time when political capacity for building these institutions is weak, due primarily to the fragmentation of potential support coalitions. Politics are stalled in particular by fractured social groups, especially business and labor, and more generally by inequality" (Donner, Schneider and Ross, 2016).

General consensus is that the only way to break out MIT "is to save and invest more, invest in education, improve infrastructure, and increase innovation, research and development (R & D)". However, the political problem has received far too little attention: "middle income countries must build strong institutions despite weak societal demand for such institutions" (Taylor, 2017).

The point of view of the OECD can be summarized as follows: "preliminary results show that to overcome the middle-income trap Latin America must prioritise policy actions to improve the rule of law, the taxation system,

① Since the 19th China's National Communist Party Congress (October, 2017) where Xi Jinping established the guideline to achieve a "moderately prosperous society in all respects" in China has been a great concern on the way to avoid the middle-income trap.

access and quality of education, investment, access to finance and economic diversification, and reduction of gender gaps" (Gurria, 2017).

In other words, the main factor that has influenced the escape of MIT has been the institutional change propitiated by a political class capable of creating the conditions for modernization, takeoff or development to take place. The Latin American countries, for decades have been debated between statist with populist proposals and liberalism with the application of measures of economic opening, and predominance of the "free" market. In both cases the objective conditions of greater investment in education, in science and technology, in infrastructure construction, etcetera, and above all, the more efficient use of the resources invested, remains a pending issue.

4. Conclusions

The national identity and foreign policy of China have a very close relationship with the design and implementation of its International Cooperation policy. In this sense, Chinese leaders have redefined the ways to integrate into CID's international efforts. This means that China does not mechanically follow the criteria of international organizations such as the OECD, but it does apply the central objectives of international cooperation supported by these organizations. So, China, has been generating its own institutional structure through which it can directly allocate its financial and technological resources.

Taking into account its own economic needs and its international policy strategy, China allocates most of its available resources for foreign aid to the least developed countries in Asia, Africa, and Latin America. A central concept that justifies this strategy is South-South cooperation. China is not considered a developed country, on the contrary in the eyes of the international community it performs as a great power.

As argued in this article, China's international cooperation goes far beyond foreign aid. In fact, it focuses much more heavily on foreign direct investment and international trade, in terms of the use of financial resources, government management and performance of Chinese enterprises abroad.

The background of China's FDI is essentially the same to that of other global and regional powers FDI. China exports capital and technology ensuring the supply of basic raw materials to maintain the country's economic growth and additionally increasing its influence, wealth, and power. In addition, China's FI fills the gaps that other countries, traditional exporters of capital and technology, have not filled.

Chinese cooperation, implemented through international trade, is supported by the promotion of global economic and trade liberalization. This strategy intends not only to reduce the transaction costs but also to foster regional and bilateral preferential and free trade agreements with all regions and countries around the world. Many types of researches and think tanks, which have analyzed the economic and geopolitical implications of this policy, support this perspective.

For China's economic foreign policy, Latin America has become a key partner, even more in terms of FDI and trade than of aid. In this sense, Latin America is vital for geopolitics, but even more vital for the geo-economy of China. The region is a major source of raw materials and the large consumer market for Chinese products, and therefore, it is clear that FDI is directed in this direction and the structure of foreign trade confirms this statement.

The Belt and Road Initiative (BRI) is nowadays the backbone of China's international cooperation. Through out this strategy China's has been influenced global finances with geopolitical implications. In this sense, the Chinese regime has increased and strengthened regional free trade agreements, created new financial institutions and influence on traditional ones.

The most important Chinese offer through the BRI is in the field of developing infrastructure, including construction of railroad, port and highway, including its financing.

Behind the great economic effort, to foster international cooperation through conectivity efforts is China's interest in strengthening its foreign direct investment policy, and expanding its trade. So, the development of connectivity taking China as a global center has a great geo-economics and geopolitics strategy. To China, raw material requirements and markets to increased its exports of technological goods and services are crucial.

China provides aid for the fight against poverty in all its manifestations as support, but not as a solution. The Chinese leadership believes that development must be based on the policies of each country, for this comes from its own experience: poverty is an internal subject that China has been solving by itself. Therefore, the Chinese cooperation with any of its modalities is not the solution to get out of the middle-income trap. The way in which China is avoiding falling into the middle-income trap is an example, though not a model as such.

Chapter 10
Chinese Funding for Development in Latin America: Geopolitical Approach and New Opportunities for Escape of the Middle-income Trap

Daniel Lemus Delgado
Carlos Cerda Dueñas

The Marshall Plan was the most relevant antecedent of international financing for development. It was the US-backed aid program for the reconstruction and economic recovery of Europe after World War II (Prado, 2002). This massive program of financial aid was allocated to 16 European countries. Between 1948 and 1951, the U.S. government transferred 13 billion USD to the devastated economies of Europe (Echeingreen and Uzan, 1992). Since then, this type of financing has been considered an essential element to achieve development. From this perspective, one way to escape the middle-income trap is to find adequate funding that allows States to finance the necessary actions for development.

The States, as well as international organizations, have foreseen different forms of financing for development[①]. Each State and institution have established their priorities and modalities of funding according to its paradigmatic vision of the best way in which these funds should operate. The paradigmatic vision of development is even more important behind of the mechanism that operates the

① The classification of external sources of financing is private and official. Official external sources are flows from third countries (official bilateral flows) or multilateral institutions. These sources include the multilateral development banks, organizations such as the International Monetary Fund or multilateral non-financial institutions such as the agencies of the United Nations system, among others. The official flows can be concessional and non-concessional. In the first case, the funding are granted under conditions that are advantageous for the recipient country in comparison with the conditions in the market. While the non-concessional flows, are those that are allowed in similar conditions to that of the markets.

loans. In this context, the model of Development Assistance Committee (DAC)[①] has been the dominant way to understand the financing for development. On the other hand, the official concessional flows are the Official Development Assistance (ODA). This assistance is the flows to developing countries that are on the list of recipient countries of the Development Assistance Committee (DAC) of the Organization for Economic Cooperation and Development (OECD) and multilateral development institutions. Three conditions are indispensable to consider a loan as financing for development. First, the main objective is to promote the development and economic well-being of developing countries. Second, it is a concessional loan. Third, the donation element is at least 25% (CEPAL, 2015).

However, in the regime of the International Development Cooperation (IDC), other non-DAC actors boost their particular vision of what kind of projects should be financed and under what circumstances and characteristics. Perhaps the emergence of the BRICS phenomenon in the new millennium has had the most significant impact on the IDC regime. The presence of these actors has meant a challenge to traditional donors, not only regarding the flows of resources but also in the conceptualization of development and the mechanisms they use to achieve (Lemus and Santa Cruz, 2015).

In this regard, the emergence of non-traditional donors has shaken the IDC regime. The new donors have raised their demands on how development financing should be understood and realized it. This group comprehends diverse countries as Saudi Arabia, Russia, Brazil, China, South Korea, Venezuela, Kuwait, and India. The approaches of this group about the financing for development are divergent. In this same way, these donors differ about the financing models, scope, interests and projects. However, these countries, particularly those included in the BRICS bloc, coincide with the aspiration to generate new schemes of financing for development based on the principles of South-South Cooperation (SSC) (Bracho, 2009).

Specifically, the growing intervention of the BRICS in related issues of IDC has evidenced how the slowly transformation of IDC regime is not a

---

① DAC is an international forum of many of the most significant funders of aid, including thirty member countries of DAC. In addition, the World Bank, International Monetary Fund, and United Nations Development Programme participate as observers. The mission of DAC is to promote development cooperation with the aim to contribute to sustainable development, including economic growth, poverty reduction and improvement of living standards in developing countries (Development Assistance Committee, 2018).

coincidence. The higher aspiration of this bloc to shape new ways of financing is proportional to the formidable economic ascent that these countries have completed during the last decade. This fact has allowed a silent change of the "rules of the game" in the field of cooperation (Woods, 2008).

The paradigmatic example is China. According to Kjøllesdal and Welle-Strand (2010), this model of cooperation is notably different and challenging for four fundamental reasons. First, the idea of the relationship between the donor country and the receptor country; indeed, this link refers a horizontal association, under the assumption that the States are equal in the international system. Second, the idea of the mutual benefit because financing development is a form of aid for both, offers and recipients. Third, the assumption that the financial aid cannot be conditioned; thus, the international assistance does not mean the renounce or condition the sovereignty. Finally, the idea that financing development is more effective when a singular actor, as the State, builds the roads and bridges of cooperation; in other words, funding for development works better when is not multilateral.

This chapter explores how new actors for financing development are emerging in Latin America and the Caribbean countries. Specifically, we analyze how the Chinese model has operated in Latin America and if model can contribute to scape to middle-income trap. In this way, in the first section we discuss different models of financial aid and the posture that China has assumed. Later, we analyze the context of the financing by Chinese institutions to support the economic growth. In this sense, we discuss the characteristics and scope of the financial aid during the years between 2006 and 2016. Finally, we conclude with the idea that the Western and the emerging models mean risks and opportunities for development.

1. The Position of China in the Conceptualization of Financial Aid

In the context of economic crises that have arisen in the countries of emerging economies and with an evident decrease in official development assistance flows, the international community recognized the need to seek new public and private sources of financing for development. The General Assembly of the United Nations approved the "Development Program" (June 20, 1997). This document established that "A strong political commitment by the international community is needed to implement a strengthened international cooperation for development as reflected in the present Agenda. The mobilization of domestic and international financial resources for development from all sources is an essential component for the comprehensive and effective implementation of the Agenda. In this connection, enhanced efforts should be made for the mobilization and provision of new and additional financial resources for the development of developing countries" (United Nations, General Assembly, 1997).

In this regard, a working group to examine the opinions of the actors of the regime of IDC was established. The purpose of this group was to develop recommendations on the formation of a high-level international intergovernmental program on the subject of financing for development. Consequently, this panel recommended a meeting at the highest level to discuss this issue. The proposal was in concordance with the Development Program. This program indicated the need to establish an intergovernmental dialogue on financing for development.

In this context, and under the auspices of the United Nations, three international conferences were convened and an extraordinary one was held. The extraordinary meeting was convened to address the challenges arising from the international economic crisis of 2008. These discussions were in the cities of Monterrey, in 2002; Doha, in 2008; New York, 2009 and, Addis Ababa, in 2015.

During these meetings, China joined the positions that the Group of 77 assumed as a block. Nowadays, this group is denominated G77 + China. Although the G77 + China has disagreed with many of the agreements reached regarding development financing, its positions have not taken a radical turn on the Addis Ababa Action Agenda. This agenda was approved by consensus, despite the fact that the G77 + China participated as a bloc with different positions that were not finally approved. In this regard, the president of the Conference, the Ugandan Sam Kutesa (2015) declared: "It is evident that the interests of all countries cannot be fully reflected in the results of a conference of this nature, but it must be appreciated that the result it is a consensus of all." China adopted the positions of a model of South-South cooperation within the deliberations (Bracho, 2015).

If the IDC is an instrument of foreign policy, it is possible to affirm that the financing by the new donors is a way to increase their regional and international presence. The main contributors of the South tend to be regional powers: China, India and Brazil. In consequence, these actors expect that the international community consider them as representatives of their neighbors in global affairs. In this sense, financing development is a tactic to win friends and gain their support in the quest to redefine a new international scenario (Walz and Ramachandran, 2011).

At present, contrary to the best practices of the DAC, China and other emerging donors frequently employ their cooperation for development—just as Western emerging donors did decades ago—as a vehicle to promote their economic interests. In this sense, ODA only recognizes activities whose primary objective is to support development. (Bracho, 2015). According to some approaches, Beijing primordially favors projects that support its commercial interests rather than development. In consequence, China could soon overtake the United States to become the world's largest donor of aid to developing countries (Lo, 2017).

However, non-traditional donors have offered their partners a range of new financing options for development. In absolute terms, the contributions provided are still meager, since they represent only eight percent of total Official Development Assistance (Zimmerman and Smith, 2011). However, the presence of these non-traditional donors challenges the power and status of traditional donors. The symbolic value of their actions and discourse is substantial. On the other hand, for the people to live in countries that received the financial aid the presence of new donors is evident because, in the most of the cases, these founds are focused in material works. Thus, the loans destined to construction of infrastructure, stadiums and hospitals—very common in this type of credits, are a visible way to show a concrete idea of development (Kragelund, 2011).

The presence of a growing flow of resources to promote development by non-traditional actors has generated suspicion and concern. For some members of the DAC, the discourse on cooperation that non-traditional donors use in international forums is no more than an ideological evasion to avoid their responsibilities as emerging donors. In contrast, some of the non-traditional actors consider that the DAC countries do not take the paradigm of South-South cooperation seriously (Bracho, 2009).

On the other hand, China is part of the BRICS group. This group is part of the so-called emerging donors. However, the countries that make up the BRICS have not necessarily followed the parameters of traditional donors. Regarding the compatibility of the BRICS with the DAC, it should be noted that there is an essential difference in the prioritization of political objectives. The cooperation for the development of the BRICS does not follow the standardized criteria of Western aid or the principles of the OECD (Morazán et al., 2012). In this debate,

"China certainly plays an extraordinary role in this agenda. To some extent, it can be argued that: China is, in fact, the only real emerging donor; the rest are hanging from the shares of China and without China, we would not have this agenda" (Bracho, 2015). The Chinese government's conceptualization of DOA is complex because it does not use the official definition of the DAC. Chinese cooperation involves a complex mix of non-concessional loans, export credits, humanitarian aid, infrastructure projects, economic investments and technical assistance in the fields of health, education, and agriculture, similar to what other donors implement that are not from the CAD, like Brazil and India (Erthal and Marcondes de Souza, 2013).

Mwase and Yang (2012) proposed the concept of "BRICS aid philosophies". They have claimed that the BRICS philosophies for financing aid differ from traditional donors in three important ways. First, the commitment of the BRICS is based on the idea of mutual benefits. Second, they tend to offer non-monetary financing without political conditionality, whether explicit or formal. However, the strategy of some of the BRICS countries is to design assistance to facilitate and complement foreign direct investment. Therefore, these practices include "aid tied". Finally, the BRICS tend to focus on micro-sustainability of individual projects while traditional donors worry more about long-term sustainability.

At the 4th BRICS Summit in New Delhi in 2012, the leaders of Brazil, Russia, India, China and South Africa considered the possibility of establishing a new development bank to mobilize resources for infrastructure and sustainable development projects in the countries BRICS as in other emerging economies, as well as in developing countries. During the 6th BRICS Summit in Fortaleza in 2014, the leaders signed the agreement establishing the New Development Bank (NDB). In this way, the member countries of the BRIC went from the discourse to concrete financing actions as a group, opening a new scenario in the IDC regime.

2. The Actors of Chinese Financing for Development

In the year of 1978, the People's Bank of China (PBC) acted as the central bank and as the only commercial bank. For 1980, in the context of the process of opening and economic reform, other state banks emerged, including the Bank of China, the Agricultural Bank of China, the Construction Bank of China and the Industrial and Commercial Bank of China. From then on, the PBC abandoned its commercial activities and limited itself to acting as a central bank. By the 1990s, new banks were established. These new financial institutions could have part of their capital in private hands. In this way, the Chinese financial system was expanded with new entities of urban, rural and regional scope (Coalición Regional, 2016)①.

Nowadays, three central institutions are involved in assistance for Chinese development: the Ministry of Commerce, the Export-Import Bank of China and the Ministry of Foreign Affairs. However, they recognize that they are not the only actors in the Chinese financial system involved in development aid activities, but they are the most important. While the Ministry of Commerce takes the lead in China's official assistance policy, both China's Ex-Im Bank and the China Development Bank (BDC) provide concessional/preferential loans and export credits for the purchase of products and services. Chinese In addition, the Ministry of Finance assigns donations to multilateral organizations and manages debt cancellation. Also, more than 20 ministries, state banks and other agencies also participate in the administration of development assistance activities, often without central coordination. To these financial institutions, it is necessary to add two multilateral banks led by China, the New Development Bank and the Asian Infrastructure Investment Bank (AIIB) (Mwase and Yang, 2012).

The Export-Import Bank of China is a state-funded and state-owned policy bank with the status of an independent legal entity. It is a bank directly under the leadership of the State Council and dedicated to supporting China's foreign trade, investment, and international economic cooperation. This bank has no official representation in Latin America, as it only has offices in Paris, an office of representation for Southern and Eastern Africa in Johannesburg, a representation for North and West Africa in Rabat and the office in St. Petersburg (The Export-Import Bank of China, n.d.).

① The China Development Bank (CDB) and the Export-Import Bank of China grant most of the international loans. In 1994, the Chinese government created the CDB and the Ex-Im Bank as "political banks", that is, as "government tools". These loans had to support the government's political objectives explicitly. Before 1994, the four major Chinese banks-Bank of China, China Construction Bank, China Agricultural Bank, and the Industrial and Commercial Bank of China-were making this type of loans. The Chinese government established the new banks with the intention that the four big banks could act like commercial banks. In this way, the government tried to reduce the moral hazard of bank managers by separating political loans from commercial ones. The creation of separate political banks would make commercial banks responsible for rational market-based loans (Gallagher, Irwin and Koleski, 2013).

China Development Bank (CDB) was founded in 1994 as a policy financial institution under the direct leadership of the State Council. It was incorporated as China Development Bank Corporation in December 2008. The State Council officially defined CHB as a development financial institution in March 2015. CDB has a registered capital of RMB 421.248 billion. Its shareholders include the Ministry of Finance of the People's Republic of China (36.54%), Central Huijin Investment Ltd. (34.68%), Buttonwood Investment Holding Co., Ltd. (27.19%) and the National Council for Social Security Fund (1.59%). CDB provides medium-term to long-term financing facilities that serve China's major long-term economic and social development strategies. By the end of 2016, its assets grew to RMB 14.34 trillion, a balance of loans of RMB 10.32 trillion. We also further enhanced our sustainability and risk management, delivering a net profit of RMB 109,667 million, ROA of 0.81%, ROE of 9.82%, and capital adequacy of 11.57%. Professional credit rating agencies including Moody's and Standard & Poor's have rated CDB at the same level as China's sovereign rate. CDB currently has 37 primary branches and 3 secondary branches on the Chinese mainland, one offshore branch in Hong Kong and five representative offices in Cairo, Moscow, Rio de Janeiro, Caracas and London, with about 9,000 staff. Its subsidiaries include CDB Capital Co.,Ltd., CDB Securities Co.,Ltd., CDB Leasing Co.,Ltd. and China-Africa Development Fund Co.,Ltd. Also, CDB is the world's largest development finance institution, and the largest Chinese bank for foreign investment and financing cooperation, long-term lending and bond issuance (China Development Bank, n.d.).

The Chinese network of development banks can be seen as a global competitor of the World Bank, the IMF, and the ADB. However, paradoxically, it would be a competitor and at the same time it gathers complementary functions. That is, as a provider of loans, IEMGs do not offer for regulatory and / or political reasons (Vadell, 2016). Despite the existence of the CBD, official aid is channeled through the Export-Import Bank of China (Gallagher, Irwin and Kolesli, 2013). Geographically, during the first years of this century, Chinese cooperation was centered on Africa (46% of its foreign aid) and its neighbors in Asia with 33% (Morazán et al., 2012).

Since 2005, the Chinese mechanisms for funding for development in Latin America have increased. Between 2005 and 2010, the Chinese state banks lent 75 billion dollars to the region, more than the World Bank, the Inter-American Development Bank (IDB) and the Bank of Exports and Imports of the United States (Erthal and Marcondes de Souza, 2013). Although these loans are considered "official aid for development", fears that the pattern used by China in Africa could be repeated in Latin America (Gallagher, Irwin and Kolesli, 2013). China's presence in Africa and its financing development model has been strongly criticized. For example, African countries wealthy in energy resources such as Angola, the Democratic Republic of the Congo and Sudan, Chinese capitals have made huge investments in infrastructure and energy. Often these projects are financed with Chinese credits that eventually will reimburse through future supplies of natural resources such as oil. This practice is known as the "Angola model" (Morazán et al., 2012). In this sense, the Angola model is a commercial exchange agreement conceived by the Chinese government, for which financial loans granted by China will pay with goods that represent a value equivalent in the international market. At the beginning of this millennium, the representatives of China approached the leaders of Angola to find a solution that would mitigate their already known energy deficit. In the understanding of the needs of this African country, China offered multimillion-dollar financing to support the reconstruction of the country, as long as they were exclusively paid with oil and according to international prices (Olguín, 2011). China exports this financing model to other African countries.

Most of the loans are for the implementation of projects executed by Chinese companies in the region. In other words, Chinese banks lend to Latin American and Caribbean countries to carry out projects implement by Chinese enterprises (Regional Coalition, 2016). Chinese loans are characterized as "non-interventionist," that is to say: they do not require a change of government or economic policies by the recipient countries in exchange for financing. In this way, Chinese banks finance countries that have external restrictions on international credit agencies or experiment conditions of political, financial, and economic risk. This situation has allowed China to increase its bargaining power in the global scenario. At the same time, China can secure natural and energy resources in the medium and long-term. In addition, this unconditional aid is an essential soft power vehicle of the People's Republic of China in Africa and Latin America (Amado, 2010)[①].

Since 2012, the Chinese government has shown its desire to increase its

---

① The international financial aid of China is unconditional and does not demand respect for the norms of good governance or respect for human rights, as do other governments and international organizations. However, the condition of accessing these loans requires that the recipient countries accept the one-China policy. This principle includes support China's position on the international stage in the cases of Taiwan and Tibet.

cooperation ties with the countries of Latin America substantially. In June 2012, during a visit to this region, Premier Wen Jiabao proposed the creation of a mechanism for cooperation between China and Latin America. Under this initiative, the Chinese government offered 1,500 million dollars in initial loans. This amount is higher than the total amount of aid that DAC allowed to Latin America and the Caribbean in 2010. The scale of this proposal demonstrates that Chinese cooperation could change the scope of development assistance in Latin America and the Caribbean similarly to what has already happened in Africa (Abdenur and Marcondes de Souza, 2013).

On the other hand, regarding triangular cooperation, China has been reluctant to participate in such arrangements (Abdenur and Marcondes de Souza, 2013). However, the China Policy Paper towards Latin America and the Caribbean notes that China is willing to deploy tripartite cooperation in LAC with extra-regional countries and international organizations as long as the projects are presented, spoiled and sponsored by the Latin American and Caribbean countries (Ministry of Foreign Affairs of China, 2016).

Nonetheless, Chinese cooperation in Latin America is advancing. On January 29, 2014, China and the countries of Latin America created the China-CELAC Forum in the city of Havana. In consequence, President Xi Jinping proposed the establishment of the China-Latin America and the Caribbean Integral Cooperation Association. The purpose of this mechanism is to promote equality, mutual benefit, and common development. This agreement traced the cooperation between both regions. The name of this mechanism is "Cooperation 1 + 3 + 6". Number 1 refers to "the plan", that is, remits the elaboration of a plan for cooperation between China, Latin America and the Caribbean, in order to guarantee full coupling and unanimity regarding development strategies. Number 3 refers to "three engines", that is, mutual support in the three areas: trade, investment, and finance. Finally, number 6 refers to cooperation in "six fields": energy, infrastructure construction, agriculture, manufacturing, science and technology, and information technology to achieve a better sectoral development.

It is a fact that the Latin American region is hungry for financing for development; however, DAC and the major financial institutions only consider Haiti a suitable country to be a recipient of aid. The other states are middle-income countries, so these countries do not receive this type of financing. Therefore, Latin American governments increasingly consider the Chinese financing aid for their development as an option. Chinese cooperation, no doubt, is an opportunity that involves risks. On the other hand, China offers copious and rapid financing for development projects in the region, but it also represents four key risks: changes in thematic priorities, displacement of donors, exclusion of civil society and regional fragmentation (Erthal and Marcondes de Souza, 2013). China tries to reverse some aspects of the negative publicity it has received internationally in its financing model (Besharati, 2013). The challenge is that these new financial links do not reproduce patterns of subordination and dependence (Slipak, 2014).

3. The Chinese Financing to Development in Latin America

China's President Xi Jinping announced determined goal of 500 billion Dollars in trade with the Latin American and Caribbean region and 250 billion Dollars of direct investment for the five-year period between 2015 and 2019 (Dollar, 2017). These promises show China's interest in having a more significant presence in Latin America. At the same times, China has shown a clear interest in participating as an observer in different multilateral organisations that covers Latin American affairs both from an economic and political perspective. That includes the Rio Group, the Inter-American Development Bank (IADB), the Latin American Integration Association (LAIA), the Economic Commission for Latin America and the Caribbean (ECLAC), the Organization of American States (OAS) and the Latin American Parliament (Hardy, 2014). Therefore, it is logical that the credits earmarked for the region in recent years reflect their increase in last years.

Another side of the coin of trade and direct investment is the financing for development (Figure 10.1). Those loans typically go to Latin American governments and parastatals, with a major part supporting infrastructure projects. Much of the remnant finances hydrocarbons and mining projects. The volume of lending has been rising over time, although with variability. The year 2010 was extraordinary, with 37.1 billion Dollars in lending to Latin American governments. In 2014, there was 22.1 billion Dollars of lending from Chinese banks to Latin American governments. This figure was more than the combined loans from the World Bank and the Inter-American Development Bank (Dollar, 2017). It is a fact that Chinese banks offer financing to a considerably diverse set of countries than the International Financing Organization and Western banks, and for different purposes (Gallagher, Irwin, and Koleski, 2012).

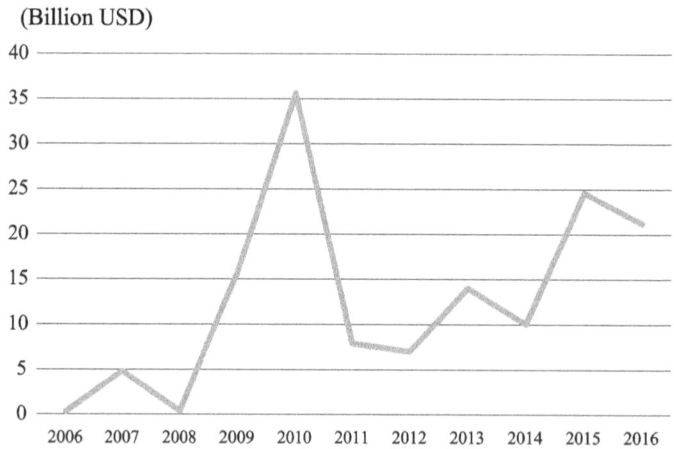

Figure 10.1 Evolution of Chinese financing for development to Latin America and The Caribe Countries (2006–2016)

Source: Based on China-Latin America Finance Database.

According to China-Latin America Data Base (2017), it is possible to affirm that CDB is the most important lender. In fact, between 2005 and 2016, this bank lent 114.3 billion USD to LAC while Ex-Im Bank gave 27 billion USD in the same period. These are the most significant Chinese financial institutions in the region. Other lenders include the State Administration of Foreign Exchange, CITIC Group, PetroChina, Sinopec, and Chinese commercial bank: China Construction Bank, Bank of China and, ICBC.

Table 10.1 Number of Loans and Amounts, 2006–2016

Country	No. of loans	Amount
Venezuela	17	62.2 billion USD
Brazil	10	36.6 billion USD
Ecuador	13	17.4 billion USD
Argentina	8	15.3 billion USD
Bolivia	10	3.5 billion USD
Trinidad and Tobago	2	2.6 billion USD
Jamaica	10	1.8 billion USD
Mexico	1	1 billion USD
Costa Rica	1	395 million USD

(Contd.)

Country	No. of loans	Amount
Barbados	1	170 million USD
Guyana	1	130 million USD
Bahamas	2	99 million USD
Peru	1	50 million USD

Source: Based on China-Latin America Finance Database.

The countries receptors of Chinese financing reflects how the geopolitical strategies are behind of this type of aids. The principal receptor of the financing is Venezuela, with 62. 2 billion USD and 17 projects, followed by Brazil with 36.8 billion USD and 10 projects; Ecuador, 17.4 billion USD and 13 projects; Argentina, 15.3 billion USD and 8 projects; and, Bolivia, 3.5 billion USD and 10 projects. When we analyze the states that received those amounts, it is evident that geopolitical reasons have been an essential element. The main loans granted were for the energy sector, the construction of infrastructure and the promotion of mining (Figure 10.2).

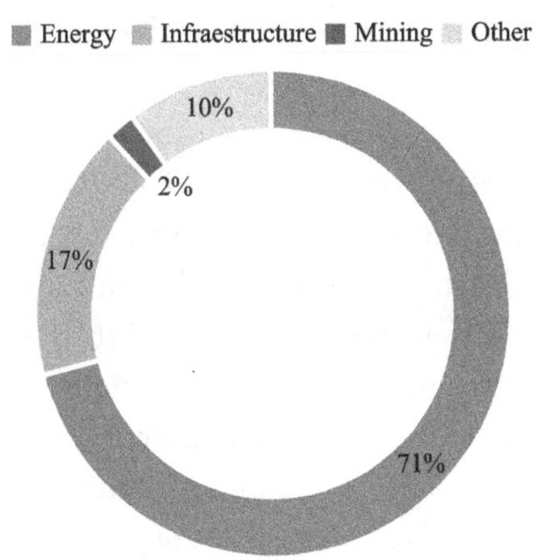

Figure 10.2 Type of loans (2006–2016)

Source: Based on China-Latin America Finance Database.

In Venezuela, in December 1998, Commander Hugo Chávez won the presidential elections at the head of a coalition of left and center-left political parties known as the Patriotic Pole. Since then, the country has become a reference point for a political and economic system that has increasingly distanced itself from the neoliberal principles promoted by the West. In this way, this country showed itself on the international stage as an alternative model in Latin America. The Venezuelan government, soon classified as undemocratic and far from the classic principles of good governance, found in China its financial ally to start up the significant infrastructure works that the country needed. On the other hand, China found in Venezuela an appropriate partner to supply the growing energy demand that China demanded more and more quantities. About the 17 projects financed by China, 12 of them went to the energy sector. In total, the amount of financing amounted to 55 billion USD.

China and Brazil has different economic conditions and close but asymmetrical relations, this make up a pair in which one has an economic direction, and the other goes through the process of conversion (Salama, 2017). Brazil is a member of the BRICS group; thus, this country is an essential partner for China in two ways. From a political perspective, Brazil is part of the new paradigms of development that we have discussed in previous sections. Therefore, the loans are part of the discourse of horizontal cooperation under the principles of South-South Cooperation. In addition, Brazil became an important supplier of raw materials for the Chinese economy. In 2016, China was the leading destination of Brazilian exports, with a value of 35.1 billion USD. The main exported product was soy.

As in the case of Venezuela, the energy sector received the most funding. The projects financed in this sector were eight. The total amount of financing was 34.3 billion USD. These loans coincided with the 13 years of left-wing government in Brazil, led by metalworker Luiz Inácio Lula da Silva and, later, by ex-guerrilla Dilma Rousseff, between the years of 2003 to 2016.

The third country that received the most funding during the period from 2005 to 2016 was Ecuador. President Rafael Correa governed Ecuador from January 2007 to May 2017. Before becoming president, Correa was Minister of Economy in 2005. In this government position, he opposed to the signing of a free trade agreement with the United States. At the same time, he sought to increase cooperation with Latin American countries. Already as president, Correa moved away from neoliberal policies and rejected the Washington Consensus. Therefore, the approach with a country like China responded to its left political orientation.

Unlike the cases of Venezuela and Brazil, the loans received by Ecuador were more balanced. Of the 13 projects financed, 6 were for the energy sector, while another 6 were in the category of others. In the first case, the amount financed was 6.09 billion USD. Other loans included finance budget deficit (2 billion USD); the construction of the road to Quito airport (80 million USD); finance annual investment plan 2015 (1.5 billion USD); some projects relationship with transportation, education and healthcare (5.3 billion USD); the construction of Yachay education complex (198 million USD), and non-discretionary and infrastructure (2 billion USD).

Finally, in the case of Argentina, the central loans to China occurred between 2007 and 2014. These investments included the development of export sector (30 million USD) and the construction of infrastructure train system (10 billion USD). In addition, China financed the construction of infrastructure to high-speed trains (273 million USD); renewable energy projects (200 million USD); energy hydroelectric dam construction (2.5 billion USD); infrastructure Belgrano loads train line (2.1 billion USD) and other purchase of cars for the metro line (162 million USD). It is important to remark that this financing was during the presidency of Cristina Fernández de Kirchner, from 2007 to 2015. As in the other cases, the Argentine government presented itself as a popular movement contrary to the dominant hegemonic model derived from economic liberalism.

4. Conclusions

The vast majority of countries in the Latin American and Caribbean region have high poverty rates and highly vulnerable social sectors. Except for Haiti, these countries do not qualify in the traditional criterion of the donors to be recipients of international aid to development. Therefore, the ODA has been significantly reduced or eliminated. The reason behind this decision is that most of the countries in the region are classified as middle-income countries. Consequently, these countries have had to resort to the new actors of financing for development and abide by their conditions.

In this sense, China offers a new source of finance for domestically appealing development projects, and with none of the policy conditionalities associated with the philosophy and norms of the financing aid from a Western perspective. At the same time, this source of financing poses and accentuates real risk for Latin American Countries if they do not have in the horizon clarity about how escape of the middle-income trap.

It is a fact that the Chinese presence in Africa and Latin America can be perceived as positive, but someone raises negative visions. China's participation in the development tasks in Latin America is considered as part of the transmission of its model of economic success (Amado, 2010). The financing granted opens the range of possibilities to access credits that contribute to development. Therefore, China is an alternative to obtain loans for countries that have it impossible due to their classification based on their income or the failure to comply with the governance standards from the Western perspective. Chinese loans focus on infrastructure and heavy industry, without covering other governmental, social and environmental purposes (Gallagher et al., 2013). However, this strong emphasis on investment in infrastructure could have influenced the new IDB strategy, which was reflected in the increase in loans for infrastructure construction (Abdenur and Marcondes de Souza, 2013). In this vision, China is considered a partner for development.

On the other hand, Chinese cooperation is considered as a competitor that does not fully take into account local needs. Moreover, the presence of China is seen as seeking to replace the traditional influence of the West in the region (Amado, 2010). Therefore, this cooperation is considered tied, and that promotes mono-exports. Traditional donors are averse to not taking into account when granting financing, the observance of good governance practices.

The criteria of measurement of the aid and the financing of projects destined to promote the development is another point that has been questioned. In the majority of the cases, they lack the element of donation of at least 25%, or by account for items not taken into account to quantify official development assistance. In this regard, only 23% of China's funding falls under the OECD's strict definition of Official Development Assistance (ODA), while 93 percent of U.S. aid falls into this category (Lo, 2017). This fact has generated that as an implicit response to this "unfair competition", a number of traditional donors have begun to relax the rules of quantification, undermining the barrier induced by CAD between what is ODA and what are commercial activities (Bracho, 2015).

At the end of the day, neither of the two models are perfect nor do they represent the possibility of escaping from the middle-income trap. In reality, it is the responsibility of the recipient of the aid to identify and implement the best projects that result in the improvement of the quality of life of its inhabitants and thus contribute to the development. Financing for development is a tool for that purpose, but it must be used with care.

Chapter 11

China and Brazil: Transitioning from the Middle-income Trap to Sustainable Development?—A Sociological Perspective on Consumption, Inequality and the Middle-income Trap

Mariana Hase Ueta
Erick Tjong
Niklas Werner Weins

Brazil and China, as emerging countries, face development challenges and can learn from each other's experiences. Brazil, like most Latin American countries has been plagued by consistently high levels of inequality, although these have been slightly decreasing in recent years. According to ECLAC and Oxfam (2016), Latin America is considered the most unequal region in the world, where the richest 10% of its population accounted for 71% of the region's wealth in 2014.

China on its turn has been experiencing a growing inequality gap. Both countries have been struggling over the years with inequality, which might compromise their strategies to promote consumption-led development. According to Piketty (2016) inequality can present impediments to the expansion of the consumption market. This article investigates the relation between inequality, market inclusiveness and the development challenges presented by the middle-income trap.

Kharas and Harinder (2011) propose that, past the stage where an economy is susceptible to falling into the poverty trap, there is a stage in which it might fall into the middle-income trap. Developing countries that have avoided the poverty trap and attained middle-income levels would then face new challenges—both economic and social—on the way to reaching advanced-income levels.

The Republic of Korea is seen as an example of the transition from growth based on a combination of resources and low-cost labor to productivity-driven growth (Lin and Treichel, 2012). At the same time, Brazil seems to have failed to avoid the middle-income trap: it is caught in a cycle in which the GDP per capita fluctuates significantly since the 1970s. This fact showcases major differences in the development policies adopted by Latin American and East Asian economies, with the latter showing higher levels of success in sustaining long-term growth (Kharas and Harinder, 2011).

What are East Asian economies' governments doing to grow from middle income to a higher stage? Three critical transitions are proposed, that can be tackled with certain policies to avoid the middle-income trap: specialization, total factor productivity increase and decentralization. In terms of social and economic development, these three factors are goals for policies that will provide the specialization of production and develop national and global brands in niche areas, as well as social-safety nets, skill-retraining programs, and the much needed middle class to consume these new products internally. As for the achievement of higher productivity levels, policymakers should provide the necessary changes in education aiming at the tertiary sector. Those policies should be broad enough to both retain and accumulate a critical mass of highly skilled professionals. Therefore, providing attractive opportunities and lifestyles in safe and liveable cities becomes an essential strategy to avoid the middle-income trap. Decentralization is an important step in addressing opportunity and income distribution gaps on a local scale, as local governments can tackle those necessities faster than central administrations (Kharas and Harinder, 2011).

Some skeptics of the middle-income trap theory do not agree with the idea of development steps, and voice criticism towards what policy makers should aim their focus at. For example, economists such as Lawrence Summers and Lant Pritchett point out that fast growth should be seen as a greater warning of a future slowdown than slow, but stable and sustainable growth. They fear that misleading signs of a slowdown can cause policymakers to try to solve the wrong problem—the absence of rapid economic growth—while there are still unresolved issues that are essential to providing long-term stability, such as insufficient investments in industrial and agricultural infrastructure (Fernholz, 2014).

According to Kharas and Harinder (2011), the complexity of modern economies requires fast decision making, and the amount of information needed combined with implementation effectiveness and the focus on results end up demanding a more pragmatic approach to policy formulation. Hout (2006) points out that, while statistical analyses have helped in understanding social change, it has been a topic all-too-often debated only within scientific disciplines, which has lead to "a triumph of mathematical expressions over verbal ones and a suspicion among some other sociologists that there was more mathematics than sociology going on". Unlike economists, sociologists "tend to perceive consumption as a social behavior tinged with certain social meaning or symbolism, instead of a mere economic act" (Tian, 2013, p.652). For that reason the communication and discussion of the contextual meaning and implications of data deserves more attention, instead of simply adopting solutions based on a one-size-fits-all recipe drawn from uncontextualized models.

China and Brazil are countries of continental dimensions and great diversity. Due to increasing relations among the BRICS and economic globalization, these countries have increased their overall dependence on market forces, but at the same time their governments are able to make economic decisions that can impact the global economy. Developing institutions that support greater economic freedom, while relying on market competitiveness will likely be determinant to their long-term success (Boskin, 2015). Kharas and Harinder (2011) point out that for avoiding the middle-income trap strong political leadership is necessary, enabling change not only in formal institutions on the upper levels, but also bringing about change in values and behaviors that go hand in hand with those policies. China has in past years shown strong government leadership capabilities, but it is yet to be known how it will influence the new middle class and its plans to becoming a high-income country.

1. Inequality and the Middle-income Trap

The dominant view currently held by institutions around the world seems to be that inequality needs to be addressed if growth is to be sustained: the World Bank's Poverty and Shared Prosperity report identified that in order to end extreme poverty by 2030, tackling inequality is crucial. In October 2017 the International Monetary Fund released a Fiscal Monitor on "Tackling Inequality" (IMF, 2017). The United Nations identified inequality as one of the challenges to be addressed by the Sustainable Development Goals, with Goal No. 10 being called "reduced inequality". Furthermore, the World Economic Forum has also been putting a stronger emphasis on inequality. Its Global Risks report of 2017 considered inequality a major obstacle to growth and one of the five major risks to the global economy (World Economic Forum, 2017).

Established economic models point out that as income distribution gets more unequal, domestic demand will grow more slowly than the GDP, causing stagnation in the absence of financial policy intervention. Both phenomena may eventually lead to the middle-income trap, as they extensively increase the debt burden on the middle and lower classes which consecutively may cause instability in the financial system (Kharas and Harinder, 2011). Kharas and Kohli (Islam, 2014) believe in the centrality of inequality in the middle-income trap discussion, and put emphasis on reducing inequality through redistribution, bringing as an example the bolster of domestic demand through debt financing in some Latin American countries.

Table 11.1 Arguments on Inequality in Relation to Growth

Arguments on Inequality in Relation to Growth	
1. "Credit constraints" and "indivisibility" of investments	Under credit constraints, inequality may render many people unable to make socially desirable investments and as a result growth may suffer. Indivisibility of investments aggravates this harmful impact, because in that case small savings cannot help much in overcoming the effects of the credits constraints
2. Electoral politics	In a situation of inequality, the median income will be lower than the mean income. As per "Median Voter Theorem", the electorate will then vote for a redistribution from high to low income people. The prospect of such redistribution will reduce the incentive to invest and will harm growth
3. Politics (not necessarily electoral)	Inequality will lead to socio-political unrest, which will scare investors away and harm growth
4. Consumption	Inequality restricts consumption demand, constrains the home market, and acts as a barrier to growth

Source: Compilation by Islam, 2014 and modified by the authors. Data Source: Alesina and Rodrik, 1994, 96; Benhabib and Rustichini, 1996; Benabou, 1996; Bertola, 1993; Galor and Zeira, 1993; Gupta, 1990; Hibbs, 1973; Kharas and Kohli, 2011; Piketty, 1997; Perotti, 1993; Persson and Tabellini, 1994; Piketty, 2017; Stiglitz, 2013; Venieris and Gupta, 1986; Apud. Islam, 2014.

According to Nazrul Islam (2014) the middle-income trap is directly related to inequality. The author defends that there is an inequality trap associated with the middle-income trap, where the high levels of income inequality hinder the reduction of inequality and ensure its persistence. He attributes the success of the "East Asian Model" to a combination of high growth rates with equitable distribution. However, China may be considered as an outlier, as the country has allowed inequality to reach high levels, similar to the ones found in the middle-income trap countries. The author suggests that inequality has become an obstacle for China's further progress, as the current macroeconomic imbalances, the decreasing efficiency of capital allocation, and the rise in social tensions, can all be traced to high inequality of income and asset distribution. Islam (2014) presents four perspectives through which it is possible to interpret the relation between inequality and growth. In the present article, we focus on the fourth perspective and investigate the relations between consumption, inequality and development.

2. China and Brazil as Unequal Countries

Many countries in the global north are discussing development and social policies in a context that differs significantly from that of developing countries, in terms of stability of institutions, favorable economic factors or relative social wealth and equality. Scandinavian countries, for instance, face very different issues relating to inequality, when compared to countries in the global south. Inequalities in many developing countries are one of the main social and economic challenges for national governments.

In all world regions, developing countries struggle with high levels of inequality. However, the case of Latin America and the Caribbean is particularly alarming. Despite relative success in reducing extreme poverty in the last decade, the region is still considered the most unequal in the world. The richest 10% of Latin America's population accounted for 71% of the region's wealth in 2014. "From 2002 to 2015, the fortunes of Latin America's billionaires grew by an average of 21% per year—an increase that Oxfam estimates is six times greater than the growth of the whole region's GDP" (Bárcena and Byanyima, 2016: 1). The Economic Commission for Latin America and Caribbean (ECLAC) and Oxfam warned that inclusive and sustainable growth should be a priority for these countries.

Brazil is no exception. Inequality is historically rooted in the country and persists despite recent economic upturns (Scalon, 2013). China, on the other hand, is in a different situation compared to Latin America's, as it is on the way to becoming more unequal mostly due to market liberalization. The following chapter discusses the evolution of inequality in China and Brazil.

Figure 11.1 shows the development of income inequality in China with data from the World Wealth and Income Database (2017a) from 1978 until 2015. Considering that China was once one of the most equal countries in the world, the developments since the Reform and Opening Policy in 1978 have contributed a great deal to rising inequality (Xie and Zhou, 2014; Li, 2016).

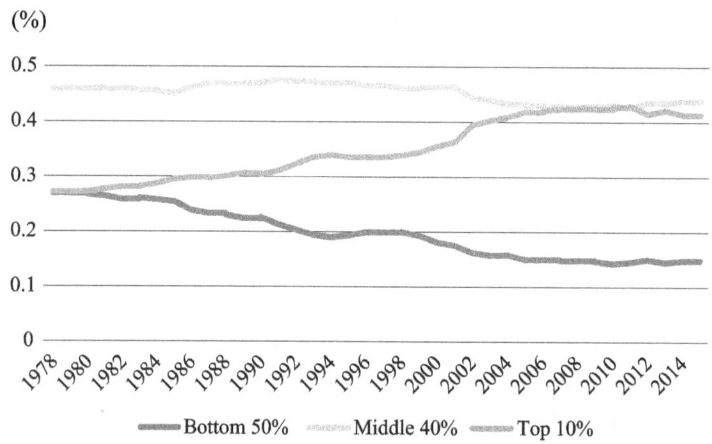

Figure 11.1 Income Inequality in China (1978–2015)

Source: WID, 2017.

However, when compared to the data available for Brazil in Figure 11.2, considering the share of pre-tax national income of the bottom 50%, middle 40% and the top 10% of society, a strong continuation of inequality can be noted. While a 2004 World Bank report points out the significance of persisting inequalities in Brazil's economic development, Bourguignon, Ferreira and Leite (2002) evaluate the country's situation as being one of "unacceptable stability". Based on those two differing scenarios, the following two sub-chapters explore each case in more detail.

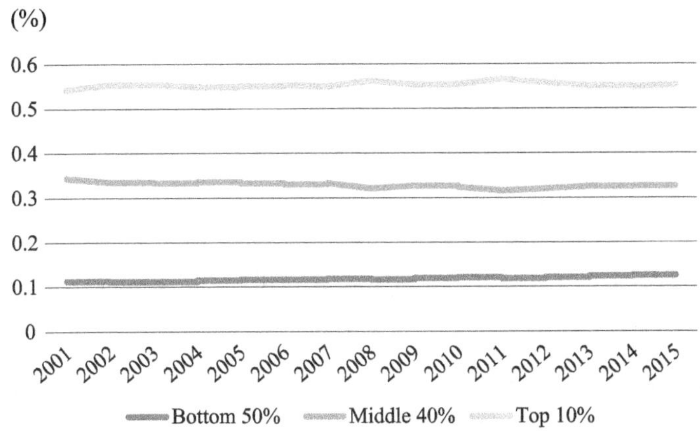

Figure 11.2 Income Inequality in Brazil (2001–2015)

Source: WID, 2017.

2.1 China's Growing Economic and Social Disparities

Since its Reform and Opening up period and the economic experiments of the 1980s, income inequality has been rising in China. Today its rate is considered high even by international standards, as can be seen in Figure 11.3 below. The U.S. Central Intelligence Agency ranked China as the world's 30th most unequal country based on the Gini coefficient—which measures income distribution in a country, from a list of 150 countries, with data from 1993 until 2016 (CIA World Factbook, 2017). The average level of household member income per capita has been rising, while the degree of socio-economic differentiation has also shown growth. During this period of economic growth and social transformation, the increase in income was accompanied by an increase in the consumption level, showing the important process through which China entered in the phase of mass consumption. However, the consumption growth did not expand at the same pace as income growth in the country. This section analyzes the development of inequality in China and its reflection in the stratification of consumption.

China's structural changes in the income inequality patterns in recent years demonstrate that "the relative distribution of the population is moving towards the two ends of the income spectrum. (...) The trend will be a serious challenge to China's goal of expanding the middle-income population (Chen, 2013).

In China, the highest 20% group has been showing a rising income trend, while the income shares of all the other groups show a general decline. In order

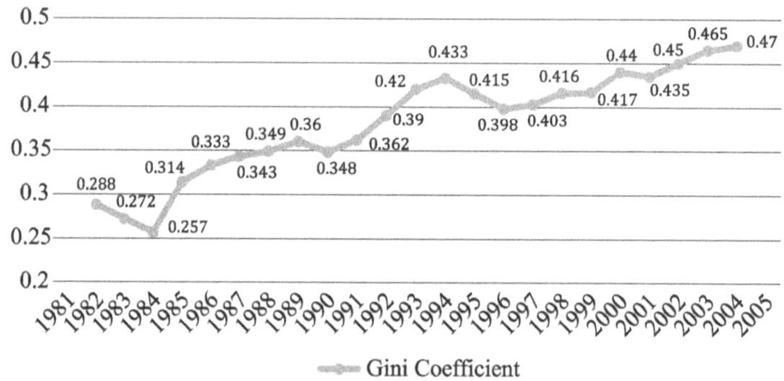

Figure 11.3 The Change in Gini Coefficient of China's Income Distribution from 1982–2005

Source: The Gini coefficient data for 1982–2006 was collected by Bi Xianping and Jiang Xinhua (2002); 2000–2005 data from annual statistics by the National Bureau of Statistics of China. Apud. Li, 2013.

to understand this process, it is important to have the year 1996 as a referential. Before this year, each strata's share showed fluctuation and the income inequality was mainly due to the increase of the proportion in the highest-income group and the decrease of the population proportion in the lowest-income group. However, after 1996 the income shares of the four lower-income groups have been declining while the income share of the highest-income group has been increasing, as a result the income ratio has been going up steadily and reaching over 22: times by 2005 (Chen, 2013). The main characteristics of income inequality in China can be analyzed through the rural-urban dichotomy and inter-regional differences (Li, 2016), as seen in Table 11.2 and Figure 11.4.

By analyzing consumption inequality between urban and rural residents, one may note a general trend of decline in the proportion of consumption attributable to rural residents, while that of the urban residents has increased. One major problem to be pointed out is the difficult access to credit in the countryside that certainly hampered increased consumption in the early 2000s (Yuan and Xu, 2015). According to Tian Feng (2013), the proportion of rural residents among the total population of the country dropped, but the proportion of rural residents' consumption dropped faster than its population. In terms of consumption stratification in the urban areas, there is a rapidly widening gap between the high income and the other income groups; and in the rural areas the gap remains relatively stable with no sign of concentration yet.

Table 11.2 Historical Panorama of Income Inequality between Urban and Rural Areas in China

Stage	Description	Urban	Rural
First Stage (1978–1984)	Gap between urban and rural income declined	Urban reform had not yet started (income of urban residents still determined by the state through planned economy)	Rural economic reform (universal implementation of the household contract responsibility system) and reform on the pricing of agricultural products and the advancement of agricultural production technologies
Second Stage (1985–1994)	Inequality between urban and rural incomes witnessed a continuous increase (income level of urban residents increased at a faster rate than rural residents)	Economic reforms on the micro level started (enterprises were allowed to raise employee wages, bonuses and benefits)	Township enterprises rapid development provided new sources of income
Third Stage (1994–1997)	Gap between the incomes of China's urban and rural residents narrowed again (non-agricultural incomes of the rural households increased at a relatively faster rate)	Large-scale public enterprises restructured (adjusted the interest relationship between the enterprises and their employees), resulting in a great number of layoffs and emergence of a new urban poor population	Rural township enterprises went through a similar reform and promoted the development of the rural non-agricultural economy
Fourth Stage (1998-present)	Urban-rural income gap in expansion	The further development of the market economy aggravated deep rooted factors of urban-rural differentiation (education disparity, migrant labor exploitation, etc.). Even though rural households' non-agricultural income has been increasing with the expansion of rural migrants labor, their income growth rate increase do not follow the faster pace of increase of the urban resident's income	
Possible Next Stage	Re-migration of the migrant workers to the countryside	Increased remittances to rural areas coincide with narrowed income inequality since 2008 due to reduction in gap between urban and rural households. Mainly due to rural migrant workers' wages increasingly more quickly than those of skilled urban workers, and to the social policies implemented in rural areas (Li, 2006: 4)	

Source: Chen, 2013; Li, 2006.

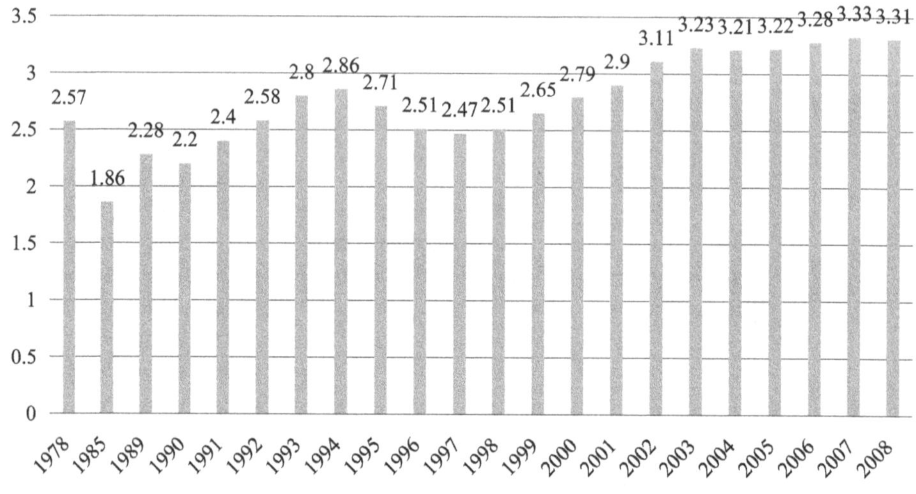

Figure 11.4 Trend of the Gap between China's Urban and Rural Income During 1978–2008

Source: *Chinese Statistical Yearbooks* (multiple years), China Statistics Press, apud. Chen, p.488, 2013.

Regarding income inequality among different regions, China can be divided into three regions that show significant development gaps: the Eastern, Central and Western regions (see Figure 11.5). Even though the inter-regional gap has not been widening as fast as the urban-rural disparity, it is important to consider the increasing development gap between the Eastern region on one side and the Central and Western regions on the other. These differences are the result of a historical process of asymmetrical investments, state policies, market opportunities and resource utilization methods that benefited most the Eastern part of the country.

"The fact that the inter-regional gap of the rural-resident income is larger than that of the urban-resident income shows that the radiation and promotion effect of urban economic development in the rural areas of the Central and Western is weaker than that of the Eastern region; an important proof on this is that the rural non-agricultural economy in the East is far more advanced than that of the Central and the West" (Chen, 2013).

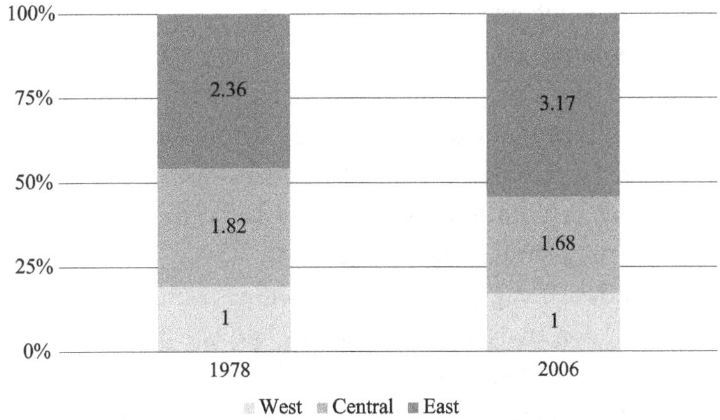

Figure 11.5 Ratio of National GDP Attributable to Eastern China, Central China, and Western China

Source: Based on data from Li, 2013, p. 64.

According to Lu Xueyi (2001) China could furthermore be divided into ten strata or classes:

Table 11.3 Ten strata of Chinese society

Strata	Proportion of the Strata*
(1) state and social administrators	1.8%
(2) private entrepreneurs	1.3%
(3) corporate managers	2.4%
(4) professionals and technicians	5.1%
(5) clerks	7.3%
(6) small proprietors	9.1%
(7) industrial workers	15.8%
(8) employees of service sectors at lower levels	11.6%
(9) agricultural workers	39.8%
(10) unemployed and underemployed people	5.7%

*According to an analysis conducted in the 2008 survey considered the highest professional stratum of any working member in a household as the representation of the household's social stratum.
Source: Chen, 2013.

The intra-stratum income inequality is also relevant to understand social and economic differentiation within the strata, especially regarding the three strata of private entrepreneurs, corporate managers, and small proprietors. While the huge intra-stratum income inequality in these strata can be explained as these groups rely on economic resources and business operations to obtain gains, the other strata that rely on professional skills and labor to obtain gains show relatively smaller intra-stratum inequalities.

Even though Tian Feng (2013) divides China into different categories of strata, his consumption analysis shows that the "private business owners" strata, which belongs to the wealthy group, is the highest and is also the only strata that has no member on either the "basic subsistence" line or poverty line. This reaffirms the evidence that this stratum benefited the most from China's social economic reforms as the "get-rich-first" group.

The author later concludes that during the maoist period, the differences in terms of income and social benefits between social strata were based on political status and occupational status. There was an egalitarian distribution and consumption system led by the state under the planned economy, where in spite of the slight income disparity between classes, the level of consumption was rather similar. The changes of the reform and opening up period brought increasing socio-economic differentiation, where "the original rather simple social structure comprising 'two classes and one stratum' (working class, peasant class, and intellectual stratum) (was) going through a dramatic transition to ten major social strata" (Tian, 2013), and also "the consumption level, consumption structure and consumption pattern of each social stratum are also undergoing increasing differentiation" (Tian, 2013).

The Chinese government has been adopting a series of measures to implement relevant policies to tackle the trend of income gap expansion between rural and urban areas, and among different regions and strata in the society. These include notably the initiatives of increasing the payment of cash transfers to rural areas, to the Western region, and to disadvantageous groups. Also, plans for a comprehensive reform of income distribution have been envisaged, through the formulation of socio-economic policies aiming to expand people's income and consumption and improving their social security net (Chen, 2013). The ability of such policies to reduce inequality in the Chinese society is yet to be evaluated.

2.2 Brazil: a Country Caught in an Inequality Trap

Brazil is the largest economy in Latin America, accounting for almost 40% of total GDP of the region. With growth rates of around 6% in the early 2000s, mostly due to its rich resource base, Brazil has been presenting both short- and long-term economic performance typical of Latin America. Since earlier decades, one of the most significant transformations in society has been the still ongoing process of transference of the labor force from the countryside to the city. Compared to 1960, when around 55% of Brazil's population was living in the countryside, nowadays the urban population makes up for 85% and is amongst the highest percentages worldwide (Scalon, 2013). During the military dictatorship, in 1965 Brazil was one of the wealthiest developing countries with a per capita income of $1,700 (in 2007 USD). By 1978 per capita GDP had reached $5,500 and average annual growth was almost 9.5% (Kharas and Kohli, 2011).

In the early 1980s Latin America entered a long period of decline and stagnation, accompanied by a de-industrialization processes, which would make Brazil surpass the per capita income of 1978 only in 1995, and for a short moment after its hyperinflation crisis (Kharas and Kohli, 2011; Scalon, 2013). Macroeconomic instability would soon wreck the country again as the East Asian crisis broke out in 1997. It was only in the mid-2000s and thanks to the commodity boom that Brazil would once more surpass its 1978 income. 30 years had gone by without any significant improvement in income levels. Still today Brazil has not been able to demonstrating a sustained fast growth as it did in the 1970s, which could assure convergence with high income economies (Kharas and Kohli, 2011).

The issue of inequality in Brazil, as in other countries of Latin America, has deep historical roots. The South American country is not only unequal in terms of income and social indicators, but also in terms of economic activity. Nobel Prize winner Amartya Sen claims that the deprivation caused by inequality and poverty cannot be understood in absolute terms. It cannot only be thought of in terms of unstable income, but must be understood in a more complex way, as a lack of basic capabilities that lead to "vulnerability, exclusion, exposure to fear and violence, lack of power, participation, and voice", which amounts to exclusion from basic rights and wellbeing (Scalon, 2013). As stated in a World Bank (2004) report on the issue, although most unequal societies like Sierra Leone, Nicaragua, the Central African Republic, Paraguay, and Guatemala "tend to be countries with a lower level of development, Brazil's level of inequality appears more prominent when compared with other middle-income countries". Its levels of inequality become even more pronounced when taking into account its size.

In a study of social classes in Brazil, Scalon (2013) points out that social mobility (considering the years 2001–2009) was very limited, with 47.6% of the urban workforce still being concentrated in manual occupations. This is reflected in the structure of Brazil's social classes. Data from the Brazilian Association of Population Studies (ABEP, 2016) distributes the population in classes ranging from A to E, with the B and C classes each divided into two sub-classifications (Table 11.4).

Table 11.4 Average Household Income Estimation for the Strata in the Brazilian Criteria, Average Household Income in BRL

Social Economic Stratum	Average Household Income
A	R$ 20,888
B1	R$ 9,254
B2	R$ 4,852
C1	R$ 2,705
C2	R$ 1,625
D-E	R$ 768
TOTAL	R$ 3,130

Source: ABEP, 2016.

Figures 11.5 and 11.6 show the percentages of those social classes in Brazil for the year 2016 with data from ABEP, differentiated by regions and for each of the country's main metropolitan regions. What can be seen is a significant difference in the distribution of classes, especially in the country's poorer northern and northeastern regions, which can be confirmed with the data on the metropolitan areas. Such stark inequality levels have led to political and cultural divides between the regions. They also define Brazilian identities regionally and within the cities, with impacts on consumer behavior.

While recent macroeconomic policies and social programs have been contributing to reduce (extreme) poverty, Brazil's high levels of inequality have still been remarkably stable, according to a report published by the World Bank

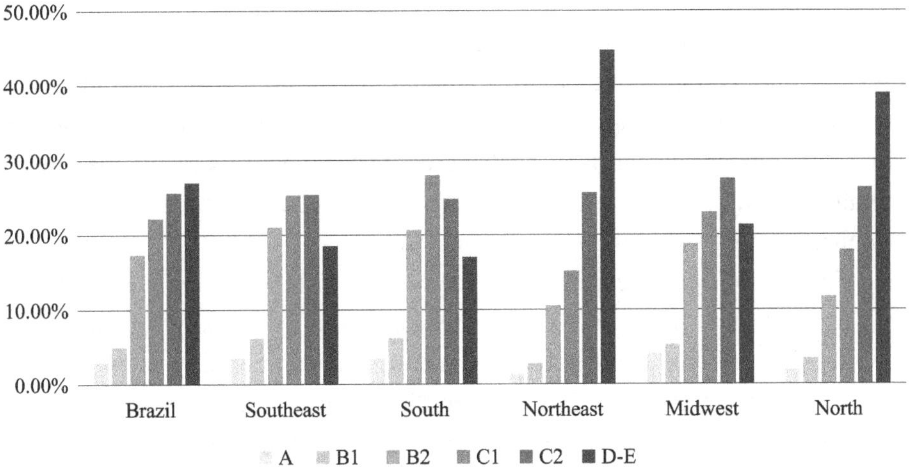

Figure 11.5 Brazilian Social Classes (from A-E) in their National and Macro-Regional Distribution. by social class.

*Data % of population in income.

Source: ABEP, 2016.

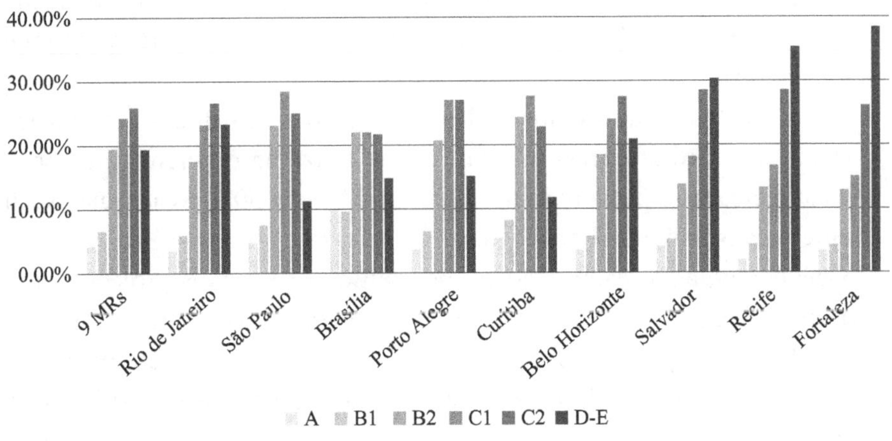

Figure 11.6 Social classes (from A-E) for 9 Brazilian Metropolitan Regions

Source: ABEP, 2016.

(2004). A ranking presented by the U.S. Central Intelligence Agency based on data on the Gini coefficient from 1993 until 2016 places Brazil as the world's 19th most unequal country, out of a list of 150 nations (CIA World Factbook,

2017). Bourguignon, Ferreira and Leite (2002) in their studies evaluate this situation as an "unacceptable stability" of Brazil's inequality. This situation is mostly due to regressive public transfers, a less equitable distribution of education, and higher wage differentials. When compared to the U.S., which is one of the most unequal industrialized countries-the CIA's above mentioned list ranks the U.S. as the world's 40th most unequal country, the report points to these three factors as follows (World Bank, 2004).

- First, public transfers are less progressive in Brazil. While most social programs are progressive, retirement pensions (especially for the public sector), consume the largest share of social spending (<50%) and, according to the World Bank, are "heavily biased in favor of higher-income groups". Furthermore, with pensions taking up more than 5% of government spending, Brazil devotes a much higher share of its resources (as compared to the U.S.) to these entitlements.
- Second, the unequal distribution of education in Brazil accounts for almost 30% of inequality. Thus, the "skill gap" in the country's labor force is quite high, even compared to other countries in the region, such as Mexico or Colombia. Only 35% of the population graduate high school (as compared to 94% in the U.S. and 52% in Mexico), reflecting a longstanding neglect in education, which has only very recently seen government action.
- Third, skills premiums (for higher qualification) in Brazil account for about one third of excess inequality. The Brazilian differential has seen great increases especially in the 1990s and is now 50% greater than such differentials in the U.S. or Mexico.

Consequently, an already unequal distribution of assets is projected into an even more unequal distribution of the labor markets, which in turn depend on each other. Skill premiums are of course partially determined by formal education (acquired skills). This development has been affected by both technological development as well as a relative shortage of highly skilled workers in the country's economy. Thus, national policies adopted in the areas of education, pensions and labor qualification have a long-standing effect of maintaining the country's high levels of income inequality.

3. Public Policies concerning Consumption in China and Brazil

Economic development is embedded in a historical and cultural context, which interacts with the macro and microeconomic policy decisions in different ways. Social and economic policies are shaped by a country's context and in turn contribute to influencing the society that produced them. When it comes to social inequalities, as mentioned above it is now widely recognized that a very polarized income distribution is harmful to growth. It might put the emerging countries at risk of not being able to attain high income levels or to meet their international obligations, such as their commitments to the sustainable development goals (Piketty, 2017).

What is still being debated, and will likely continue to be, is if debt financing of consumption and similar measures will ultimately prove to be economically sustainable, and if they can be seen as short-term solutions or, on the contrary, as the reason behind future crises. It is however less disputed that a high degree of inequality is harmful for a country that aims to graduate from the middle-income level to a high-income one and to move from low-wage, labor-intensive manufacturing to a highly productive, technologically sophisticated production and exports (Lin, 2012).

Policy recommendations from authors including Kharas and Kohli (2011), Stiglitz (2013) and Piketty (2017) point out how policies for consumption stimulus or expanded access to credit can support this process. The case of China, which is at the crossroads of becoming a consumer society, but which until recently understood itself as a labor-intensive production country, presents highly interesting considerations about this transition. Brazil, as a historically unequal society that in past decades has had to deal with several economic crises, has already made the transition to a consumption focused economy. How far this decision has the potential to combine economic sustainability with more socially equitable growth is discussed below.

Inequality should be a focal topic for developing countries in the discussion of their development issues. Hout (2006) points out how the "run-up in social inequality in many nations over the last 20 years has led to a variety of social and economic problems". According to the author, claims are made "that cross-sectional inequalities overstate the problems because today's inequalities are undone by tomorrow's social mobility". Hout's affirmations criticize the optimism about social mobility as "misplaced". While social mobility does occur, it is far from perfect, even in the most open societies of Western Europe.

On average, a person's place in society maintains a strong, positive correlation with social origins—between 0.25 and 0.40 in rich countries. Furthermore, most mobility that occurs reflects occupational upgrading and economic growth that affects everyone, regardless of their social origins. While this may mask some of the social consequences of inheritable privilege, it does not negate them.

3.1 Inequality in Chinese Policies: the Way Out of the Trap

Over the past decades China has come to be known as the factory and growth miracle of the world since its first experiments during the Reform and Opening Period with venture capital and export-oriented growth policies (Kuijs and Wang, 2005; Li, 2016). In the face of a changed global environment that has been shaken by several economic and financial crises at regional and global levels, as well as a dramatically changed domestic situation with an ever-more stable and urban middle class, Beijing's policy makers are now turning to domestic consumption and innovation as a means to maintain high levels of growth (Lardy, 2006).

One of the most significant marks beginning this transformation process can be seen in the "denunciation and termination of the party line 'taking the class struggle as the key link'" and Deng Xiaoping's declaration to focus on "making economic construction central". They were accompanied by major reforms of CCP language concerning social classes, "uniting all forces to meet future challenges" and overcoming the revolutionary-against-counter-revolutionary divide. The resulting profound changes in ownership structures gave rise to a rapidly growing non-publicly-owned economy and a new social strata of private business owners. The unprecedented rate of urbanization and rapid industrialization transformed one fifth of a billion peasants into "new workers" in China's growing East coast and inland metropoles. At the same time there was significant growth of an urban middle stratum that would eventually form the backbone of a consumption-driven economic system. All this was also accompanied by major demographic changes as the ones caused by stringent birth control and the One Child Policy since the 1970s (Li, 2013), but also by a sharp rise in inequality, particular in a rural-urban divide. While the urban Gini coefficient in the early 1980s was a mere 0.16, those rates have risen to high levels of around 0.5 in recent years (Xie and Zhou, 2014; Li, 2016). As previously mentioned, China is now ranked among the world's 30 most unequal countries.

The changes in interest patterns caused by reforms including the sharing of revenues and expenses between the central and local governments, resulted in private, foreign-funded, and township enterprises forming their own independent interests (see e.g. Wong, 1991). The "tax-for-profit" and "disbursement-to-loan" policies have significantly changed the functioning of the economy, notably of the state-owned enterprises that long dominated the post-reform Chinese economic landscape and that had enjoyed easy access to funds and credit (Zhigang, Vercueil and Boyer, 2017). The implications of Deng's dictum "let some get rich first" were combined with increasing competition and regionally diverging interests between cities and provinces, thus gave rise to relative inequality (Zacharias, 2007; Li, 2016).

While in the 1980s household consumption averaged slightly more than half of the country's GDP, this share fell from an average of 46% in the 1990s, to 38% in 2005 and only 36% in 2015. This is one of the lowest shares of any major economy, compared to a world average of around 60% in the UK and India and relatively high 70% in the U.S. (Lardy, 2006; Hsu, 2015). Differentiations in residents' employment and income statuses enlarged income inequality, and lowered consumption's contribution to economic growth, while in the same period capital investment accounted for over half of China's economic growth (Zhigang, Vercueil and Boyer, 2017).

In December 2004 the Chinese leadership decided to shift its policies from investment and export-led development to consumption-driven growth. At the 2006 the then the Premier then Wen Jiabao reinforced this intent and affirmed that it does not mean that the leadership seeks to slow the rate of economic growth. The primary goal was to change the structure of demand and to raise the efficiency of investments. The government believed that rapid growth was more likely to prove sustainable if generated by expanding consumption by Chinese households and less by surging investment by Chinese companies and a "ballooning global trade surplus" (Lardy, 2006).

Since this decision the government has started to implement policies for rural and low-income households, including agricultural subsidies and exemptions from agricultural fees. Regressive taxes had been a huge burden on rural households in the 1990s when they accounted for 10% of this group's average income. According to Li (2016) these exemptions and reforms towards progressive taxation had an overall positive impact on the reduction of the growing income inequality between rural and urban areas. Gradually and experimentally implemented since the 1990s, the cash transfer program Dibao was a policy initiative to guarantee a minimum income for poor and low-income households. It was expanded very rapidly to cover rural as well as urban areas and in 2013 included some 54 million people (Golan, Sicular and Umapathi, 2014). Furthermore, initiatives such as the health insurance "New Rural Cooperative Medical Scheme" and the "New Rural Pension Scheme" were rapidly expanded. By the end of 2013 more than 800 million rural people were inscribed in this health insurance, covering almost 99% of China's rural areas. Golan, Sicular and Umapathi (2014) point out the program's indirect effects on rural incomes (Li, 2016).

While Li (2016) evaluates the government's economic policies as a move "to equal sharing of the outcomes of growth and a harmonious society" and from "stimulating investment and export growth to encouraging an increase in consumption", Lardy (2006) holds that the transition toward consumption-driven growth was off to a slow start and that it is "likely to be substantially delayed" as consumption stimulus, e.g. in the housing sector it is yet to take effect (Hsu, 2015).

Since the Reforming and Opening up of China and with the adoption of more market oriented policies, the country has seen a sharp rise in inequality from its former wealth distribution. The growth model of extremely rapid industrial development in the Eastern coastal cities and later in bigger inland cities has certainly exacerbated the rural-urban divide. However, it has to be noted that the Chinese government has undertaken efforts to reduce those developments. With the change of its growth model, many of the several hundred million migrant workers are likely to migrate back to their countryside homes and bring with them both money and a changed mindset. The future effects on family relations, health and social security financing (Dreger and Zhang, 2014) as well as the ageing of society after three decades of strict family planning are still to be seen.

In combination with increasingly consumption-led growth, the implications are now not only economically relevant, but start to call attention of social and environmental sciences. China's new consumption model must be accompanied by radical changes in energy generation, solid waste, and natural resource management. Also, in order to ensure a socially and environmentally sustainable society, a renewed understanding of the nature-society-relationship and of the human identity within a vulnerable natural system of finite resources must be adopted, as proposed in the Ecological Society doctrine.

3.2 Brazil's Consumption-based Growth Strategy to Escape the Middle-income Trap

Brazil is, according to many, the typical case of a country struggling with the middle-income trap. As discussed above, in the course of the past century, the country went from a sustained and accentuated growth in the 1960s and 1970s to a period of overall stagnation from the 1980s to the 2000s. The latter period of stagnation impeded it to raise living standards to a level compared to the ones enjoyed in high income economies. Recent economic booms have been supported by commodity prices and have led to an expansion of consumption, but these periods tend to come to an abrupt end (Kharas and Kohli, 2011). This growth pattern raises the question on whether the expansion of the Brazilian middle class and the increased consumption levels in the country experienced in the 2000s are a sign that millions have indeed been lifted out of poverty and entered the middle class, as observed by Nassif (2017), or whether it is only the effect of a temporary economic bonanza. According to Nassif, 24 million people moved above poverty levels between 2003 and 2009, but after the crisis, in 2015 alone an estimated 3.7 million Brazilians went back to poverty (Caleiro, 2016).

A main cause for the middle-income trap is the higher wage levels in middle-income countries, which no longer allow middle income groups to enjoy a comparative advantage for the production of low-skill, labor-intensive goods. At the same time, middle income countries are often unable to compete with high income countries in the production of technologically advanced goods. Lin and Treichel (2012) define the middle-income trap as the inability to move from low value-added industries to high value-added ones, which is observed in several countries across Latin America.

To tackle this issue, Brazil has been adopting a strategy that is mainly based on consumption-led growth. This strategy relies on the country's market size and industrial base to promote growth based on domestic demand. As a matter of fact, successive governments have been adopting a series of measures to stimulate domestic demand: throughout the 2000s, public banks such as the National Bank for Economic and Social Development (BNDES), the Bank of Brazil (BB) and the Caixa Econômica Federal, a publicly-owned financial institution, have been irrigating the market with credit in order to promote consumption. Government consumption stimulus packages are commonly based on tax reductions, subsidies for housing and social programs. In 2009, a total of USD 20.4 billion was injected by the government into the economy, partially to counter the effects of the global financial crisis (Ferrari Filho and Paula, 2015).

Interestingly, a continuous trend of policies adopted to stimulate demand can be verified, in spite of changes in government. In December 2011, the then Workers' Party ("Partido dos Trabalhadores" or PT) government launched a series of measures to boost consumption, including exemptions and reductions of a tax on industrial goods (IPI), temporary exemptions of certain contributions on companies' profits (PIS/COFINS) for some goods, increased access to credit and the expansion of the government's housing subsidies, implemented through the "Minha Casa, Minha Vida" program (Federal Government of Brazil, 2011). Five years later, in January 2016, the new Temer administration announced that BRL 83 billion would be allocated to promote consumption and investments through an expanded access to credit (Federal Government of Brazil, 2016).

Brazil has therefore been focusing on a consumption-based growth strategy, as a means to generate growth via domestic demand. On the one hand, demand is stimulated with access to credit and tax cuts, while social programs are implemented to reduce extreme poverty and inequality. The focus on demand could be partially explained as a result of the country's collective perception of consumption as a central concept for one's class identity. People perceive themselves as belonging to the middle class through their consumption patterns, mainly by owning a home (O'Dougherty, 2002). It might thus appear natural to policy makers that development can be achieved by alleviating extreme poverty and stimulating consumption by the middle class.

However, according to some authors, while the consumption led-growth policy has demonstrated its relevance, this strategy will not be sufficient for the country to escape the middle-income trap. It is crucial to create a competitive economy through innovation and export-led growth, as demonstrated by the cases of East Asian economies such as Japan, Korea or Singapore. During their different economic development stages, these economies have all shifted from an agricultural-based economy to a services- and high-technology-based one. By increasing the shares of higher value goods and services in their GDP, East Asian economies were able to sustain higher living standards in the long-term. If Brazil does not succeed in diversifying its industrial base, it risks facing an increased deindustrialization process (Tjong, 2014), partially due to competition from Chinese manufactured goods (Lin and Treichel, 2012).

Brazil risks being trapped within middle-income levels for a long period if the issues of the extreme inequality and lacking productivity and competitiveness are not properly addressed. To improve its living standards beyond middle income levels, Brazil must thus combine adequate social policies with the promotion of a more productive and competitive economy more productive and competitive economy. On the relations between the middle class, consumption, and development, it might be argued that the middle class can contribute to sustaining development in the long term, but not if its role is restricted to being the country's credit-based consumers when times are good for the economy.

4. Conclusions

Over the past decades, China and Brazil have experienced an increase of the overall national income accompanied by a trend of expansion of the domestic consumer market. However, to better understand this process it is necessary to focus on the construction of new subjectivities in the changing context of these unequal societies. As both countries move from production-led policies to consumption-led ones, it is important to understand the transformation of the citizen from Worker to Consumer. It is not enough to create a discourse of the "democratic inclusion" of the citizens in the consumer market, it is imperative to look deeper into the new inequality and segregation dynamics that emerge from this process.

Consumption—as a source of power, agency and imagination—goes beyond the act of purchasing, playing a central role in modern subjectivity delimitating the individual boundaries while acting as a link of social belonging: "it is an act that at the same time imprison and free the individuals from the social structures through which they transit" (Pinheiro-Machado and Scalco, 2014: 7).

Inequality, consumption and economic growth are complex matters that involve not only economic analyses, and demands that researchers understand that monetary redistribution is not the only way to promote equality and social justice. "Inequalities have a number of different causes, derivations, and imbrications that cannot be reduced to the economic realm. (...) Among inequality's numerous dimensions are distributing empowerment, not only economic, but also cultural, and political, among others." (Costa and Scalon, 2013).

Over the past two decades, Brazil implemented a series of social policies to stimulate consumption and reduce extreme poverty, which have successfully led to a sharp narrowing of the income inequality gap. However, the recent gains in social equity now seem threatened by the country's current economic and political crisis. Inequality in the country presents a multidimensional and multifaceted nature, and its rigid class structure leads to the reproduction of inequalities through the unequal provision of opportunities. This scenario poses additional difficulties to the long-term success of Brazil's fight against inequality.

On its turn, China's policy has been one of shifting its economic growth from a model driven by investments and exports to a new model based on domestic private consumption. As a potential result of this policy, consumption is expected to become crucial for future GDP growth. Nonetheless, this process faces a number of obstacles, such as the historically high savings rate, driven in particular by the low level of social security and a highly regulated financial market, as well as the urban-rural disparity (Dreger and Zhang, 2014). To better understand this process, it is imperative to focus on the contexts and the experiences of the agents involved in such transformations. China's previous development cycle had its price competitiveness in export markets paid for by low wage growth. Now the citizen that was once signified as a worker (production-citizen) has to occupy a new place in society as a consumer (consumption-citizen). "When the subject of production strives to reemerge in the chain of the symbolic world, it is a process of negative hallucination, the 'I' of production has to enter a process of identification or subjectification with the 'other' of consumption" (Ngai, 2003).

Even though consumption is something both countries want to boost in their strategies to achieve sustained economic growth, we should be careful with what Pun Ngai points out as a "democratic show", a consumer "revolution" in which all could participate. Consumption can reinforce pre-existing socially unequal structures and even create new forms of segregation, as the author observed in her ethnography among the *dagongmei*, who are women migrant laborers from the countryside that moved to the urban centers in mid-1990s. These individuals got caught in a complex power struggle, at the same time that they pursued to enhance their cultural capital and broaden their horizon in the city through consumption, they faced discrimination and humiliation when trying to contest new consumption spaces, as they were not recognized as "qualified" to integrate these power dynamics.

The emergence of new inequality dynamics can also be observed in Brazil, as Pinheiro-Machado and Scalco (2014) observed in the "rolezinhos" phenomenon—characterized by big groups of young individuals from lower income groups strolling around shopping malls and other elite consumer centers—elucidates the inclusion of the peripheries in the consumption market and contests old social structures. However, these events caused commotion among the elite consumers that traditionally occupied these spaces and shop owners, who even tried to deny the right of these young consumers to circulate in the shopping malls. This phenomenon unleashed a convoluted debate on inclusion and the reproduction of old inequalities, such as race segregation, and new inequalities as the democratic "right to the city".

Chinese and Brazilian investments in a consumption-based development project, expanding credit in the case of Brazil, or improving social security in the case of China, might not be enough for the success of this project. Adopting a consumption-led development model to avoid the middle-income trap will only succeed if we look at the individuals undergoing this transformation process and the construction of new subjectivities in this context. It is imperative that a sustainable and inclusive development strategy goes beyond the macro-economy and through an anthropological perspective and an ethnographic sensibility understand the perspectives of the agents involved in the contradictions and paradoxes of development. Development must be understood in a holistic way, as it is not only expressed through a country's income level. Whether led by economic growth or crisis, changes in economic levels affect how individuals interact and perceive each other, how they produce and consume goods and services, and how they see their position in society as a source of class identity.

This article aimed at contributing to the discussions on the middle-income trap and its potential challenges for development in China and Brazil, by adopting a broader perspective on this topic. It could be argued that the challenges posed by the middle-income trap go beyond the economic growth; it also impacts social and class structures, by affecting the level of inclusion and social justice and a country's environmental sustainability. An example of this holistic understanding of development might be China's recent 13th Five Year Plan, which presented projects that demand interdisciplinary debate, in which intercultural contributions could lead to creative solutions.

In conclusion, we would like to contribute to the debate on middle-income trap and development challenges by proposing a more integrated approach to this matter: we should go beyond a mere economic perspective of sustainable growth, isolated from other considerations. The implications of consumption-driven growth for inequality and income levels must be studied by an approach that integrates social sustainability, particularly in the spheres of inclusion and social justice, and also environmental sustainability.

Chapter 12
Climate Change in Brazil and China: Impacts, Political Responses and Challenges

Mariana Delgado Barbieri
Leila da Costa Ferreira
Fabiana Barbi

If initially greenhouse gas emissions were seen as an eminent environmental problem, the complexity of the phenomenon has transformed this question in one of the great challenges of the 21st century: it is an issue that besides affecting environmental, economic, political matters, also affects development and public health. Emissions and their immediate consequence—climate change, challenge the survival of the human species and each report from the International Panel on Climate Change (IPCC, 2007; IPCC, 2013) consolidates this threat.

Policies to contain greenhouse gas emissions (GHG) directly influence the relation between production and consumption and, in this sense, China and other countries face huge challenges when trying to balance production and maintenance of economic growth with reduction of emissions.

The high GHG emissions increased throughout the 20th century because of anthropogenic activities that had an exponential increase in the case of China and Brazil from the 1980s on. These emissions are promoting global warming from the high concentration of pollutants in the atmosphere, changing the functioning of ecosystems, increasing ocean levels, leading to desertification, a greater occurrence of hurricanes, typhoons and cyclones, rising temperatures in several parts of the globe, etc. (Beck, 2010; Giddens, 2010; Ferreira and Barbi, 2012).

These changes in the global system increased environment risks of this time, in which modernity radicalization, advances in science and technology, economic development and industrialization produce new risks and must be faced globally, considering climate change affects everyone and cannot be understood from a local perspective or an isolated phenomenon (Beck, 2010).

In this sense, to deal with environmental issues in the 21st century, there is need to think about new political and economic strategies to mitigate emissions and promote adaptations, which today we know as inevitable, after all, even if the emissions stopped, we would suffer the consequences of climate change for many years (Barbi and Ferreira, 2016).

This chapter aims to understand the nature of GHG emissions in China and Brazil; discuss the major economic and social impacts of climate change in the two countries; and, organize the political actions of the countries, nationally and internationally in a list. For this we use primary data (emissions reports; legislation; National Plans) and secondary data, from a literature review.

This study is the result of research undertaken in LABGEC (Laboratory of Social Dimensions of the Global Environmental Changes in the Global South) from NEPAM (Center for Environmental Studies and Research), of the State University of Campinas/Brazil, coordinated by the Professor Leila da Costa Ferreira, Phd., who investigates climate change in countries from the Global South, especially Brazil, China, and Mozambique. We do not aim to carry out a comparative analysis between the countries, but to discuss a wider sociological question—global environmental changes, from reflections that emerge from an empirical basis, and that allow us to understand the problem of overcoming the middle-income trap, from a perspective focused on the environmental issue and the human impacts on nature. Thus, we want to work the different dimensions of environmental issues, from the interdisciplinary and holistic vision of the phenomenon.

1. Greenhouse Gas Emissions in China and Brazil

China is the country with the highest GHG emission in the world: responsible for 29% of global emissions in 2015, it surpassed the United States in 2007 (IEA, 2015). The increase in emissions was extremely high, growing 300% between 1990 and 2010.

This growth comes from deep social changes in the country promoted from the *Four Modernizations Plan* of 1978, which included China in the global economic context. The *Four Modernizations Plan* sought to develop agriculture, industry, defense, science and technology, stimulating international reinsertion to make China a major world power by 2050 (Gamer, 1999; Leite, 2013). Deng Xiaoping said the goal was to quadruple GDP, in addition to absorbing foreign investment, technology and science, opening China to the world with the so-called *open-door policy* (Hsü, 2000). High emissions are directly associated with the burning of fossil fuels, mainly coal, that is still China's energy matrix, corresponding to more than 60% of the annual energy production (Liu, 2015) and consuming more than 50% of global production of coal. The use of coal as the main source of energy has been decreasing slowly with the higher use of renewable energy sources such as wind power and solar energy, which started receiving greater support and investments from the government as of the 11th National Energy Plan, considering the 13th Five-Year Plan (2015–2020) established a reduction goal of 18% of GHG emissions. Besides the development of wind and solar energy, the plan also wanted to double the power generation capacity from hydropower plants, in addition to the construction of more than 30 nuclear power plants, an energy option full of controversies pronounced after the accident of Fukushima, in Japan, in 2011 (Basso and Viola, 2014).

The quick increase in GHG emissions since the 1980s is associated with deep transformations in China: the strong industrialization (manufacturing globalization), urbanization, changes in soil use, population increase, emergence of a new middle class (Shapiro, 2012).

The inclusion of China in the globalized market was due to the exportation of manufactured goods of low value. The high increase in the production demanded a high increase in energy obtained from the burning of coal. The industrial and energy sectors have become the major GHG emitters, followed by cement production and by transports directly associated with urbanization and changes in the profile of population distribution (Shi and Zhang, 2006).

Cement industry has expanded to allow the construction of cities to house a huge amount of people from the countryside. Such process was the biggest in history, with the displacement of more than 300 million people (He, 2006). Consequently, the number of constructions and the use of cement followed this movement. The cement industry has been considered a significant contributor to global warming, being one of the main industrial emitters of CO_2 (Rehan and Nehdi, 2005). China produces almost half of the cement produced worldwide, generating increases in the burning of coal for the production of energy for cement manufacturing, and producing large amounts of CO_2 and other heavy metals, such as thallium, cadmium, mercury and lead (Gerth,

2010).

The massive population displacement from the countryside to the city had several consequences on the social structure and functioning of Chinese society. In 1980, 80% of Chinese lived in the countryside. Today, 53% live in the city and 47% in the countryside (United Nations, 2014). Quick changes has led to a greater ecological pressure. After all, the bigger the size of the urban centers, the greater the consumption of energy, fuel, water, generating greater air pollution from the emission increase of GHG and other gases and particles.

The expansion of cities over the 1980s and incorporation of new lifestyles come from globalization and the opening of China to the world. A new middle class arises with Western consumption and life patterns, which are: having a car, having heating and air conditioning in all the rooms of the house, consuming more superfluous goods and meat, and producing more waste and residues, thus directly contributing to the increase of GHG emissions—the main responsible for climate change (Shapiro, 2012; Zhang and Ong, 2008).

The car market in China is already the largest in the world, surpassing the United States with more than 17.2 million cars sold in 2010 (Shapiro, 2012). The luxury goods market also expands significantly, accounting for over 20% of the world's consumption of jewelry, watches, clothes, shoes, a clear example of integration in the Western culture incorporated by China through the increased use of internet and new social media, in addition to increases in Chinese people international trips and higher number of foreigners in China.

What we observe is the presence of a global movement, in which life patterns are imported by China. However, because of the modernization promoted since the 1980s, China becomes a huge exporter of risks, a direct reference to Ulrich Beck's work that states that scientific and technological development produces new post-industrial risks globally (that affect everything and everyone), are imperceptible, untold and unpredictable. Among the produced risks, we have the ones regarding ecology, such as environmental and climate changes, the main focus of this chapter (Beck, 2010; Ferreira, 2017).

> *Climate change is the most urgent, deep and serious part of environmental crisis of the 21st century. It is urgent because there is little time for us to stabilize the concentration of greenhouse gases at acceptable levels in the atmosphere. It is serious because it increases desertification, water resources and biodiversity crisis significantly. In addition, it destroys great part of the existing infrastructure, damages economic activities and severely affects poor populations of the planet. And it is deep because there is still no technological solution for it (Beck, 2010, p. 10).*

Despite China standing out when it comes to climate change and emission of GHG (being considered a climate power because of high GHG emissions), Brazil features the 7th position in the emission volume rank (OC, 2017), also being internationally recognized for its pro-activity.

Unlike China, Brazilian emissions are historically based on the use of soil and on farming. However, in the last decade, it was possible to observe a new emission configuration due to emissions from energy generation, according to what we see in Figure 12.1:

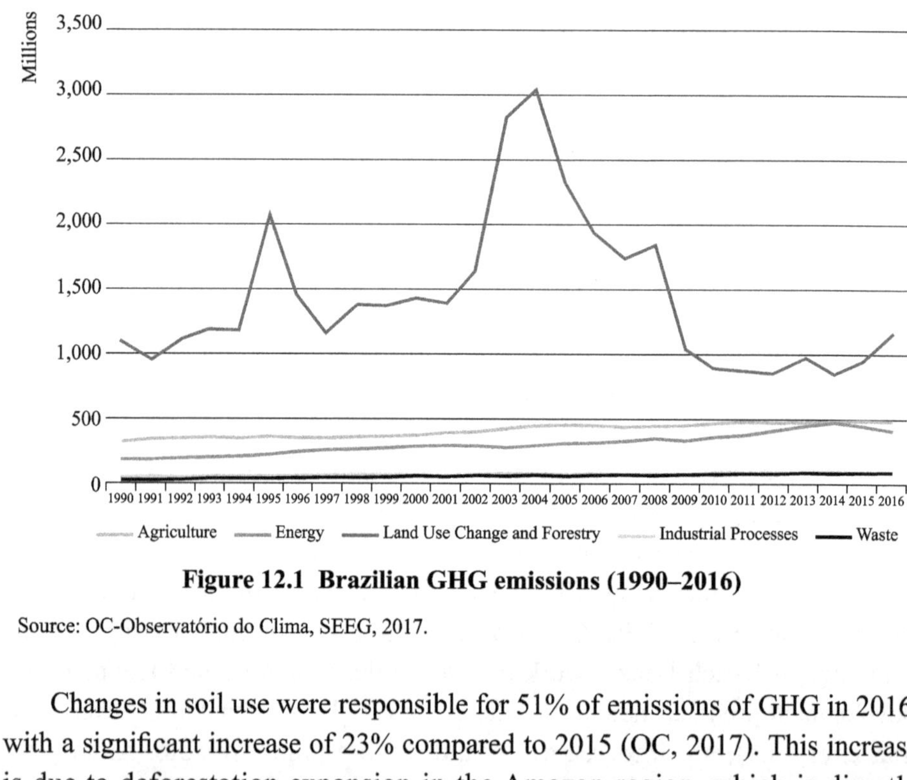

Figure 12.1 Brazilian GHG emissions (1990–2016)

Source: OC-Observatório do Clima, SEEG, 2017.

Changes in soil use were responsible for 51% of emissions of GHG in 2016, with a significant increase of 23% compared to 2015 (OC, 2017). This increase is due to deforestation expansion in the Amazon region, which is directly associated with the increase in commodity exports, such as soybeans and cattle, to China and other countries. In 2009, China became the main trading partner of Brazil (Mortatti, Miranda and Bacchi, 2011) and recent changes in Chinese legislation of agricultural products might encourage this partnership even further. Since May 2017, there is no more minimum price wage for Chinese agricultural products, which has discouraged the Chinese domestic production but stimulated Chinese imports. In this sense, Brazil benefits commercially and economically, thus exporting more feed grains, meat, fruits, vegetables and other commodities. However, the damages to the environment are significant because the increase in demand leads to increased deforestation and expansion of Brazilian agriculture.

In case of climate change, besides deforestation promoting GHG emissions, it devastates an important carbon sink: the forests. Carbon sinks are elements that can absorb more carbon than they are capable of emitting, such as forests, soil and water. Reducing forest areas leads to more climate changes, and in the case of the Amazon forest, it directly affects its regions, as it is the case of the Brazilian Southeast. The reduction in steam supply to the atmosphere affects the formation of air rivers that influence the amount of rainfall in the Southeast of the country. This is just one example among several deforestation consequences that can lead to major changes in the planet's climate (Nobre, 2014).

Unlike China, Brazil shows an emission distribution pattern of agricultural countries, the agriculture and livestock sector being the second largest in GHG emission. When considering the sector of soil changes and the agriculture and livestock sector together, they both represent more than 70% of emissions. It is interesting to observe that Brazil's emissions have increased at a time of serious economic recession, "Brazil becomes the only major economy in the world to increase pollution without generating social wealth" (OC, 2017, p. 2).

In Brazil, the energy sector, a big emitter in China, is only the third biggest emitter, because the Brazilian energy matrix is mainly based on hydroelectric generation, which leads to lower emissions when compared to coal, commonly used in China. Reduction in emissions which occurred in 2016 through energy generation is directly associated with the use of wind and solar energy; the recovery of water reservoirs levels after the drought of 2014, which led to the higher use of thermal power plants in 2014 and 2015; and economic recession.

In large cities, such as Rio de Janeiro and São Paulo, emission setting is different: industries and the burning of fossil fuels are mainly responsible for emission. Together, these two cities emit 3% of the total of GHG in the country.

The distinct nature of Brazilian and Chinese emissions clearly show that mitigation policies of countries need to be different, despite their consequences being the same at a global level (climate change), the local level will suffer in different ways, as we will see in the net topic.

2. Economic and Social Impacts of Greenhouse Gas Emissions in China and Brazil

Human activity is identified as the main responsible for the increase in GHG emissions since industrial revolution, with an increase of more than 70% of emissions between 1970 and 2004. There is strong scientific evidence that global warming is mainly caused by the increase in the concentration of GHG, such as: carbon dioxide (CO_2), methane (CH_4), nitrous oxide (N_2O) and halocarbons. The intensification of the emission of these gases increases the greenhouse effect, a natural phenomenon that allows the survival of the human species by controlling the temperature on the Earth's surface. However, anthropogenic emissions have turned the greenhouse effect into a problem, increasing the temperature in the continents and oceans, the sea level from polar ice caps melting, growth and emergence of deserts, intensification of typhoons, cyclones and hurricanes, changes in precipitation and temperature climatic patterns (IPCC, 2007; IPCC, 2013). The destruction of ozone layer, which reduces the amount of solar radiation that reaches the surface of the earth (troposphere), makes the planet absorb a greater amount of solar radiation and retain more heat.

People are starting to feel the effects of climate change around the world and science has been more and more dedicated to understand this problem. In addition, government policies, the public and private sectors, non-governmental organizations have been concerned with the consequences of these transformations that affect many aspects of human life.

If at the beginning of the discussion and reflection on the problem the developed countries were seen as responsible for implementing mitigation policies considering they were the major GHG emitters, because of industrial development since the 19th century, today most countries participate in international agreements and develop their national plans for mitigation and adaptation to climate change, given the impacts that they have already felt around the world.

It is always important to note that when dealing with the climate change, we are dealing with a global phenomenon. This way, pollution consequences in China, for example, are not restricted to its political border at the local level. It is known that California is directly affected by toxic gases and particulate materials produced in China that get carried away by the wind to the American coast (Ewing et al., 2010). Similarly, besides emitting GHG gases that intensifies global warming, Amazon deforestation also affects rainfall formation in Brazil and other countries of South America, which has an direct impact on the agricultural production and power generation. For being a global phenomenon, there is the need for a global administration of climate, as we will see in the last part of the chapter.

The temperature increase has already been felt in the late 20th century, which was the warmest period since the beginning of measurements in 1880, and projections indicate that until the end of the 21st century, there will be a minimum warming of 2°C. According to the most pessimistic projection of IPCC, the RCP 8.5 projection, we might see an increase of 6°C before 2100. This increase of temperature will bring several consequences regarding economy, society, health, food safety, etc.

The last IPCC report (IPCC, 2013) points out that climate change must affect directly the agricultural production, reducing fertile areas and affecting the reproduction of species and twinning. There will be an agricultural reconfiguration of countries. This framework might aggravate hunger in the poorest countries that still suffer from scarcity of food. The value of commodities might rise, making basic goods more and more expensive for human consumption. Research conducted by David Lobell and team identified the effects of climate changes in agricultural crops increased around 20% of commodity prices in the global market between 1980 and 2008 (Lobell, Schlenker and Costa-Roberts, 2011).

With a reduction of 2% in agricultural productivity and the increase of 14% in demand until 2050 because of population growth (Nahur *et al*, 2015), hunger might be widely debated, after all, the countries at the South of the globe might be the most affected ones. In places where there is hunger and poverty already, it will be intensified, showing that despite the impacts of climate change being global, not all individuals will experience it in the same way—the wealthy ones will suffer less impact. In this situation, Brazil and China will be widely affected.

In Brazil, the cultures of rice (in the Southeast) and soybean (Central region) will be the most affected, as well as corn cultures throughout South America and Central America. The semi-arid in Northeast of Brazil can turn into an arid region, because of the warmer climate in the future, that would directly affect subsistence agriculture, the way population with low levels of social and economic development survive. The reduction in water availability (which is already low) and the fall in health population indexes might lead people to migrate.

In China the problem will be even greater, considering that large regions will be affected by drought, which will demand an increase in irrigation. However, China already suffers today with a low water availability/per capita (Shapiro, 2012). Different agricultural species will not be able to adapt to climate change at the same pace they occur, which might reduce its availability and change its cultivation areas. In the case of Brazil, we verified that temperate climate fruits such as grapes, pears, peaches and apples might have its crop reduced; however, a more tropical culture like sugar cane has been expanding to southern areas of the countries that used to be colder.

Changes in the temperatures of oceans and water acidifications (because of the higher amounts of CO_2 in the oceans) also alter fish offer, considering that they migrate in the search for more adequate temperatures for their own survival and reproduction, directly affecting populations whose fishing is still the main economic activity.

The presence of drought coupled with the decrease in the offer of food and drinking water might intensify the occurrence of environmental refugees, i.e., individuals that will have to abandon their homes because of the environmental conditions of the region where they live. United Nations predict that by 2050 there will be more than 250 million environmental refugees all over the world, as a consequence of climate change—most of them coming from poor countries. It is a major humanitarian crisis (UNHCR, 2008).

The decrease of fertile soil in China and the search for agricultural, energetic and mineral resources developed "new colonial relations" between China and several countries in Africa, Asia and South America. China is interested in new suppliers and areas for cultivation and extraction, and several countries wanted Chinese investments to deal with the economic crisis that affects several economies since the late 2000s. Voracious demand for commodities means ensuring the maintenance of Chinese economic growth; in this game, China starts to directly influence product prices and trading rules (Moyo, 2013).

This scenario of food shortages, environmental refugees, reduction of economic growth might reverse the trend of poverty reduction, creating new levels of poverty in many countries, thus increasing social inequality. An increase of 2.5°C in the 21st century might lead to an economic loss from 0.2% to 2% of global income; besides this loss, there will be more expenses to contain the global warming effects (Nahur et al, 2015).

Besides the increase in poverty, the lack of food and the high price of commodities, climate change will directly affect human health. Epidemiological studies show that air pollution increases the risk of heart disease, lung cancer, causing increased mortality. The WHO (World Health Organization) reported that in 2015 there were over 7 million deaths associated with environmental pollution and climate change (WHO, 2015). The changes in the precipitation levels and rising temperatures change the distribution of vectors of disease, accelerating the spread of diseases such as malaria, cholera, dengue, and zica fever.

In Brazil, in 2016, viruses transmitted by Aedes aegypti killed 734 people, accounting for almost 2 million cases of dengue, zica fever and chikungunya. The Lancet Countdown Report identified that global warming increases the transmission capacity of these mosquito-borne diseases—there was an increase of 9.4% in disease transmission capacity since 1950 (Watts et al, 2017).

In China, the biggest public health problem is pollution, which killed more than 366,000 people in a year. However, this number might reach 1.3 million deaths by 2030 if pollution indexes remain the same. In addition, more than 45% of the deaths in China are associated with cerebro-cardiovascular diseases that are strongly influenced by temperature increase, elevating mortality risk groups, such as the case of older adults and small children.

To avoid these consequences, there is need for implementing mitigation measures in an effective way and promoting these adaptations to deal with the current global warming effects, the greatest challenge when it comes to climate change.

3. Chinese and Brazilian Climate Change Policies

When it comes to national policies, discussions on climate change have been a part of the Brazilian and Chinese political agenda for more than ten years. But there is still a number of important issues to be solved in the next few years, which might guide the political and economic action of the countries.

The theme is full of uncertainties and scientific research provides several perspectives on the probable negative impact caused by climate change: coastal flooding due to sea level rise; intensity increase of extreme climate events; negative impacts in human health, in infrastructure and the environment; decrease of water quality (IPCC, 2013; Ferreira, 2017). The role of environmental sociology and interdisciplinary research must be to observe the human and social dimension of climate change, which is often neglected because this problem is commonly seen as a physical phenomenon. To think about human and social dimensions means to recognize that socioeconomic inequality is a big obstacle for adaptation policies considering that less favorable populations become more vulnerable to the effects of climate change and there is need to think beyond the mitigation policies aimed at emission reduction. It is necessary to understand that countries in the South of the globe have their own demands, such as: the need for sanitation, income distribution, access to drinking water, adequate housing, eradication of hunger—which are associated with mitigation and adaptation policies in a future with less impact or impacts with fewer dimensions.

Most part of the theoretical production on climate change comes from the Northern countries and corroborates with the notion that there is a geopolitics of knowledge, according to Mignolo (2004). If the North has theoretical experience, the South has practical experiences. This division between North and South is not merely geographic, it is a sociology metaphor for developed, underdeveloped and developing countries. There is need for more theoretical production conducted by the global South to incorporate their social and human elements into the climate and physical debate, considering that the most affected countries would be the ones placed in global South and that global policies are mainly conduced in the global North, not recognizing the risks of the first modernity (social inequality, income distribution, unemployment, diseases) (Beck, 2010) as important in the debate on the risks of the second modernity, especially the ecological ones. In this aspect, China is associated with the global South for being in development only in the last two decades.

When it comes to climate changes, China had two milestones in 2007: it was a year that the emission of greenhouse gases surpassed the USA emissions for the first time and the year when China approved its National Climate Change Plan. In this year, China also changed in international negotiations, by showing to understand the importance of climate change and being open to negotiations. In COP 15, the country establishes voluntary goals for emission reduction, despite not taking the responsibility of other developed countries (United States, European Union and Japan) that could compromise their economic development goals.

Among the developing countries, China was the first one to present a Climate Change Plan. To strengthen the Plan and enhance the debate on the topic, the country created several research centers and allowed the disclosure of pollution data in the national media.

The National Climate Change Plan was the result of legislation and plans developed and improved since the 1990s. Environmental policies date back to the 1970s, after the Conference of the United Nations (UN) in Stockholm, when the UN was encouraged to create a governmental document that stimulated environmental protection and pollution reduction. In 1979, a legal base was started with the implementation of the Law of Environmental Protection, a response to air pollution, water pollution, and the disposal of solid waste. In 1989, this law is reviewed and expanded, thus establishing four principles: coordination of environmental protection, pollution prevention, the responsibilities of the polluting countries, and the importance of environmental management.

In 1992, China participated in Rio 92, a United Nations Conventions that proposed Agenda 21, a program that defended a new and environmental aware development pattern by conciliating environmental protection, social justice and economic efficiency. Among the developing countries that signed the agreement, China was the only one who actually drew up a plan and initiated implementation.

Agenda 21 and China's internal issues, such as the exponential increase of air pollution, water contamination, intensification of environmental disasters, international pressures, and China's participation in trade agreements, such as the World Trade Organization, encouraged the development of new laws and the creation of Ministries and departments to deal with environmental issues. The increase in China's emissions over the 90s led to an increase in social and historical responsibility, which made China change its position regarding international agreements and national plans, considering the environmental dimension as essential for the country's future development. With that "in China, climate changes are seen as a subject both associated with a strategy for sustainable national development and international collaboration" (Moreira and Ribeiro, 2017).

It is possible to recognize 3 phases in the development of environmental policies in China: (1) the first refers to the creation of a command system by establishing the Environmental Protection Bureau (EPB) in 1974, later incorporated into the Ministry of Urban and Rural Construction. (2) the second one was the adoption of environmental policies and instruments of environmental administration with the creation of the National Environment Protection Agency (NEPA) in 1990, becoming a State Environment Protection Agency in 2003. From 2002 on, several social actors, such as NGOs (non-governmental organizations), recognize the importance of their participation, thus attending Rio+10 in Johannesburg as autonomous entities. (3) the third one was the incorporation of scientific approaches for environmental protection and development by defining an agenda focused on environmental administration with the government's encouragement and permission for disclosure of information, in addition to the change in the conduction of national policies: economic development and environmental protection considered equally; to do so, there is need to search for a model that integrates State, market, and civil society in the national policies (Raman, 2016; Barbi, 2015).

China has one of the world's most advanced environmental legislation, despite presenting an implementation gap resulting from their own political organization that hindered its implementation. The central government must guide an environmental policy and the local government must conduct appropriate measures to local conditions. In this sense, a major obstacle is the prioritization of economic development at the expense of environmental protection. Another difficulty is the lack of technical knowledge by many monitoring employees, as well as the existence of a complex bureaucratic system, and the lack of transparency in the projects locally implemented.

The Chinese central government has been showing in recent years the relevance of environmental administration. However, because of the territorial dimension, the characteristics of each location, and the several stages of development of each region of the country, a single model of economic development, modernization and sustainable development was inappropriate, evidencing the need for an environmental administration that connects the central leaders of the country to the local leaders of different sectors to better understand the needs of a certain locality and the best way to promote the protection of the environment, the mitigation of emissions, and adaptation to climate change.

Similarly to China, Brazil started its environmental policies from the United Nations Conference in 1972 with the formation of the Secretaria de Estado do Meio Ambiente (SEMA) [Environment State Department] in 1973. In the Stockholm Conference, despite taking the lead among the "third world" countries, Brazil recognized that the environment could be a great obstacle for modernization. In this sense, Brazil's initial position defended the idea that the economic development could not be sacrificed because of the environment and that "first world" countries, the ones that most contributed to environmental degradation, should be responsible for it and pay for the costs of the environmental problem (Guimarães, 2011; Ferreira, 2017).

In the years that followed the Conference, Brazil did not change its attitude regarding the need for development at any cost regardless of the environmental consequences. Although some policies have been created to fight the contamination of urban areas, its effective implementation was hindered by other government plans that encouraged the heavy industry and strong economic development, for example. Even after its transition to democracy, Brazil did not change its position regarding environmental policies, remaining focused on its own economic development.

However, in 1987, hopes were renewed with the creation of the Ministry of Housing, Urbanism and Environment. Environmental issues were expected to be part of governmental discussions, however, they appear in the Constitution of 1988 in a chapter entirely dedicated to them, pointing out a series of new regulations, contributing to the state and local administrations by giving them fiscal and political strength. The period between 1970 and 1980 was the first phase of environmental concerns in Brazil, in which we see a low internalization of environmental problem and its week implementation.

Rio 92 became a historical landmark in the Brazilian environmental policy. The Conference contributed to the dissemination of environmental issues in the Brazilian society and the State showed a more globalized attitude by supporting international agreements, the creation of Agenda 21, and recognizing the problem as something global that must be seen as a priority in the international agenda. Similarly to China, Brazil has openly defended that wealthy countries should pay for higher costs, considering the idea of common but different responsibilities—climate policies should be according to historical responsibility.

The President of Brazil, Itamar Franco (1992 1994) consolidates the Ministry of the Environment, which obtained success when promoting environmental concerns in the Brazilian government. At the end of the 1990s and the beginning of the 2000s, there was a larger internalization of environmental problematic with the creation of different organs and systems to promote the needed environmental policies. In 2002, the government launched the Brazilian Agenda 21 with the participation of different social sectors, encouraging the action of local and state governments in the promotion of sustainable development.

Regarding the specific climate change policies, the first government action was the creation of the *Fórum Brasileiro sobre Mudança Climática* (FBMC)

[Brazilian Forum on Climate Change] in 2000 to inform and mobilize the society to the debate on environmental and climate changes. In 2007, it created the *Comitê Interministerial sobre Mudança do Clima* (MIC) [Interministerial Committee on Climate Change] to plan and implement a national plan for climate change. Such a plan was approved in 2009, establishing a national climate change policy thanks to the collaborative work between the civil society, organizations, research institutions and public authorities. In the same year, the *Painel Brasileiro de Mudanças Climáticas* (PBMC) [Brazilian Climate Change Panel] was created according to IPCC models aimed at gathering, synthesizing and evaluating scientific information on Brazilian climate change, and producing reports and varied information to help in the decision-making process on the matter (Barbi, 2015).

In COP 15 (15th Conference of Convention Parts-Climate Change Framework of the United Nations in Copenhagen), Brazil has adopted the voluntary goal of reducing greenhouse gases to 38/36.1%, i.e., 9% of total emissions projected for 2020 (Governo do Brasil, 2009). These goals were approved by the National Congress and are part of the National Policy on Climate Change (Law 12.187/2009), defining the principles, guidelines and tools to reach this goal (Nahur *et al*, 2015). This reduction goal was the result of pressure exerted by civil society and the private sector, considering the government did not want to define quantified emission goals (Ferreira, 2017).

In 2010, new laws were approved, creating sectoral plans of mitigation and adaptation to climate changes, aiming to stimulate a low-carbon economy, thus reducing emissions and ensuring the population's long term well-being.

In 2016, the National Plan of Adaptation to Climate Change was established thanks to the collaboration of the civil society, the private sector, and the State government to promote the reduction of vulnerability caused by climate changes, by focusing on the management of risks associated with these changes. Eleven sectors were involved in the elaboration of the plan: agriculture, water resources, food and nutritional safety, biodiversity, cities, risk management of disasters, industry and mining, infrastructure, people and vulnerable populations, health and coastal areas.

Despite being a national plan, each city is encouraged to draw up its own plan of adaptation, considering the effects of climate change might be stronger at local levels, to reduce the impacts that might arise in the near future. There is need for recognizing that climate changes intensify the already existing vulnerabilities, that is why the main focus of the cities should be the promotion of sanitation, sustainable urban drainage, housing, slope retaining structures, improvements in the water and sewerage systems.

Despite the fundamental importance of this Adaptation Plan, its implementation is still low. This plan is part of the contributions that Brazil has sent to the United Nations as part of the global efforts to combat climate change. Greater efforts must be conducted to achieve the programmed goals, considering that emissions increased in 2016 and that the chance of Brazil achieving the reduction of GHG proposed in 2009 is even smaller.

4. Conclusions: Climate Change Challenges

Global climate changes imply a big challenge: it is necessary to brutally reduce the emissions, but we also have to adapt ourselves to the effects brought by these changes (Barbi & Ferreira, 2016). The current levels of emission allow us to state that severe consequences will be felt in the next decades. The urgency of the action is associated with the lack of efficient actions in the last decades, despite the development of several national plans and global agreements.

Climate changes have been discussed for over 20 years, but little was actually done to decrease the emissions. Emissions have been increasing annually, and the warning signal was already given. Despite the reduction in emissions thanks to global economic crisis of 2007/2008, the tendency is for emissions to keep increasing around 2.2% per year. Industrialization, population growth and increases in energetic demands are the responsible for the increase emission in the 21st century. As a consequence, the occurrence of extreme phenomena has been more and more intense; the strong heat waves that reached Europe and the United States in the summer of 2017, temperatures above 50°C in Asia, intense hurricanes in Caribbean, drought in East Africa, monsoon floods, are events closely related to climate change.

The current challenge is to develop a low-carbon economy, which demands new investment patterns in clean energy, such as wind and solar energy. The governments need to be willing to participate actively in their process of transformation to low-carbon economies by attracting investments, decreasing the taxes of key sectors, and creating research and technology centers. Climate changes bring new opportunities to countries willing to promote an economy based on environmental respect, social inclusion and development (Albuquerque and Ferreira, 2013).

To achieve emission reduction goals does not mean to stop the country's economic growth, considering it would not even affect the gross domestic product (GDP): the real challenge is to combine mitigations with economic and social development, and climate changes contribute to the discussion of new development patterns and new technology. China is probably a great example to be followed: the country has been strongly investing in science and technology, being the main producer of photovoltaic panels to generate solar energy. China's challenge is to stop basing its economic growth in the production of cheap manufactured goods from the use of low technology and cheap work force and try to produce alternatives to address the challenges of climate change, but also making it possible to overcome the middle-income trap through a sustainable and socially responsible growth. The idea is to develop international partnerships, to get investments in innovation and education, enabling effective advances in environmental administration and the achievement of the proposed mitigation goals.

If the necessary measures for adaptation and mitigation are not taken, there is a risk that countries will face economic stagnation and large financial losses, being trapped in the middle-income trap. In China, economic losses due to pollution and environmental impacts are estimated to have been between 7% and 20% of GDP over the period 1985–2005 (Diamond, 2005). The cost of health care is also very high, as is the social cost, with more than 366,000 deaths per year due to pollution. This number can reach more than 1.3 million deaths in 2030 (Shuxiao, 2016). The losses estimated annually due to the intensification of extreme events are more than U.S. $ 32 billion (Liu, 2014), a very high value to be ignored and not to promote effective changes. We have as a consequence of climate change the intensification of the losses (caused by the intensification of extreme phenomena, increase of environmental damage, etc.) and the increase of the expenses (with public health, with water depollution, with construction of channels for irrigation, etc.) which may lead to an imbalance in the countries' internal accounts and the need for new strategic directions to maintain social, productive, economic and financial equilibrium (Hu, 2017).

Brazil, which is already impacted by climate change, but to a lesser extent, can reduce its GDP by 0.5% to 2.3% by 2050 due to the consequences of climate change, according to projections made in a study conducted by the University of São Paulo (Margulis, Dubeux, Marcovitch, 2011). In addition, poverty may increase because of the greater vulnerability of the poor to the effects of climate change. If this is confirmed, the middle-income trap can be a reality, since the domestic consumer market may shrink, food items become more expensive, hindering economic development and overrunning of the middle-income trap.

Another serious consequence of climate change is the decrease in water availability, which affects the population and also agricultural and industrial production, as well as the increase in acid rains, desertification, the decrease in arable land, results of the changes promoted by the increase in greenhouse gas emissions that directly influence the economic development and progress of any country. China may be held hostage to these consequences, having to spend money to mitigate these impacts, reducing the amount of other more strategic areas. Investment in new technologies and the adequacy of the energy matrix is essential so that China, as well as Brazil, will continue to develop, with relative energy autonomy and with less greenhouse gas emissions. In this sense, Brazil's investment in biofuels, as in the case of ethanol, is an example of new ways of being taken, stimulating economic growth and technological innovation.

For being a global problem, matters regarding environmental administration need a new meaning to approach multiple social spheres, actors, and political institutions. Environmental administration demands a multi-scale, multi-actor and multi-level action to deal with climate change. Multi-scale administration comprises the scales of the problem of adaptation to climate change, responsibility awareness for adaptation at several administration levels, and the ways to deal with the tension between the administration scale and the problem of adaptation (Dewulf et al, 2015). It is an effective administration strategy directly associated with multi-level administration, i.e., environmental administration, to find solutions for a complex and transverse problem that must considered by several levels of the public sector (local, regional, state, national, transnational and global) that despite implementing their own adaptation and mitigation policies, end up affecting all the other levels (Dewulf et al, 2015; Newell et al, 2012).

The multi-actors administration concerns the allocation of public and private responsibilities in the interaction between public and private actors, and in the specific roles developed by non-governmental organizations and civil society. When treating of these multiple actors, we not only refer to the state/government (the public sphere), but also to companies/market, science/centers of research, media, society/NGOs, all of these being essential actors in environmental administration, whose actions are associated with each other and the establishment of partnerships and support networks (Dewulf et al, 2015).

In this sense, Brazil and China, and other countries of BRICS (Brazil,

Russia, India and South Africa) must strengthen their mutual cooperation and enjoy the opportunities to learn with one another, to exchange experiences and impressions to improve environmental administration. One of the most important cooperation areas among the countries of BRICS is the field of sustainable development, environmental management and environmental administration. Countries from BRICS also suffer with the bad side of globalization, such as poverty, inequality, social tensions, and should get together to discuss better ways to develop and solve issues regarding health problems, hunger, energy, environment, as well as food security, energy security, and drinking water. By working together they might promote global administrations actions to meet their needs for sustainable economic and social development.[①]

① The authors thank Espaço da Escrita—Coordenadoria Geral da Universidade-UNICAMP-for the language services provided.

Conclusions

One of the most critical challenges in China, as well as most Latin American governments, is finding and implementing a formula to escape the middle-income trap (MIT). This book aims to analyze how China and Latin America can support, stimulate, and learn together how to overcome MIT. Currently, as mentioned by González and Lemus, the economies of Latin America show a productivity growth that has been decreasing for decades. On the other hand, China after two decades of high growth faces the challenge to continue developing without falling into MIT. Therefore, from different paths, China and Latin America have reached the same crossroads: how to guarantee an inclusive economic growth that allows overcoming the MIT. González and Lemus to illustrate the significant challenge that MIT represents for emerging economies, explain that of the 101 existing middle-income economies in 1960, by 2008 only 13 became high-income economies.

China recognizes the strategic nature of its ties with Latin America, as demonstrated by the development agenda established in the China-CELAC Cooperation Plan. China has also recognized the need to reshape this relationship by identifying new growth areas suitable for Latin America, in addition to the commodity trade that used to be the cornerstone of this partnership. Cortes discusses how Latin America can take advantage of China's support to carry out a development strategy. The challenge is to generate long-term productive and competitive growth in the region. It must be sufficient to overcome MIT in a socially inclusive manner, offering innovation policies based on the accumulation of human capital and advanced technological infrastructure. Cortes argues that the economic relationship between China and Latin America can be redesigned based on new areas in which both parties can work, focusing mainly on innovation capabilities. Innovation has proven to be the engine of development in the high-income countries that escaped MIT. Latin American nations must achieve the skills and knowledge demanded by world markets, participate in innovative and value-creating activities, and build a national mentality focused on continuous training and improving their human capital to boost innovation processes.

Similar to Cortes, Feldmann concludes that to overcome MIT it is necessary to develop innovations and technology, but unlike Cortes, he proposes that the formation of large Latin American multinational companies in the technology sector are required. Latin American countries must find a way to create a group of large multinationals to enter the very restricted group of developed nations. Indeed, Latin America has some powerful companies, but almost always works in sectors that were important in the 19th century, and became irrelevant in this 21st century. Being a global player in industries such as bakery, beverages, cement, mining, agriculture, fish or steel is not bad, but it is not enough, says Feldmann. The recent growth of exports has occurred mainly in the sectors of agriculture, fish, and mining. This means more deforestation for the export of wood and more land available for agriculture and livestock.

Latin American companies, as Feldmann explains, need to operate in an adequate legal framework that is not politicized or with corrupt practices. It also requires a strong capital market and modern financial services with higher levels of savings. In general, in Latin America, credit is very difficult to obtain and the mechanisms for long-term financing are scarce. Solving macroeconomic problems is a necessary condition, but it is not enough to increase competitiveness. It is essential that we also pay attention to the specific issues of the company, acting as soon as they appear and assisting in what makes it relevant to increase international competitiveness, concludes Feldmann.

One of the most robust forms of cooperation and integration are the Free Trade Agreements (FTA). Borquez says that FTA between China and Latin America seek to deepen the level of cooperation in the region. Binetti analyzed the evolution of relations between Mercosur and China with a focus on the development of Mercosur members (Brazil, Argentina, Uruguay, and Paraguay). In doing so, it seeks to highlight the strengths and weaknesses of Mercosur as an integration mechanism, and propose ways, in which members can reform the bloc to promote integration, build a shared policy towards China and take advantage of current opportunities to exit MIT. Binnetti maintains that the block had been stalled for years before China became an important trading partner. The emergence of China, however, provided a significant challenge that some social, political and economic actors within the Mercosur nations used as an excuse to protect their particular interests and preserve the status quo. The members of Mercosur must unite and design an integration mechanism for the 21st century, which has the institutional and technical tools necessary to channel China's interest in industrial development, trade in services and innovation. China has shown many signs of its willingness to diversify its relations with the Mercosur countries, away from the pattern of trade in commodities for manufactures. The inclusion of Argentina and Brazil within the Belt and Road Initiative (BRI), as well as China's multimillion-dollar funds for industrial innovation and technological improvement in Latin America, are explicit testimonials to this.

As explained by Hernández, China's international cooperation is related to its foreign policy, and this, according to the historical national project of its leaders to turn China into a world power. Currently, the BRI is the backbone of China's international cooperation and a way to define China's identity in the global system. Latin America has joined the BRI mechanism, including external aid. China's cooperation, Hernández continues, includes commercial objectives and direct foreign investment.

China has been generating its institutional structure through which it can directly allocate its financial and technological resources. China allocates most of its available resources for foreign aid to the less developed countries of Asia, Africa, and Latin America. China's international cooperation focuses much more on foreign direct investment and international trade. For China's economic, foreign policy, Latin America has become an essential partner, even more regarding foreign direct investment and trade than aid. In this sense, Latin America is vital for geopolitics, but even more so for the geo-economy of China. The region is an important source of raw materials and the vast consumer market for Chinese products.

Through the BRI initiative, China has had an influence on global finance with geopolitical implications. In this regard, the Chinese regime has increased, and strengthened regional FTA created new financial institutions and influenced traditional ones. Chinese leaders believe that development should be based on the policies of each country since this comes from their own experience: poverty is an internal issue that China has been solving on its own. Therefore, Chinese cooperation with any of its modalities is not the solution to leave MIT. The way in which China is avoiding falling into the middle-income trap is an example; although it is not a model as such, Latin America will have to develop its model, conclude Hernandez.

Borquez focuses on the China-Chile FTA case. He analyzes how this FTA has become a more complex instrument thanks to the new clauses incorporated gradually, emphasizing the development of financial, and technological and scientific research cooperation. In this context, the China-Chile FTA emerges as an alternative of cooperation that allows small economies such as Chile to advance on the road to development. This is what has happened with the case of China and Chile, which through the signing of an FTA have deepened the level of relations, from the mere economic exchange to the search for complex cooperation.

Borquez explains that it is important to note that China has demonstrated its capacity to extend its influence through FTA with countries with an ideologically moderate profile and that historically have been close to the United States (Chile, Costa Rica and Peru). The merit of China has been that in a short time it has understood that Latin America is not a similar sociopolitical unit, for which the country has been articulating cooperation devices based on different profiles of nations. In this line, it is observed that the coming years will strengthen this trend since China is negotiating FTA with three new countries in the region (Colombia, Panama and Uruguay). It has marked a movement in the Latin American geopolitical puzzle where China not only manages to attract the attention of ideologically close countries like Venezuela and Ecuador but is also establishing different highly binding projects with more pragmatic countries.

Within the subject of the FTAs, Zhou, Valderrey and Montoya analyze a potential scenario in which Mexico and China collaborate through the FTA. They develop a comparative review of the impact of a potential FTA for both economies, finding that this would yield positive results for both countries. Unfortunately, Mexico, like most economies in Latin America, meets the requirements to remain within MIT. China is in a very different situation, even with the ability to leave MIT and guide Latin America. China, in fact, is currently moving from manufacturing to an economy of services. In the process, it is creating opportunities for companies in different countries of the Latin American region, for sustained growth. Therefore, comment Zhou, Valderrey and Montoya, China and Mexico must explore different mechanisms that lead to their consolidation and growth of their economies. Some areas where the country could use significant improvements are education, R & D and infrastructure. In addition, the growing presence of China in Latin America can eventually become a long-awaited change of leadership (USA to China) for these economies. After all, many decades of American leadership in the region have not been enough to bring Latin American nations to sustained prosperity.

Continuing with the analysis of the China-Mexico relationship and following the proposal of Feldmann that discusses the importance of developing multinational companies in Latin America, Cervantes and Hartmann analyze the entry to China of four Mexican MNEs. These companies, opposed to what the traditional International Business theory predicts, have not only migrated to culturally similar and physically close countries, but have also entered countries that are very distant physically and culturally, such as China. The main challenges that Mexican multinationals have faced are: fierce competition, cultural differences (even in the palate), different regulatory systems, strong fluctuations in demand; and, in addition, a general ignorance of the Chinese regarding Mexico, its culture and its products. However, these companies were not intimidated by being outsiders and found ways to deal with the challenges presented in China. Everyone is aware of the enormous potential not only of China, but also of its position as a gateway to East and Southeast Asia. Economists agree that Asia is the region of the world with the greatest growth potential in the coming years. All MNEs in Latin American countries need clear strategies, agility to adapt to changing circumstances and discipline in execution. At this point, some in-depth studies would be welcome to identify those elements that could be replicated by other companies, as well as the errors that should be avoided. As Feldmann explains, the developed and strong multinationals in Latin America are fundamental to overcome the MIT.

In addition, Regalado, Montoya, and Zapata analyze the effect of multinational enterprises. Nevertheless, at difference of Cervantes and Hartmann they studied the impact of the Chinese Multinationals in Latin America.

González and Lemus propose a different path to overcome the MIT, the creative economy. They argue that the creative economy has the potential to generate income and jobs while promoting social inclusion, cultural diversity and human development. In fact, creativity, knowledge and greater access to information are powerful engines of economic growth and a privileged way to promote development in a globalized world. In short, in the age of enormous globalization, creativity and knowledge have become an essential element to achieve economic growth and social development. Many facts indicate that the creative economy is positive for developing countries. González and Lemus analyze the creative economy in China from the perspective of creative cities. They explained how the Chinese experience could be an example that inspires newfound opportunities to achieve economic growth in the countries of Latin America. The Chinese show the importance of public policies that support the transformation of traditional economic activities into creative economic activities. The Chinese experience of the creative industries illustrates how these activities could be implemented in Latin American countries, argue Gonzalez and Lemus.

In a different line of analysis, Lemus and Cerda analyze the topic of International Cooperation for Development (IDC). Explaining that the emergence of non-traditional donors has shaken the IDC regime, and they propose China as a paradigmatic example, they argue that China's cooperation model is markedly different and challenging. The importance of Chinese support to Latin America has been strong, as an example, they mention that in 2014, there were $ 22.1 billion of loans from Chinese banks to Latin American governments. This figure was more than the combined loans of the World Bank and the Inter-American Development Bank, explain Lemus and Cerda. On January 29, 2014, China and the countries of Latin America created China-CELAC. Chinese President Xi Jinping announced a target of 500 billion dollars in trade with the Latin American and Caribbean region and 250 billion dollars of direct investment during the five-year period (2015–2019), explain Lemus and Cerda. China offers Latin America a new source of financing for development projects, and without any of the policy conditions associated with the philosophy and rules of financial aid from a Western perspective. Chinese loans focus on infrastructure and heavy industry, without covering other governmental, social and environmental purposes. In this vision, China is considered a partner for development. At the end of the day, no model of International Cooperation for Development is perfect or the total solution to escape from MIT. In reality, it is the responsibility of the recipient country to identify and implement the best projects that result in the improvement of the quality of life of its inhabitants and thus contribute to development, conclude Lemus and Cerda.

Hase, Tjong, Werner, and Junqueira, analyze the MIT from a different perspective, the consumption. They conduct a comparative study between Brazil and China. They explain that recently, Brazil and China have been investing in domestic consumption as a way to prevent an economic slowdown. They made a comparative analysis of the policies adopted by each government to stimulate consumption and its impacts on growth and income distribution. China and Brazil move from policies directed by production to those directed by consumption, it is important to understand the transformation of the citizen from worker to consumer. Hase et al. argue that it is not enough to create a discourse on the "democratic inclusion" of citizens in the consumer market, it is imperative to deepen the new dynamics of inequality and segregation that arise from this process.

Chinese and Brazilian investments in a development project based on consumption, the expansion of credit in the case of Brazil or the improvement of social security in the case of China may not be sufficient for the success of this project. The adoption of a consumption-based development model to avoid MIT will only be successful if we look at the individuals who undergo this transformation process and the construction of new subjectivities in this context. It is imperative that a sustainable and inclusive development strategy goes beyond macroeconomics and, through an anthropological perspective and an ethnographic sensitivity, understand the perspectives of the agents involved in the contradictions and paradoxes of development, conclude Hase et al.

Finally, in a more different approach, Delgado, da Costa, and Barbi, analyze the challenges of global climate change and relate it to the MIT. Specifically, they aim to identify the nature of greenhouse gas emissions in Brazil and China, the impacts of climate change and government responses to the problem. Delgado et al., explain that countries must balance economic development with the mitigation of greenhouse gas emissions. Environmental governance should be promoted at different levels (local, national and global) with the participation of several extracts from society in the search for responsible environmental development. Brazil and China, the main emitters of greenhouse gases, play a fundamental role in the formulation and application of public policies of adaptation and mitigation, thus contributing to a sustainable future. If the necessary measures for adaptation and mitigation are not taken, there is a risk that countries will face economic stagnation and great financial losses, being trapped in MIT.

In this book thc MIT problem has been analyzed in an integral way and observed from very different angles. The authors of this book propose that countries trapped in MIT must implement innovation policies based on the accumulation of human capital and the advanced technological infrastructure. It is also important that Latino American countries support the development of the creative economy, and stimulate consumption in their internal markets. Other important work avenue for Latin American countries is to promote the development of multinational companies and facilitate access to international markets, specifically in the Latin American and Chinese markets. Furthermore, the countries of Latin America have to rely, intelligently and using money in projects that generate great value and social impact, in international cooperation projects, such as the China-CELAC Cooperation Plan. They should also rely on the large loans that Chinese banks and institutions are granting to the region. Another very effective form of cooperation and development is the FTA (free trade agreements) (success case is the China-Chile FTA). Additional, Latin American governments must take advantage of the interest that China is showing in the region, as well as the inclusion of some of the region countries in the great Chinese project of the BRI. Finally yet importantly, attention to the environment is paramount, China and Latin America must support each other in the fight against the emission of greenhouse gases, as well as in the fight against the impacts of climate change.

None of the lines suggested in this book is presented as the great panacea or solution. Working in all of them with intelligence, effort and honesty, governments, companies and citizens, all together can leave the MIT and move to higher economic and social welfare levels.

References

Introduction. The Middle-income Trap: A puzzle from different perspectives.

Agenor P., Canuto, O. & Jelenic, M, (2012), *Avoiding Middle-Income Growth Traps*, Washington D.C.: World Bank.

Ayiar S., Duval R., Puy D., Wu Y. & Zhang, L., (2013), *Growth Slowdowns and the Middle Income Trap*, Washington, DC: International Monetary Fund.

Richard F. Doner, R & Schneider, B.S., (2016), "The Middle Income Trap: More Politics than Economics", *World Politics*, Vol. 68, No. 4, pp.608-644

Egawa A., (2013), "Will Income Inequality Cause a Middle-income Trap in Asia? Bruegel Working Paper", http://bruegel.org/wp-content/uploads/imported/publications/WP_2013_06.pdf.

Eichengreen B., Park D. & Shin K., (2013), *Growth Slowdowns Redux: New Evidence on the Middle-income Trap*, Cambridge, MA: National Bureau of Economic Research.

Felipe, J., Kumar, U. & Galope R., (2014), *Middle-income Transitions: Trap or Myth?* Tokyo: Asian Development Bank.

Gill, I. & Kharas, H., (2007), *An East Asian Renaissance. Ideas for economic Growth*. Washington D.C.: World Bank.

Ginsburg, T., (2014), Law and Development of Middle-Income Countries: Avoiding the middle-income trap, in T. Ginsburg & R. Peerenboom, *Law and Development of Middleincome Countries: Avoiding the Middle-income Trap*, New York: Cambridge University Press, pp. 246-269.

Glawe. L. & Wagner. H., (2016), The middle-income trap: Definitions, Theories and Countries Concerned—A Literature Survey. *Comparative Economic Studies*, Vol. 58, No.1, pp.507–538.

Jankowska A., Nagengast A. & Ramon J., (2012), *The Product Space and the Middle-income Trap: Comparing Asian and Latin American Experiences*. Paris: OECD.

Kharas, H. & Kohli, H., (2011), What is the Middle Income Trap, Why do Countries Fall into It, and How Can It Be Avoided?, *Global Journal of Emerging Market Economies*, Vol. 3, No.1, pp.281–289.

Pruchnik, K. & Zowczak, J., (2017), middle-income trap: Review of the Conceptual Framework. Tokyo: Asian Development Bank Institute.

Spence, M., (2011), *The Next Convergence. The Future of Economic Growth in a Multispeed*

World, New York: Farrar, Straus and Giroux.

Woo, W. T., (2014), "The Major Types of Middle-income Trap That Threaten China", in W.R. Woo, M. Lu & J.D. Sachs, eds., *A new economic growth engine for China: escaping the Middle-income Trap by not doing more of the same*, Singapore: World Scientific pp.3-39.

World Bank, (2012), China 2030: Building a Modern, Harmonious, and Creative High-Income Society. Retrieved February 3, 2018, from http://documents.worldbank.org/curated/en/781101468239669951/pdf/762990PUB0china0Box374372B00PUBLIC0.pdf

World Bank, (2016), World Bank list of economies (September). Retrieved February 7, 2018, from https://datahelpdesk.worldbank.org/knowledgebase/articles/906519–world-bank-country-and-lending-groups

World Bank, (2017), World Development Indicators 2017. Retrieved February 7, 2018, from https://openknowledge.worldbank.org/handle/10986/26447

World Bank. (n/d). The World Bank in Middle Income Countries: Overview. Retrieved February 13, 2018, from http://www.worldbank.org/en/country/mic/overview

World Economic Forum, (2018), The Global Competitiveness Report 2017–2018. Retrieved February 4, 2018 from http://www3.weforum.org/docs/GCR2017–2018/05FullReport/TheGlobalCompetitivenessReport2017%E2%80%932018.pdf

Chapter 1. Post-China Boom Development: Policy Priorities for Latin America in the Way Out of the Middle-income Trap

Agénor, P.R., & Canuto O., (2012), *Middle-Income Growth Traps*, Washington D.C.: The World Bank Group.

Agénor, P.R., Canuto, O., & Jelenic, M., (2012), *Avoiding Middle-Income Growth Traps*, Washington D.C.: The World Bank Group.

China-CELAC Forum, (2015), Cooperation Plan (2015–2019), Beijing, http://www.chinacelacforum.org/eng/zywj_3/t1230944.htm.

Dingrmans, A., (2016), "Trying to stay ahead of the curve in Chile's economic development: exploring a way out of the middle-income trap through pragmatic export development", *Development Policy Review*, Vol.34, No.5, pp.643-669.

Economic Commission for Latin America and the Caribbean, (2015), Latin America and the Caribbean and China: Towards a new era in economic cooperation. Santiago: United Nations.

Economic Commission for Latin America and the Caribbean, (2016a), *Estado de la banda ancha en América Latina y el Caribe 2016*. Santiago: United Nations.

Economic Commission for Latin America and the Caribbean, (2016b), *Relaciones Económicas entre América Latina y el Caribe y China: Oportunidades y Desafíos. Santiago*: United Nations.

Elson, A., (2014), Dragon among the Iguanas. *Finance and Development*, Vol. 51, No.4, pp.44-46.

Gallagher, K. (2016). *The China Triangle: Latin America's China Boom and the Fate of the Washington Consensus*. New York: Oxford University Press.

Garrett, G, (2004), "Globalization's Missing Middle", *Foreign Affairs*, *83*(6) 84-96.

Gereffi, G, (2014), "Global value chains in a post-Washington Consensus world", *Review of*

International Political Economy, Vol. 21, No.1, pp.9-37.
Gómez, D., (2016), "How can Latin America escape its middle-income trap? World Economic Forum", ,https://www.weforum.org/agenda/2016/09/how-can-latin-america-escape-its-middle-income-trap/
Lanteigne, M, (2013), *Chinese Foreign Policy: An introduction*. Abingdon, Oxon: Routledge.
OECD/CAF/ECLAC, (2016), Latin American Economic Outlook 2017: Youth, Skills and Entrepreneurship. OECD Publishing: Paris. doi: http://dx.doi.org/10.1787/leo-2017–en
Ohno, K, (2009), Avoiding the middle-income trap—renovation industrial policy formulation in Vietnam. *ASEAN Economic Bulletin*, *26*(1) 25-43.
Paus, E, (2014), Latin America and the Middle Income Trap, ECLAC-Financing for Development Series 250, Santiago: United Nations, http://repositorio.cepal.org/bitstream/handle11362/36816/S2014300_es.pdf?sequence=1 & isAllowed=y
Paus, E, (2017), Escaping the Middle Income Trap: Innovate or Perish, ADBI Working Paper 685. Tokyo: Asian Development Bank Institute, https://www.adb.org/publications/escaping-middle-income-trap-innovate-or-perish
Shambaugh, D, (2016), *China's Future*. Cambridge: Polity Press.
Stiglitz, J., Lin J., and Monga, C, (2013). "Introduction: The Rejuvenation of Industrial Policy", in J. Stiglitz, and J., Lin eds., *The Industrial Policy Revolution: The Role of Government beyond Ideology*, pp. 1-15, New York and London: Palgrave Macmillan.
Watson, C, (2017), "Concentrated Interests: China's Involvement with Latin American Economies", In J. deLisle, & A. Goldstein, eds., *China's Global Engagement: Cooperation, Competition and Influence in the 21st Century*, pp. 123-154. Washington, DC: Brookings Institution Press.

Chapter 2. The Lack of Large Local Enterprises as an Important Explanation for the Middle-income Trap in Latin America

Arbix, G., (1998), *Inovar ou inovar: a indústria entre o passado e o futuro*, São Paulo: Papagaio, 2007 its problems and its promise. Boulder, CO: Boulder Publishers.
Besanko D, Dranove D, Shanley M & Schaefer S. A, *Economia da Estratégia*, Porto Alegre: Bookman; 2006.
Brito Cruz, C. H, (2004), "A universidade, a empresa e a pesquisa", http://www.ifi.unicamp.br/~brito/artigos/univ-empr-pesq-rev102003b.pdf
WIPO, Cornell University & INSEAD, "The Global Innovation Index 2016", from: http://www.wipo.int/edocs/pubdocs/en/wipo_pub_gii_2016.pdf
Dicken, P., (1998), *Global Shift*, New York, NY: The Guilford Press.
Fairbanks, M., & Lindsay, S., (2000), *Arando o Mar: Fortalecendo as fontes ocultas de crescimento em países em desenvolvimento*, Rio de Janeiro, RJ: Qualitymark.
Freeman, C., & Soete, L., (1997), *The economics of Industrial Innovation*, Cambridge, MA: MIT Press.
Galbraith, J. K., (1978), *O Novo Estado Industrial*, São Paulo, SP: Pioneira.

Hobsbawm, E., (1999), *Era dos Extremos-o Breve Seculo XX-*, São Paulo: Companhia das Letras.

Larrain, J., (2014), "Modernity and Identity: Cultural Change in Latin America", in R. Gwynne & C. Kay eds., *Latin America transformed: Globalization and Transformation*, pp. 22–38, Abingdon, Oxon: Routledge.

Macilwain, C., (1998), "Latin America steps up its science tempo", Nature, 391, 524–525.

Malecki, E., (1997), *Technology & economic development*, London: Longman.

Markovich, S.J., (2012), "Promoting Innovation through R & D", https://www.cfr.org/backgrounder/promoting-innovation-through-rd.

Millan, B., & Concheiro, A., (2000), *Mexico 2030: Nuevo siglo, nuevo pais*, Mexico: Fondo de Cultura Económica.

Organization for Economic Cooperation and Development, (2016), *OCDE statistical database*, from http://www.oecd.org.

Porter, M., & Stern, S., (2002), Inovação e localização de mãos dadas, *HSM Manage*, Vol.30, No.1, pp.118–125.

Quijano, J.M., (1998), *Empresas, innovación y empleo*, Caracas: Sela.

Riemschneider, B., (2016), "2016 Global R & D Funding Forecast Predicts Continued Moderate Growth", https://www.rdmag.com/article/2016/03/2016–global-rd-funding-forecast-predicts-continued-moderate-growth

Sagasti, F., (1981), *Ciencia, tecnologia y desarollo latinoamericano*, Mexico: Fondo de Cultura Económica.

Sbragia, R., (2006), *Inovação: Como vencer este desafio empresarial*, São Paulo, SP: Clio.

Stiglitz, J., & Walsh, C., (2003), *Introdução à microeconomia*, Rio de Janeiro, RJ: Campus.

Chapter 3. Free Trade Agreements as Mechanisms of Wide-ranging and Multi-layered Cooperation: China and the Deepening of Relations with Chile

Alt, J., Frieden, J., Gilligan, M.J., Rodrik, D., & Rogowski, R, (1996), "The political economy of international trade: enduring puzzles and Agenda for Inquiry", *Comparative political studies*, Vol. 29, No.6, pp.261-281.

Baldwin, D., (1980), "Interdependence and power: a conceptual analysis", *International Organization*, Vol.34, No.4, pp.471-506.

Cohen, B., (1990), "The political economy of International trade", *International organization*, Vol.44, No.2, pp.261-281.

Copeland, D., (1996), "Economic Interdependence and War: A Theory of Trade Expectations", *International Security*, Vol.20, No.4, pp.5-41.

Collier, P., (2008), *The Bottom Billion: Why the Poorest Countries are Failing and What Can Be Done About It*, Oxford: Oxford University Press.

Gartzke, E., Li, Q. & Boehmer, C., (2001), "Investing in the Peace: Economic Interdependence and International Conflict", *International Organization*, Vol.55, No.2, pp.391-438.

Gilpin, R., (1987), *The political economy of International Relations*, Princeton: Princeton University Press.

Haggard, S. & Simmons, B., (1987), "Theories of international regimes", *International Organization*, Vol.41, No.3, pp.491-517.

Hast, S., (2014), *Spheres of Influence in International Relation: History, Theory and Politics*, Oxford: Routledge.

Haugaard, M., (2012), "Rethinking the four dimensions of power: domination and empowerment", *Journal of Political Power*, Vol.5, No.1, pp.33-54.

Haugaard, M., (2015), "Concerted Power Over", *Constellations*, Vol.22, No.1, pp.147-158.

Hoekmaan, B. & Kostecki, M., (2009), *The Political Economy of the World Trading System: The WTO and Beyond*, Oxford: Oxford University Press.

Keohane, R. & Nye, J., (1977), *Power and Interdependence: world politics in transition.* Boston: Little-Brown.

Krasner, S., (1976), "State Power and the Structure of International Trade", *World Politics*, Vol.28, No.3, pp.317-347.

Krugman, P, (2012), "The Theory of Trade Agreements, Economic Integration, Size of Economies, Trade Costs and Welfare", in S. Snorraso ed., *Asymmetric Economic Integration*, pp.9-46, Berlin: Springer-Verlag.

Little, R. (2007). *The Balance of Power in International Relations: Metaphors, Myths and Models.* Cambridge: Cambridge University Press.

Marchand, M., (1994), "The political Economy of North-South Relations", in R. Stubbs, & G. Underhill eds., *Political Economy and the Changing Global Order*, pp.289-301, Toronto: McClelland and Stewart.

Morgenthau, H., (1960), *Politics Among Nations: the Struggle for Power and Peace.* New York: Knopf.

Niu, H., (2015), A new Era of China-Latin America Relations. *Anuario de Integración Coordinadora Regional de Investigaciones Económicas y Sociales*, No.11, http://www.cries.org/wp-content/uploads/2016/02/03-Niu.pdf.

Ragin, C., (2014), *The Comparative Method: Moving Beyond Qualitative and Quantitative Strategies*, Berkeley: University of California Press.

Waltz, K., (1979), *Theory of International Politics*, New York: McGraw Hill.

Shixue, J., (2010), "China's First Latin American Policy Paper is a road map for future relations", *China.org Magazine*, http://www.china.org.cn/opinion/2010–11/05/content_21281787.htm.

Zajonc, R., (1965), "Social Facilitation", *Science*, Vol.149, No.3681, pp.269-274.

Zeng, K., (2016), "China's Free Trade Agreement Diplomacy", *The Chinese Journal of International Politics*, Vol.9, No.3, pp.277–305.

Zissimos, B., (2004), "Review of The Economics of the World Trading System" , *Economic Journal*, Vol.114, No.496, pp.338-340.

Chilean General Directorate of International Economic Relations-Direcon, (2003), Tratado de Libre Comercio Chile-Estados Unidos, http://www.sice.oas.org/TPD/CHL_USA/Studies/DIRECONTLC_s.pdf.

Direcon, (2015), *Análisis de las relaciones comerciales entre Chile y China en el marco del tratado de libre comercio*, http://www.sice.oas.org/TPD/CHL_CHN/Studies/FTAreview_

Aug2015_s.pdf.

Direcon, (2017), Chile se convirtió en el principal exportador de fruta a China en 2016. *La tercera Newspaper*, http://www.latercera.com/noticia/chile-se-convirtio-principal-exportador-fruta-china-2016/.

OECD, (2018), *Production Transformation Policy Review of Chile: Reaping the Benefits of New Frontiers*. Paris: OECD Development Pathways, http://www.oecd.org/publications/production-transformation-policy-review-of-chile-9789264288379–en.htm.

MOFCOM, (2008), "Supplementary Agreement on Trade in Services of the FTA between China and Chile", http://fta.mofcom.gov.cn/chile/xieyi/xieyizhengwen_en.pdf.

SCPRC, (2008), "First China's Policy Paper on Latin America and the Caribbean", http://www.gov.cn/english/official/2008–11/05/content_1140347.htm.

SCPRC, (2016), "Second China's Policy Paper on Latin America and the Caribbean", http://english.gov.cn/archive/white_paper/2016/11/24/content_281475499069158.htm.

WTO, (2017), RTA data base. Retrieved July 12, 2017, from https://rtais.wto.org/UI/PublicAllRTAList.aspx.

Chapter 4. Mercosur and China: Partnerships, Challenges and Opportunities

Beef Central, (2018), "Competitor watch: China extends Argentina's access for chilled beef and lamb", https://www.beefcentral.com/trade/competitor-watch-china-extends-argentinas-access-to-chilled-beef-and-lamb/.

Bekerman, M., Dulcich, F., & Moncaut, N., (2014), "La emergencia de China y su impacto en las relaciones comerciales entre Argentina y Brasil", *Problemas del Desarrollo*, Vol.45, No.176, pp.55-82.

Berrettoni, D., (2013), "Las asimetrías estructurales en el MERCOSUR: Balance a 20 años de iniciado el proceso de integración", *Relaciones Internacionales*, Vol.22, No.45, pp.1-23.

Cambero, F. & Sherwood, D., (2018), "China invites Latin America to take part in One Belt, One Road", https://www.reuters.com/article/us-chile-china/china-invites-latin-america-to-take-part-in-one-belt-one-road-idUSKBN1FB2CN.

Castaño, F. & Piñero, F.J., (2016), "*La Política Automotriz del MERCOSUR (PAM): Evolución y Actualidad* ", Paper presented at 7th International Relations Conference of the Universidad de La Plata, Argentina.

Estevadeordal, C., Mesquita M. & Kahn, T., (2014), *LAC Investment in China: A New Chapter in Latin America and the Caribbean-China Relations*, https://publications.iadb.org/bitstream/handle/11319/6599/LAC_investment_in_China_ENGLISH.pdf?sequence=1 & isAllowed=y.

Gallagher, K. P., & Myers, M., (2016), "China-Latin America Finance Database", Washington: *Inter-American Dialogue*.

Hashmi, M. A., (2017), "A Critical Analysis of Mercosur Countries' Trade Relationships with the United States and China", *International Business Research*, Vol.10, No.1, p.163.

Infocampo, (2017), China redujo aranceles para la importación de alimentos: "Es una oportunidad para Argentina", Retrieved from http://www.infocampo.com.ar/china-redujo-aranceles-para-laimportacion-de-alimentos-es-una-oportunidad-para-argentina/

Jenkins, R., & de Freitas Barbosa, A., (2012), "Fear for manufacturing? China and the future of industry in Brazil and Latin America", The China Quarterly, Vol.209, pp.59-81.

Malamud, A., (2013), "El Mercosur: misión cumplida", *Revista SAAP*, Vol.7, No.2, pp.275-282.

Ministerio de Relaciones Exteriores de Paraguay, http://www.mre.gov.py/tratados/public_web/ConsultaMercosur.aspx.

Mander, B., Pearson, S. & Rathbone, J. P., (2016), "Argentina's economic rise fuels rivalry with Brazil", *Financial Times*, https://www.ft.com/content/93370c6e-0e06-11e6-9cd4-2be898308be3.

Niebieskikwiat, N., (2016), "Acuerdos de comercio con China: Macri los quiere dentro y no por fuera del Mercosur", *Clarín*, https://www.clarin.com/politica/acuerdos-comercio-china-macri-mercosur_0_H1qe4IUkx.html.

OECD/ECLAC/CAF, (2015), *Latin American Economic Outlook 2016: Towards a new Partnership with China*, Paris: OECD Publishing.

Paikin, D., & Dulcich, F, (2017), "El sexto socio del MERCOSUR: Un estudio sobre la penetración importadora china y su impacto en el comercio intrarregional", *Revista Perspectivas de Políticas Públicas*, Vol.6, No.12, pp.395-414.

Rebossio, A., (2014), "Una comparación social entre Mercosur y Alianza del Pacífico", *El País*,http://blogs.elpais.com/eco-americano/2014/03/una-comparaci%C3%B3n-social-entre-mercosur-y-alianza-del-pac%C3%ADfico.html.

Reuters, (2015), "Automotriz Chery Socma cierra en Uruguay por crisis en Brasil y Argentina", https://lta.reuters.com/article/businessNews/idLTAKBN0O42IN20150519

Russell, R., & Tokatlian, J. G., (2016), "Contemporary Argentina and the rise of Brazil", *Bulletin of Latin American Research*, Vol.35, No.1, pp.20-33.

El Cronista (2010), "Sin avances entre Argentina y China por aceite de soja", *El Cronista*, http://www.cronista.com/economia/Sin-avances-entre-Argentina-y-China-por-aceite-de-soja---20100604–0107.html.

Tribunal Permanente de Revisión, http://www.tprmercosur.org/es/sol_contr_laudos.htm.

Zelicovich, J., (2015), "El MERCOSUR a 20 años del Protocolo de Ouro Preto: un balance de la dimensión comercial", *Revista Latinoamericana de Desarrollo Económico*, Vol.24, pp.97-120.

Chapter 5. China-Mexico FTA: Overcoming Trade Barriers to Escape the Middle-income Trap

Díaz Dapena, A., Fernández Vázquez, E., Garduño Rivera, R., & Rubiera Morollón, F., (2015), *Does Trade Imply Convergence? Analyzing The Effect of NAFTA on The Local Convergence in Mexico*, Mexico, D.F. CIDE.

Domingues, E. P., Haddad, E. A., & Hewings, G., (2008), "Sensitivity Analysis in Applied General Equilibrium Models: An Empirical Assessment for MERCOSUR Free Trade Areas Agreements", *The Quarterly Review of Economics and Finance*, Vol.48, No.2, pp.287-306.

Fox, A., Serge, S. & Tsigas, M., (2015)., *Predicting the effects of NAFTA with the BDS, GTAP, and EK models*. U.S. International Trade Commission.

Hearn, A. H., (2015), "Mexico, China, and the Politics of Trust", *Latin American Perspectives*, Vol.42, No.6, pp.120-139.

Hills, C. A., (2014), "NAFTA's Economic Upsides: The View from the United States", *Foreign Affairs*, Vol.93, No.1, p.122.

KPMG, (2015). *China Outlook 2016*, KPMG Global China Practice.

Li, C. & Whalley, J., (2014), "China and the Trans-Pacific Partnership: A Numerical Simulation Assessment of the Effects Involved", *The World Economy*, Vol.37, No.2, pp.169-192.

Lin, J. Y., & Treichel, V., (2012), *Learning from China's Rise to Escape the Middle-income Trap-A New Structural Economics Approach to Latin America*, Washington, D.C. World Bank.

Mendoza, J., (2016), "The Potential Impact of the Trans-Pacific Partnership on the Mexican Trade with China and Korea", *Asian Journal of Latin American Studies*, Vol.29, No.2, pp.1-28.

Nakajima, T., (2002). An Analysis of the Economic Effects of Japan-Korea FTA: Sectoral Aspects. *The Journal of Econometric Study of Northeast Asia*, Vol.4, No.1, pp.1-16.

Nan, Yin, (2017), "El comercio electrónico ayudará a construir 'ruta de la seda digital' entre China y América Latina y el Caribe", *Xinhua*, http://spanish.xinhuanet.com/2017–11/12/c_136746846.htm.

Petri, P. A. & Plummer, M. G., Zhai, F., (2014). "The TPP, China and the FTAAP: The case for convergence", in T. Guoqiang & Petri P.A.,eds., *New Directions in Asia-Pacific Economic Integration*, pp. 78-89, Honolulu: East-West Center.

Pruchnik, K. & Zowczak, J., (2017), *Middle-income Trap: Review of the Conceptual Framework*. Tokyo: Asian Development Bank Institute.

Sánchez, M. G. L., Regalado, S. C., Bravo, R. G., & Guzman-Anaya, L., (2016), *Economic impact of Economic Partnership Agreement Mexico–Japan*, Tokyo: The Institute for Economic Studies Seijo University.

Schott, J. J., (2016). Overview: Understanding the Trans-Pacific Partnership, in C., Cimino-Isaacs & J.J. Schott eds., *Trans-Pacific Partnership: An Assessment*, pp. 9-22, Danvers, MA: Peterson Institute for International Economics.

Siriwardana, M., & Yang, J., (2008), "GTAP Model Analysis of the Economic Effects of an Australia–China FTA: Welfare and Sectoral Aspects", *Global Economic Review*, Vol.37, No.3, pp.341-362.

Solís, M., & Katada, S. N., (2015), "Unlikely Pivotal States in Competitive Free Trade Agreement Diffusion: The Effect of Japan's Trans-Pacific Partnership Participation on Asia-Pacific Regional Integration", *New Political Economy*, Vol.20, No.2, pp.155-177.

Song, G. & Wen, Y., (2012), China's Free Trade Agreement Strategies, *The Washington Quarterly*, Vol.35, No.4, pp.107-119.

Tukker, A., & Dietzenbacher, E., (2013), "Global Multiregional Input-output Frameworks: an Introduction and Outlook", *Economic Systems Research*, Vol.25, No.1, pp1-19.

Walmsley, T., Aguiar, A., & Narayanan, B., (2012), *Introduction to the Global Trade Analysis Project and the GTAP Database*, No. 3965, Center for Global Trade Analysis, Department of Agricultural Economics, Purdue University.

Chapter 6. The Multimexicans in China

Agencias en Beijing., (2006), "El osito Bimbo va a la conquista de China", *Crónica*, http://www.cronica.com.mx/notas/2006/269835.html.

Alfa., (2017), "Informe Anual 2016", https://www.alfa.com.mx/down/informes/InformeAnual16.pdf.

Anderson, B., (2010, Sep 17), "Bimbo 'destraba' las puertas de China", *Expansión*, http://expansion.mx/expansion/2010/09/03/bimbo-china-expansion?internal_source=PLAYLIST.

Aulakh, P. S., (2007), "Emerging Multinationals from Developing Economies: Motivations, Paths and Performance", *Journal of International Management*, Vol.13, pp.235-240.

Automotive News China, (2013), "Nemak launches 2nd engine component plant", http://www.autonewschina.com/en/article.asp?id=10664.

Automotive World, (2016), "Nemak Successfully Consummates the Acquisition of Cevher Döküm Sanayii A.Ş", https://www.automotiveworld.com/news-releases/nemak-successfully-consummates-acquisition-cevher-dokum-sanayii-s/.

Cantwell, J., (2009), "Location and the Multinational Enterprise", *Journal of International Business Studies*, Vol.40, pp.35-41.

Cavusgil, S. T., (1980), "On the Internationalization Process of Firms", *European Research, 8*, 273-281.

CNN Expansion, (2015a), "Interactive Ranking 2014, the 500 Companies most Important in Mexico", *CNN Expansion*, http://www.cnnexpansion.com/rankings/interactivo-las-500/2014.

CNN Expansion, (2015b), "Las 100 mexicanas más globales del 2015", *CNN Expansión*, https://expansion.mx/especiales/2015/01/13/las-100-mexicanas-mas-globales-2015.

Corona O., (2009), "Softtek Mexican proudly 100%", *Infochannel*, http://www.infochannel.com.mx/softtek-100-mexicana-orgullosamente.

Coronado, S., (2017), "Nemak negocia con clientes para nueva planta en China", *El Financiero*, http://www.elfinanciero.com.mx/monterrey/nemak-negocia-con-clientes-para-nueva-planta-en-china.html.

Czinkota, M. R., (1982), *Export development strategies: U.S. promotion policy*, New York: Praeger.

Cuervo-Cazurra, A., (2011), "Selecting the Country in which to Start Internationalization: The Non-sequential Internationalization Argument", *Journal of World Business*, Vol.46, pp.426-437.

Cuervo-Cazurra, A., (2012), How the Analysis of Developing Country Multinational Companies helps Advance Theory: Solving the Goldilocks Debate, *Global Strategy Journal*, Vol. *2*, pp.153-167.

Cuervo-Cazurra, A., & Ramamurti, R., (2014), "*Understanding Multinationals from Emerging Markets*", Cambridge: Cambridge University Press.

Cuervo-Cazurra, A., & Ramos, M., (2004), "Explaining the Process of Internationalization by Building Bridges among Existing Models", in S. W. Floyd, J. Roos, C. D. Jacobs, & F. W. Kellermanns, eds., *Innovating Strategy Processes*, pp. 111-122, London: Blackwell.

Cuervo-Cazurra, A. & Montoya, M., eds., (2018), *Mexican Multinationals: How to Build*

Multinationals in Emerging Markets, Cambridge University Press.

Díaz, U., (2016, May 17), "Crece Interceramic in China", *Reforma*, http://www.reforma.com/aplicacioneslibre/articulo/default.aspx?id=845560 & md5=664291b4cd3892527b14a4b64d53e2da & ta=0dfdbac11765226904c16cb9ad1b2efe & po=4

Dunning, J., (1977), Trade, location of economic activity and the MNE: A search for an eclectic theory, in B. Ohlin, P.-O. Hesselborn, & P. M. Wijkman, eds., *The International Allocation of Economic Activity* (pp. 395-418). London: Palgrave Macmillan.

Economista, (2015), "Desaceleración golpea exportaciones en China", *América Economía*, https://www.americaeconomia.com/economiamercados/comercio/desaceleracion-golpea-exportaciones-mexicanas-china

EFE., (2010, Jun 10), Mexicana Interceramic firma memorando de cooperación con socia china Kito: China-Mexico. *Mis finanzas en línea*, http://www.misfinanzasenlinea.com/noticia.php?nid=15765

El Economista., (2017), "Interceramic inauguró obra en Chihuahua con 100 mdp", *El economista*, https://www.eleconomista.com.mx/estados/Interceramic-inauguro-obra-en-Chihuahua-con-100-mdp-20170908–0064.html.

Forbes, (2006), The World's Biggest Public Companies, http://www.forbes.com/lists/2006/18/Rank_1.html.

Forbes, (2016), The Global 2000, http://www.forbes.com/lists/2010/18/global-2000–10_The-Global-2000_Country.html.

Forbes, (2017), The World's Biggest Public Companies, https://www.forbes.com/global2000/list/4/#tab:overall.

García, S., (2017), Chihuahua, el plan de Interceramic para duplicar ventas en 5 años *El Financiero*, http://www.elfinanciero.com.mx/empresas/chihuahua-el-plan-de-interceramic-para-duplicar-ventas-en-anos.html

Guillén, M. F., & García Canal, E., (2009), The American Model of the Multinational Firm and the "New" Multinationals from Emerging Economies, *Academy of Management Perspectives*, *23*, 23-35.

Guillén, M. F., & García-Canal, E., (2013), *Emerging Markets Rule*, New York: McGraw-Hill.

Hennart, J.-F., (2009), Down with MNE-centric theories! Market Entry and Expansion as the Bundling of MNE and Local Assets, *Journal of International Business Studies*, Vol.40, pp.1432–1454.

IHS SupplierInsight., (2013), Nemak begins production at second plant in China, http://www.ihssupplierinsight.com/news/22610/nemak-begins-production-at-second-plant-in-china.

Interceramic., (2005), Informe Anual 2004, https://interceramic.com/inversionistas/reportes/informes-anuales.

Interceramic, (2017), "Informe Anual 2016", from https://interceramic.com/inversionistas/reportes/informes-anuales.

Johanson, J. & Vahlne, J. E., (1977), "The Internationalization Process of the Firm: A model of Knowledge Development and Increasing Foreign Market Commitments", *Journal of International Business Studies*, Vol.8, pp.23-32.

Knowledge@Wharton, (2013), "Mexican Multinationals Target China's most Adventurous Consumers", http://knowledge.wharton.upenn.edu/article/mexican-multinationals-target-chinas-most-adventurous-consumers/.

Kogut, B. & Zander, U., (1992), "Knowledge of the Firm, Combinative Capabilities, and the Replication of Technology", *Organization Science*, Vol.3, pp.383-397.

Kruger, U., (2014), "Bimbo, un caso de éxito latinoamericano en China Retrieved from *SinoLATAM*", http://www.sinolatamforum.com/opiniones_detalle/0-m151-238/bimbo-un-caso-de-exito-latinoamericano-en-china.

Latin Trade., (2014), "Grupo Bimbo: Todo empieza con entender al consumidor", *Latin Trade*, http://latintrade.com/es/grupo-bimbo-todo-empieza-con-entender-al-consumidor/.

Liu, R., (2015), "Los primeros diez productores de cemento en China", *Spanish People Daily*, http://spanish.peopledaily.com.cn/n/2015/0310/c92121–8860832–10.html

Luo, Y., & Tung, R. L., (2007), "International Expansion of Emerging Market Enterprises: A Springboard Perspective", *Journal of International Business Studies*, *38*, 481-498.

Mathews, J. A., (2006), "Dragon Multinationals: New Players in 21st Century Globalization", *Asia Pacific Journal of Management*, *23*, 5-27.

Milenio., (2017), "Bimbo planea expandirse en China", *Milenio*, http://www.milenio.com/negocios/bimbo-china-asia-oriente-pekin-mexico-negocios-milenio-noticias_0_941306154.html.

Mitchell, R., (2007), "Mexico, Latin America and the Battle to be the Next India", *Computerworld*, http://www.computerworld.com/article/2477683/it-management/mexico--latin-america-and-the-battle-to-be-the-next-india.html.

Nemak, (2017), "Annual Report 2016", http://investors.nemak.com/phoenix.zhtml?c=253659 & p=irol-reportsannual.

Nemak, (2017), "Investor Presentation", http://investors.nemak.com/phoenix.zhtml?c=253659 & p=irol-presentations.

Nemak Careers, (2014), "Chongqing", http://careers.nemak.com/interior-pages/our-regions/asia/chongqing.aspx#Overview.

Nemak Careers, (2014), "Nanjing", http://careers.nemak.com/interior-pages/our-regions/asia/nanjing.aspx#Overview.

Nemak Careers, (2014). "Shanghai", http://careers.nemak.com/interior-pages/our-regions/asia/shanghai.aspx#Overview.

Ng, B., (2017), Obesity: the big, fat problem with Chinese cities, *The Guardian*, https://www.theguardian.com/sustainable-business/2017/jan/09/obesity-fat-problem-chinese-cities.

Notimex, (2017), "Interceramic invertirá 80 mdd en planta de producción en Guanajuato", *Milenio*, http://www.milenio.com/negocios/interceramic-inversion_mexico-guanajuato-planta_produccion-loseta-ceramica-milenio_0_919708389.html.

Our Mobile Planet, (2013), "*Our Mobile Planet Data Download* ", *With Google*, http://think.withgoogle.com/mobileplanet/es/downloads/.

Quesada, J. A., (2011), "*Casos de empresas exitosas en Mexico y a nivel global* ", Mexico: Instituto Mexicano de Ejecutivos de Finanzas.

Ramamurti, R., (2012), "What is Really Different about Emerging Market Multinationals?", *Global Strategy Journal*, Vol.2, pp.41-47.

Ramírez, M., (2014), "Anuncia Lamosa lucha contra dumping chino", *El Norte*, https://norte-monterrey.vlex.com.mx/vid/anuncia-lamosa-lucha-dumping-chino-497517662.

Ramírez, M., (2016), "Impone SE cuotas a pisos chinos", *El Norte*, 17.

Ramírez, Z., (2004), "Empresario Alfredo Harp duplicaria en 48% inversiones bursátiles", *Noticias Financieras*, 1.

Rugman, A., (2010), "Do We Need a New Theory to Explain Emerging Market MNEs?", in K. P. Sauvant, ed., *Foreign Direct Investments from Emerging Markets: The Challenges Ahead*, pp.89-93, New York: Palgrave McMillan.

Rugman, A. M., & Verbeke, A., (1992), "A Note on the Transnational Solution and the Transaction Cost Theory of Multinational Strategic Management", *Journal of International Business Studies*, Vol.23, pp.761-771.

Sánchez, A., (2016), "Nemak quiere doblar apuesta por China y diversificarse", *El Financiero*, http://www.elfinanciero.com.mx/empresas/nemak-quiere-doblar-su-apuesta-por-china-y-diversificarse-mas.html.

Siegel, J., (2009), "Grupo Bimbo", Harvard Business School case 9-707-521.

Softtek., (2007), "NFVZone Softtek finalizes acquisition of China's IT United", http://www.tmcnet.com/usubmit/2007/08/20/2874627.htm.

Softtek, (2008), "Softtek Introduced Softtek Asia with Expansion of Global Delivery Center in China", https://www.softtek.com/es/sala-de-prensa/comunicados-de-prensa/softtek-introduce-softtek-asia-con-la-expansion-del-centro-global-de-entrega-en-china.

Softtek, (2009, July 28), "Softtek abre nuevo Centro Global de Servicios en Wuxi, China", https://www.softtek.com/es/sala-de-prensa/comunicados-de-prensa/softtek-abre-nuevo-centro-global-de-servicios-en-wuxi-china.

Softtek., (2013), "Softtek abre su primer Centro de Excelencia para Servicios de Movilidad Empresarial en Beijing, China", https://www.softtek.com/es/sala-de-prensa/comunicados-de-prensa/softtek-abre-su-primer-centro-de-excelencia-para-servicios-de-movilidad-empresarial-en-beijing-china.

Softtek., (2017), "¿Quiénes somos?", http://www.softtek.com/es/acerca-de-softtek/iquienes-somos.

Suárez Ramírez, A., (2016), "El Grupo Bimbo, una década en China", *ChinaHoy*, Retrieved from http://www.chinatoday.mx/eco/news/content/2016–11/29/content_731563.htm.

Valtierra Gallardo, S., (2013), "*Innovación y tecnología en la industria y su relación con la vinculación académica*", Mexico: Academia de Ingeniería, A.C.

Wilkins, M., (2009), "The History of the Multinational Enterprise", in A. R. Rugman, ed., *The Oxford Handbook of International Business, 2nd ed*, pp-3-38, Oxford, UK: Oxford University Press.

Zapata, L., & Hartmann, A. M., (forthcoming), "Automotive components: Metalsa vs. Nemak. In A. Cuervo-Cazurra & M. A. Montoya, eds., *Mexican Multinationals: How to Build Multinationals in Emerging Markets*. Cambridge, UK: Cambridge University Press.

Zhang, W., (2011), "Al pan, pan y a Bimbo", *ChinaHoy*, http://www.chinatoday.mx/eco/clae/content/2011–07/26/content_379348.htm.

Chapter 7. Strategies for the Construction and Internationalization of Chinese Brands Aimed to the Latin American Market

Aldama, Z., (2014), "Coches chinos en rutas sudamericanas", *El País*, https://elpais.com/economia/2014/10/31/actualidad/1414758249_485100.html.

Armony, A. C., & Strauss, J. C., (2012), "From Going Out (zou chuqu) to Arriving In (desembarco): Constructing a New Field of Inquiry in China–Latin America Interactions", *The China Quarterly*, Vol.209, No.1-17.

Baraya Rubiano, A., (2015), "Se dispararon las ventas de motos en Colombia durante el 2014", *Motor*, http://www.motor.com.co/actualidad/tecnologia/dispararon-ventas-motos-colombia-2014/20681.

Barredo, A., (2016), "BYD, la Tesla china, se come el mercado eléctrico mundial. *Hipertextual* " , https://hipertextual.com/2016/07/byd-tesla-coche-electrico.

BBC Mundo, (2014), Xiaomi, "la empresa emergente más valorada del mundo". *BBC Mundo*. Retrieved from http://www.bbc.com/mundo/noticias/2014/10/141030_tecnologia_perfil_empresa_xiaomi_ig.

BlueFocus, (2016), *China's Global Brands 2016*, Beijing: BlueFocus.

BYD Autos, (2017), "*BYD*", http://www.byd.com/la/auto/es/index.html.

Collado, C., (2016), "Los teléfonos de OnePlus no llegarán a Latinoamérica oficialmente, al menos de momento", *Andorid4All*, https://andro4all.com/2016/10/oneplus-no-llegaran-latinoamerica.

Cuartas, E., (2017), "Xiaomi crecerá a través de venta de smartphones en tiendas físicas", *Enter*, http://www.enter.co/cultura-digital/negocios/xiaomi-crecera-a-traves-de-venta-de-smartphones-en-tiendas-fisicas/.

Cubadebate., (2016), "Comienzan en Cuba operaciones con tarjetas bancarias chinas de la UnionPay", *Cuba Debate*, http://www.cubadebate.cu/noticias/2016/01/19/comienzan-en-cuba-operaciones-con-tarjetas-bancarias-chinas-de-la-unionpay/.

Eclass., (2010), *BYD: Construyendo futuro*, https://comunidad.eclass.com/articulo/5891/byd-construyendo-futuro.

Egido, A., (2013), "Haier, un grupo chino, una marca mundial", *Eada Business School*, http://www.distribucionactualidad.com/haier-un-grupo-chino-una-marca-mundial/.

Fan, Y., (2006), "The globalisation of Chinese brands", *Marketing Intelligence & Planning*, Vol.24, No.4, pp.365-379.

Fetscherin, M., & Sardy, M., (2008), "Chinese Brands: the Build or Buy Considerations", *International Journal of Chinese Culture and Management*, Vol.1, No.4, pp.418-438.

Fornes, G., & Butt-Philip, A., (2014), "Chinese Outward Investments to Emerging Markets: Evidence from Latin America". *European Business Review*, *26*(6), 494-513.

Gao, P., Woetzel, R., & Wu, Y., (2003), "Can Chinese brands make it abroad?", *The McKinsey*

Quarterly Vol.4, pp.54-65.

Glowik, M., (2016), *Market Entry Strategies : Internationalization Theories, Concepts and Cases of Asian High-Technology Firms: Haier, Hon Hai Precision, Lenovo, LG Electronics, Panasonic, Samsung, Sharp, Sony, TCL, Xiaomi*, Berlin: De Gruyter Oldenbourg.

Haier, (2015), "*About Haier*", http://www.haier.net/ve/mergepage/about_haier/.

IPMark, (2013), *Haier, una marca en construcción*, http://ipmark.com/haier-una-marca-en-construccin/.

He, P., (2012), *Chinese brands and branding strategies*, Hertfordshire: University of Hertfordshire.

Hase-Ueta, M., Tjong, E., Werner-Weins, N. and Junqueira-Schmidt, F., (2018), "China and Brazil: Transitioning from the middle-income trap to Sustainable Development? A Sociological Perspective on Consumption, Inequality and the Middle-income Trap", in Lemus, D., Cervantes, M., and Montoya, M., eds. *Development and the National Middle-income Trap: China-Latin America*, Beijing:China Social Sciences Press.

Hollis, N., (2013), "Is China ready to build global brands?", https://www.brandingstrategyinsider.com/2013/11/is-china-ready-to-build-global-brands.html#.Wft-xFvWypo.

Jialing., (2014), *Estrategia de posicionamiento*. Retrieved November 11, 2017, from http://www.jialingcolombia.co/compania/.

Jianhui, H., (2013), "*Empresas multinacionales de países emergentes: el caso de las empresas automovilsíticas de china* (master's thesis)", Universidad de Oviedo, Spain.

Kithany, D., (2016), "Turbulence Expected from Haier's Planned Acquisition of GE Appliances", *HIS Markit*", https://technology.ihs.com/571914/turbulence-expected-from-haiers-planned-acquisition-of-ge-appliances.

Labbrand., (2015), "*Growth of Branding in China*", http://www.labbrand.com/brandsource/growth-branding-china.

Massiero, G., Ogasavara, M. E., Jussani, A. C., & Risso, M. L., (2016), Electric vehicles in China: BYD strategies and goverment subsidies, *Revista de Administração e Inovação*, Vol.13, No.1, pp.3-22.

Morris, David., (2016), "China UnionPay's Commercial Card Growth Strategy: First Asia, then the World!", https://www.packagedfacts.com/Content/Blog/2016/03/01/China-UnionPay%E2%80%99s-commercial-card-growth-strategy-First-Asia-then-the-world.

Nardali, S., (2017), "Systematic Literature Review on Born Global Firms", *Yonetim ve ekonomi*, Vol.24, No.2, pp.563-578.

Paus, E., (2017), "Escaping the Middle Income Trap: Innovate or Perish", ADBI Working Paper 685, Tokyo: Asian Development Bank Institute, https://www.adb.org/publications/escaping-middle-income-trap-innovate-or-perish.

People Daily, (2016), "UnionPay apunta al mercado financiero de América Latina", *Xinhua*, Retrieved from http://spanish.peopledaily.com.cn/n3/2016/0512/c31620–9056819.html.

Rodríguez, D. A., Santana, M., & Pardo, C. F., (2015), "*La motocicleta en América Latina: Caracterización de su uso e impactos en la movilidad en cinco ciudades de la región*", Bogotá: Corporación Andina de Fomento-CAF.

Romero, M. M., Rodríguez Escudero, A. I., Rodríguez Pinto, J., & Temprano García, V., (2017), "Caso práctico: OnePlus. Desarrollo de estrategias y retos de una empresa 'born global'", *Harvard Deusto Márketing y Ventas*, Vol.142, pp.56-64.

Segura Martín, P., (2017), "Xiaomi desembarca oficialmente en Latinoamérica (sí, también en Chile)", https://pisapapeles.net/xiaomi-desembarca-oficialmente-en-latinoamerica-si-tambien-en-chile/.

Tan, K., (2017), "Generic Internationalization Strategies of Emerging Market Multinationals: The Case of Chinise Firms", *Advances in Economics and Business*, Vol.5, No.2, pp.83-94.

TODOAutos, (2017, November 22), "BYD presenta la más grande flota de taxis eléctricos en América Latina", *TODOAutos*, http://www.todoautos.com.pe/portal/autos/172-noticias/6374–byd-e6-biotaxis-colombia.

Xiaofei, D., (2014), "Los autos chinos en América Latina", *China Today*, http://www.chinatoday.mx/eco/clae/content/2014–06/20/content_625220.htm.

Xiaomi, (2017), "Home: All products", http://www.mi.com/en/list/.

Xinhua, (2016), "Con vehículos eléctricos, China se destaca en Salón Internacional del Automóvil de Bogotá. *America Economía*", https://www.americaeconomia.com/negocios-industrias/con-vehiculos-electricos-china-se-destaca-en-salon-internacional-del-automovil.

Chapter 8. Chinese Creative Cities as a Path to Escape of the Middle-income Trap

Agénor, P.R., (2017), "Caught in the Middle? The Economics of Middle-income Traps. *Journal of Economics Survey*", Vol.31, No.3, pp.771–779.

Analistas Económicos de Andalucía., (2017), *Cultura y Desarrollo: Impacto socioeconómico de Málaga 2016*, Málaga: Economía Andaluza.

Araujo, R. M, (2015), "La economía creativa, una fuente creciente de desarrollo", *Hospitalidad ESDAI*, Vol.27, pp.7-28.

Banco Interamericano de Desarrollo., (2014), "El impacto económico de las industrias creativas en las Américas", Banco Interamericano de Desarrollo, http://idbdocs.iadb.org/wsdocs/getdocument.aspx?docnum=38370643.

Barboza, D., (2010), "China Passes Japan as Second-Largest Economy", *The New York Times*, http://www.nytimes.com/2010/08/16/business/global/16yuan.html?pagewanted=all.

Barrowclough, D. & Kozul-Wright, Z., (2008), "Voice, Choice and Diversity through Creative Industry: towards a New Agenda to Development", in D. Barrowclough & Z. Kozul-Wright, *Creative Industries and Developing Countries Voice, Choice and Economic Growth*, p. 3-35. London: Routledge.

Boccella, N. & Salerno, I., (2016), "Creative Economy, Cultural Industries and Local Development", *Procedia-Social and Behavioral Sciences*, Vol.223, No.291–296.

Cai, F., (2012), "There a 'Middle-income Trap'?", Theories, Experiences and Relevance to China, *China and World Economy*, Vol.20, No.1, pp.49-61.

Cunningham, S. D., (2007), "The Creative Economy: Patterning the Future", *Dialogue: Academy of the Social Sciences in Australia*, Vol.26, No.1, pp.15-23.

CEPAL, (2008), *Structural Change and Productivity Growth 20 Years Later: Old Problems, New Opportunities*, CEPAL: Santiago de Chile.

El Informador, (2017), "China busca que la cultura sea pilar de su economía hacia 2020", *El Informador*, https://www.informador.mx/Economia/China-busca-que-la-cultura-sea-su-pilar-economico-en-2020–20170508–0140.html.

European Institute for Comparative Cultural Research, (2008), *Mobility Matters: Programmes and Schemes to Support the Mobility of Artists and Other Cultural Professionals*, http://www.mobility-matters.eu/web/files/14/en/Final_Report_-_Mobility_Matters___ERICarts.pdf.

Florida, R., (2011), "Understanding the Creative Economy in China. University of Toronto: Martin Prosperity Institute", http://martinprosperity.org/media/CreativeChina_EnglishVersion.pdf.

Fung, A., (2016), "Strategizing for Creative Industries in China: Contradictions and Tension in Nation Branding", *International Journal of Communication*, Vol.10, pp.3004–3021.

Gerffi, G., (1990), "Paths of Industrialization: An Overview", in G. Gerffi and Wyman D.L., ed., *Manufacturing Miracles: Paths of Industrialization in Latin America and East of Asia*, pp. 3-31, Princeton, NJ: Princeton University Press.

Grams, D. & Warr, M., (2003), *Leveraging Assets: How Small Budget Arts Activities Benefit Neighborhoods*, Chicago, IL: Richard H. Driehaus Foundation and the John D. and Catherine T. MacArthur Foundation.

Hartley, J., (2005), "Creative industries", in J. Hartley, ed., *Creative industries*, pp. 1-40, Oxford, U.K: Blackwell Publishing.

Haw, S.G., (2007), *Beijing, a Concise History*, London: Routledge.

International Monetary Fund, (2017), "*World Economic Outlook, October 2017, Seeking Sustainable Growth: Short-Term Recovery, Long-Term Challenges*", Washington: International Monetary Fund.

Keane, M., (2010), "Great Adaptations: China's Creative Clusters and the New Social Contract", *Continuum: Journal of Media & Cultural Studies*, Vol.23, No.2, pp.221-230.

Landry, C., (2000), *The Creative City: A Toolkit for Urban Innovators*, London: Earthscan Publications.

Landry, C., (2006), *The Art of City Making*, London: Earthscan Publications.

Levickaitė. R., (2011), "Four Approaches to the Creative Economy: General Overview", *Business, Management and Education*, Vol.9, No.1, pp.81–92.

Lemus, D., (2011), *Innovación a la china: la larga marcha del gigante asiático hacia el liderazgo mundial*, Madrid: Lid Editores.

Levickaite, R., (2012), "Interlinks of Cultural and Creative Economies through Creative Products and Services", *Mokslas: Lietuvos Ateitis*, Vol.4, No.3, pp.256-261.

Mungello, D.E., (1994), *The Forgotten Christians of Hangzhou*, Hawaii: University of Hawaii Press.

Murphy, A. B., (2012), "China's Cultural and Creative Economy: An Introduction", *Eurasian Geography and Economics*, Vol.53, No.2, pp.179-181.

Navickas, V. and Malakauskaitė, A., (2009), The Impact of Clusterization on the Development of Small and Medium-sized Enterprise (SME) Sector. *Journal of Business Economics and Management*, Vol.10, No.3, pp.255–259.

O'Connor, J., (2009), "Introduction: Creative Economies", in L. Kong y J. O′Connor, eds., *Creative Economies, Creative Cities. Asian-European Perspectives*, pp. 1-5, New York: Springer.

Oliveira, J. S., (2014*)*, *La Industria Creativa como recurso de desarrollo económico: el caso del grupo Cland*, Sevilla: Universidad de Sevilla.

Patience, M., (2014), "La apuesta de China por una industria creativa", *BBC*, http://www.bbc.com/mundo/noticias/2014/01/140121_china_taotao_creatividad_finde.

Piedras, E., (2010), "Mexico: Tecnología y Cultura Para un Desarrollo Integral", in A.C. Fonseca Reis, ed, *Economía Creativa como estrategia de desarrollo: una visión de los países en desarrollo*, pp. 150-167, Sao Paulo: Itao Cultural.

Rosas, M. C., (2012), "¿Una economía creativa?. *América latina en Movimiento*", https://www.alainet.org/es/active/52124.

Santos-Duisenberg, E., (2008), "La Economía Creativa: ¿Es una Opción de Desarrollo Factible?", In A.C. Fonseca Reis, ed, *Economía Creativa como estrategia de desarrollo: una visión de los países en desarrollo*, pp. 54-76, Sao Paulo: Itao Cultural.

Ramanathan, S., (2008), "La Economía Creativa como Estrategia de Desarrollo: La Perspectiva Hindú", in A.C. Fonseca Reis, ed, *Economía Creativa como estrategia de desarrollo: una visión de los países en desarrollo*, pp. 204-223, Sao Paulo: Itao Cultural.

Ren, X., (2008), "Architecture as Branding: Mega Project Developments in Beijing", *Built Environment* Vol.34, No.4, pp.517-531.

Scott, A. J., (2008), *Social Economy of the Metropolis: Cognitive-Cultural Capitalism and the Global Resurgence of Cities*, Oxford: Oxford University Press.

Taylor, M., (2017), The Politics of Latin America's Middle income Trap, Washington, Council of Foreign Relations, https://www.cfr.org/blog/politics-latin-americas-middle-income-trap.

The World Bank and Development Research Center of the State Council, PRC., (2013), *China 2030: Building a Modern, Harmonious, and Creative High-Income Society*, Washington, D.C.: The World Bank, http://documents.worldbank.org/curated/en/781101468239669951/pdf/762990PUB0china0Box374372B00PUBLIC0.pdf.

The World Bank, (2017), *Global Economic Prospect: A Fragile Recovery*, Washington, D.C.: The World Bank, http://www.worldbank.org/en/publication/global-economic-prospects.

Trápaga, Y., (2012), La producción alimentaria en China y Mexico. Dos historias contrapuestas del subdesarrollo. In Dussel, E., ed., *Cuarenta años de la relación entre Mexico y China: acuerdos, desencuentros y futuro*, pp. 249-260). Mexico, D.F.: Universidad Nacional Autónoma de Mexico.

Thiruchelvam, S., (2014), "The Future of Chinese Arts and Creative Industries", *Forbes*, https://www.forbes.com/sites/sthiruchelvam/2014/11/24/the-future-of-chinese-arts-and-creative-industries/#2f1a3cf13980.

Valderrey, F. and Lemus, D., (2017), "New Silk Road and International Business Diplomacy", *Comillas Journal of International Relations*, Vol.10, pp.47-64.

UNCTAD, (2008), "*Creative Economy Report 2008. The Challenge of Assesing the Creative Economy: towards Informed Policy-making*", http://unctad.org/en/docs/ditc20082cer_en.pdf.

UNCTAD, (2010), "*Creative Economy Report 2010. A Feasible Development Option*", http://unctad.org/en/Docs/ditctab20103_en.pdf.

UNESCO, (2013), "*Creative Economy Report 2013: Special Edition. Widening Local Development Pathways*", http://www.unesco.org/culture/pdf/creative-economy-report-2013.pdf.

UNESCO., (2016), *Creatives Cities for Sustainable Development*, https://fr.unesco.org/creative-cities/sites/creative-cities/files/creative%20cities%20for%20web.pdf.

Wuwei, L., (2011), *How Creativity is Changing China*. London: Bloomsbury Academic.

Xiang, H., (2014), "Introduction: 2011–2015: Principles of National Cultural Strategy and Cultural Industries Development", in H. Xiang and Walker, P.A., eds., *China Cultural and Creative Industries Reports 2013*, pp. 1-9, London: Springer.

Yao, Z., (2015), "How Can China Avoid the Middle Income Trap? *China and World Economy*", Vol.23, No.5, pp.26-42.

Zhang, Z. & To, C., (2004), "How do Industry Clusters Success: a Case Study in China's Textiles and Apparel Industries", *Journal of Textile and Apparel, Technology and Management*, Vol.4, No.2, pp.1-10.

Zhong, D., Zhang, Z. and Zhang, Y., (1997), "From Wenmingxi (Civilized Play) to Yingxi (Shadowplay): The Foundation of Shanghai Film Industry in the 1920s", *Asian Cinema*, Vol.9, No.1, pp.46-64.

Zhou, Z., (2014), *A Study on Globalizing Cities: Theoretical Frameworks and China's Modes*, Hackensack, NJ: World Century Publishing Corporation.

Chapter 9. The China's International Cooperation, a Pathway to Escape the Middle-income Trap in Latin America?

AidData, (2017), "AIDDATA: By the Numbers: China's Global Development Footprint, The clearest look yet at Chinese official finance worldwide", http://aiddata.org/china.

Alonso, J.A. & Glennie, J., (2015), "What is development cooperation?", *Development Cooperation Forum*, New York: ECOSOC, U.N., http://www.un.org/en/ecosoc/newfunct/pdf15/2016_dcf_policy_brief_no.1.pdf.

Avendano, R., Melguizo, A. & Miner, S., (2017), "Chinese FDI in Latin America: New Trends with Global Implications", Washington, D.C: *Atlantic Council*, http://publications.atlanticcouncil.org/china-fdi-latin-america/.

Brautigam, D., (2011), "Aid 'With Chinese Characteristics': Chinese Foreign Aid and Development Finance Meet the OECD-DAC Aid Regime", *Journal of International Development*, Vol.23, No.5, pp.752-764.

Buckley, P.J., Clegg, J., Cross, A.R., Liu, X., Voss, H. and Zheng, P., (2007), "The Determinants of Chinese Outward Foreign Direct Investment", *Journal of International Business Studies*, Vol.38, No.4, pp.499-518.

CNDR, (2015), Perspectivas y acciones para promover la construcción conjunta de la Franja

Económica a lo largo de la Ruta de la Seda y de la Ruta de la Seda Marítima del Siglo XXI, http://www.fmprc.gov.cn/esp/zxxx/t1252441.shtml. Acceso: 18/02/2017.

Delfsma, W. & Duyters, G., (2009), "*Multinationals and Emerging Economies. The Quest for Innovations and Sustainability*". Chentelham, U.K.: Edward Elgar.

Donner,F.R. & Schneider, B.R., (2016), "The Middle-income Trap: More Politics than Economics", *World Politics*, Vol.68, No.4, pp.608-644.

Elek, A., (2015), China takes the lead on economic integration. *East Asia Forum*, http://www.eastasiaforum.org/2015/07/07/china-takes-the-lead-on-economic-integration/.

European Commission, (2017), "China, Policy, news, events and bi-lateral science and technology agreements with China. Europe Union", Brussels, http://ec.europa.eu/research/iscp/index.cfm?pg=china.

Gurria, A., (2017), "The Middle income Trap in Latin America: ongoing OECD-World Economic Forum partnership", http://www.oecd.org/ development/middle-income-trap-in-latin-america-ongoing-oecd-wef-partnership.htm.

Griffiths, J., (2017), China's New World Order: Xi, Putin and Others Meet for Belt and Road Forum, *CNN*, http://edition.cnn.com/2017/05/13/ asia/china-belt-and-road-forum-xi-putin-erdogan/.

Mussacchio, M., (2015), "Mexico ante el ascenso de China en el plano internacional", in A. Girón, A. Vargas & Pulido, G, eds., *China y Mexico. Un diálogo cultural dese la Humanidades y la Ciencias Sociales*, pp. 285-296, Mexico, D.F.: Universidad Nacional Autónoma de Mexico.

HKTDC Research., (2016), "The Belt and Road Initiative", https://beltandroad.hktdc.com/sites/default/files/imported/ beltandroadbasics/hktdc_1X0K715S_en.pdf.

Inge, K., Grunberg, I. & Stern, M., (1999), *Global Public Goods: International Cooperation in the 21st Century*, New York: The United Nations Development Programme.

OECD, (2018), *Net ODA (indicator)*, https://data.oecd.org/oda/net-oda.htm.

ONU Mexico, (2016), *Objetivos de Desarrollo Sostenible*, http://www.onu.org.mx/agenda-2030/objetivos-del-desarrollo-sostenible/.

Perlez, J. & Huang, Y., (2017), "Behind China's $1 Trillion Plan to Shake Up the Economic Order", *The New York Times*, https://www.nytimes.com/2017/05/13/business/china-railway-one-belt-one-road-1-trillion-plan.html?hp & action=click & pgtype=Homepage & click Source=story-heading & module=photo-spot-region & region=top-news & WT.nav=top-news & _r=0.

State Council Information Office, (2011), "China's Foreign Aid", www.chinanews.com/gn/2011/04–21/2989430.shtml.

State Council Information Office, (2014), "China's Foreign Aid'", http://news.xinhuanet.com/english/china/2014–07/10/c_133474011.htm

Shepard, W., (2017), "I Spend Two Years on China's Belt and Road, and This is What I Found", *Forbes*, https://www.forbes.com/sites/wadeshepard/2017/05/13/i-spent-two-years-on-chinas-belt-and-road-and-this-is-what-i-found-part-1/#71f2e5354b68.

Stallings, B., (2017), "Chinese Foreign Aid to Latin America. Trying to Win Friends and Influence People", in M. Myers, Margaret & C. Wise,, eds., *The political Economy of China-Latin*

America Relations in the New Millennium. Brave New World ,pp. 69-90, New York: Routledge.

Sun, Y., (2014), "Africa in China's New Foreign Aid White Paper", *Brookings*, http://www.brookings.edu/blogs/africa-in-focus/posts/2014/07/16-africa-china-foreign-aid-sun.

Taylor, M., (2017), "The Latin America's Middle-income Trap", https://www.cfr.org/blog/politics-latin-americas-middle-income-trap.

Wilson, E J., (2008), "Hard Power, Soft Power, Smart Power", *The ANNALS of the American Academy of Political and Social Science*, Vol.616, No.1, pp.110-124.

Xinhua, (2014), "China concede 14.410 millones de dólares para ayuda al extranjero entre 2010 y 2012", *Xinhua Español*, http://spanish.xinhuanet.com/china/2014–07/10/c_133474508.htm.

Xinhua, (2016), "Full text of China's Policy Paper on Latin America and the Caribbean", *Xinhua*, http: //www.china.org.cn/world/2016–11/24/content_39777989.htm.

Zhang, Y., Gu, J. & Yunnan, C., (2015), *China's Engagement in International Development Cooperation: The State of the Debate*, Beijing: Institute of Development Studies/Tsinghua University.

Chapter 10. Chinese Funding for Development in Latin America: Geopolitical Approach and New Opportunities for Escape of the Middle-income Trap

Abdenur, A and Marcondes de Souza, D., (2013), "Cooperación china en América Latina. Las implicaciones de la asistencia para el desarrollo", *Revista Íconos*, Vol.47, 69-85.

Amado, C., (2010), "A China e a cooperação Sul-Sul", *Revista Relaçôes Internacionais*, Vol.26, 39-46.

Besharati, N., (2013), *Common Goals and Differential Commitments. The Role of Emerging Economies in Global Development. Discussion Paper*, Bonn: Deutsches Institut für Entwicklungspolitik.

Bracho, G., (2009), "La identidad de los países de renta media y de Mexico desde la perspectiva de la OCDE", En C. Ayala, & J. A. Pérez, eds., *Mexico y los países de renta media en la cooperación para el desarrollo: ¿hacia dónde vamos?* ,pp. 287-315, Mexico, D.F: Instituto Mora.

Bracho, G., (2015), *In Search of a Narrative for Southern Providers. The Challenge of the Emerging Economies to the Development Cooperation Agenda. Discussion Paper*, Bonn: Deutsches Institut für Entwicklungspolitik.

China Development Bank, "About CDB", http://www.cdb.com.cn/English/gykh_512/khjj/.

Coalición Regional., (2016), *Papel de los Bancos Nacionales de Desarrollo en la estructura del financiamiento regional en América Latina*, Bogotá: Coalición Regional por la Transparencia y la Participación.

Development Assistance Committee., (2018), *Development Assistance Committee DAC*, http://www.oecd.org/development/developmentassistancecommitteedac.htm

Dollar, D., (2017), "China's Investment in Latin America", *Geoeconomics and Global Issues Paper*, Vol.4, pp.1-19.

Echeingreen, B. and Uzan, M., (1992), The Marshall Plan: Economic Effects and Implications for

Eastern Europe and the Former USSR, *Economic Policy*, Vol.7, No.14, pp.13-75.

Gallagher, K., Irwin, A. and Koleski, K., (2012), *The New Banks in Town: Chinese Finance in Latin America*, Washington, DC: The Inter-American Dialogue.

Gallagher, K., Irwin, A. and Koleski, K., (2013), "¿Un mejor trato? Análisis comparativo de los préstamos chinos en América Latina", Mexico, D.F: Universidad Nacional Autónoma de Mexico.

Hardy, A., (2014), *The World Turned Upside Down: The Complex Partnership Between China and Latin America*. Singapore: World Scientific Publishing.

Kjøllesdal, K. and Welle-Strand, A., (2010), "Foreign Aid Strategies: China Taking Over?", *Asian Social Science*, Vol.6, No.10, pp.3-13.

Kragelund, P., (2011), The Rejuvenation of Non-traditional Donors Development Cooperation with Africa, *Development and Change*, Vol.42, 585-607.

Kutesa, S., (2015), *Statement at the Closing Plenary of the Third International Conference on Financing for Development*, http://www.un.org/pga/160715_statement-at-closing-plenary-of-the-third-international-conference-on-financing-for-development/.

Lemus, D. and Santa Cruz, A., (2015), "La política de la cooperación internacional para el desarrollo: los países argamasa y el caso de Mexico como proceso de localización normativa invertida", *Relaciones Internacionales*, Vol.48, pp.59-85.

Ministerio de Relaciones Exteriores de China., (2016), *Documento sobre la Política de China Hacia América Latina y el Caribe*, http://www.fmprc.gov.cn/esp/zxxx/t1418256.shtml

Morazan, P., Knoke, I., Knoblauch, D., and SchäfeR, T., (2012), *The Role of Brics in the Developing World*. Brussels; European Parliament.

Mwase, N. and Yang, Y., (2012), *BRICs' Philosophies for Development Financing and Their Implications for LICs*, Washington: International Monetary Fund.

Olguín, P., (2011), "El compromiso de China con el desarrollo del tercer mundo: el caso Angola", *Revista Estudios de Asia y África*, Vol.46, No.3, pp.589-649.

Prado, J., (2002), "El Consenso de Monterrey: ¿Una alternativa al esquema tradicional de financiación al desarrollo?" *Relaciones Internacionales*, Vol.88, pp.69-83.

Salama, P., (2017), "Brasil y China: caminos de fortalezas y desconciertos". *Revista Problemas del Desarrollo*, Vol.188, No.48, pp.9-28.

Slipak, A., (2014), "América Latina y China: ¿Cooperación Sur-Sur o 'Consenso de Beijing'?", *Revista Nueva Sociedad*, Vol.250, pp.102-113.

Stuenkel, O., (2015), *The BRICS and the Future of the Global Order*. Lanham: Lexington Books.

Teixeira, J., (2016), "A Influência Chinesa nos Processos de Integração na América Latina", *Revista Intellector*, Vol.12, No.24, pp.223-225.

The Export-Import Bank of China, "Brief Introduction", http://english.eximbank.gov.cn/tm/en-TCN/index_618.html.

United Nations, (1997), "Resolution Adopted by the General Assembly", http://www.un.org/documents/ga/res/51/ares51-240.htm

Vadell, J., (2016), "La Red de Bancos de Desarrollo de China (RBDC) y sus implicaciones para América latina", *Voces en el Fénix*, Vol.56, pp.30-38.

Walz, J. and Ramachandran, V., (2011), "Brave New World: A Literature Review of Emerging Donors and the Changing Nature of Foreign Assistance", Washington, D.C.: Center for Global Development.

Woods, N., (2008), "Whose aid? Whose influence? China, Emerging Donors and the Silent Revolution in Development Assistance", *International Affairs*, Vol.84, pp.1205–1221.

Chapter 11 China and Brazil: Transitioning from the Middle-income Trap to Sustainable Development?—A Sociological Perspective on Consumption, Inequality and the Middle-income Trap

ABEP, (2016), *Brazilian Criteria 2015 and social class distribution update for 2016*, São Paulo: Associação Brasileira de Empresas de Pesquisa.

Aglietta, M., & Bai, G., (2016), "China's 13th Five-Year Plan. An Economic Impact Assessment In Pursuit of a 'Moderately Prosperous Society'", *CEPII Policy Brief*, Vol.12, No.12, pp.1–16.

Bárcena, A., & Byanyima, W., (2016), "Latin America is the World's Most Unequal Region", *ECLAC*, https://www.cepal.org/en/articles/2016–latin-america-worlds-most-unequal-region-heres-how-fix-it.

Boskin, M. J., (2015), "Can the BRICS Escape the Middle-income Trap?", *World Economic Forum*, https://www.weforum.org/agenda/2015/06/can-the-brics-escape-the-middle-income-trap/.

Bourguignon, F., Ferreira, F., & Leite, P., (2002), *Ex-Ante Evaluation of Conditional Cash Transfer Programs: The Case of Bolsa Escola*, Washington D.C.: World Bank.

Caleiro, J. P., (2016), "Crise empurra 3,7 milhões de volta para fora da classe C. *Exame*", http://exame.abril.com.br/economia/noticias/crise-empurra-milhoes-de-volta-para-fora-da-classe-c.

Canuto, O., (2014), "What's Holding Back Brazil?", *Project Syndicate*, http: // www.project-syndicate.org/commentary/otaviano-canuto-identifies-several-growth-traps-that-have-stopped-brazil-s-ascent-to-high-income-status?barrier=accessreg.

Cavusgil, S. T., & Kardes, I., (2013), "Brazil: Rapid Development, Internationalization, and Middle Class Formation", *Internext*, Vol.8, No.1, pp.1–16.

Central Intelligence Agency, (2017), *The World Factbook*, https://www.cia.gov/library/publications/the-world-factbook/rankorder/2172rank.html.

Chen, G., (2013), "Structural Characteristics and Trends of Income Inequality in China", in P. Li, M. K. Gorshkov, C. Scalon & K. L. Sharma, eds., *Social Stratification in the BRIC Countries: Change and* Perspective, pp. 481-498, Singapore: World Scientific.

Costa, L. G., & Scalon, C., (2013), "Income Inequality and Social Stratification in Brazil: Key Determining Factors and Changes in the First Decade of the 21st Century", in P. Li, M. K. Gorshkov, C. Scalon & K. L. Sharma, eds., *Social Stratification in the BRIC Countries: Change and* Perspective, pp.421-438, Singapore: World Scientific.

Dreger, C., & Zhang, Y., (2014), "Prospects for Consumption-Based Growth in China", *DIW Economic Bulletin*, Vol.2, No.2, pp.3-6.

Federal Government of Brazil, (2011), "Governo adota pacote de estímulo à economia", http://www.brasil.gov.br/governo/2011/12/governo-adota-pacote-de-estimulo-a-economia.

Federal Government of Brazil, (2016), "Governo lança medidas para injetar R$ 83 bi na economia e incentivar o crescimento", http://www.brasil.gov.br/governo/2016/01/governo-lanca-medidas-para-injetar-r-83-bi-na-economia-e-incentivar-o-crescimento.

Ferrari Filho, F., & Paula, L. F., (2015), "A Critical Analysis of the Macroeconomic Policies in Brazil from Lula da Silva to Dilma", *Brazilian Keynesian Review*, Vol.1, No.2, pp.218–227.

Fernholz, T., (2014), "The Myth of the Middle-income Trap", *Qurtz*, https://qz.com/310657/the-myth-of-the-middle-income-trap/.

Golan, J., Sicular, T., & Umapathi, N., (2014), *Any Guarantees? China's Rural Minimum Living Standard Guarantee Program* Washington, D.C: World Bank.

Hout, M., (2006), "Economic Change and Social Mobility", in G. Therborn, ed., *Inequalities of the World*, p. 119-135, London: Verso.

Hsu, S., (2015), "China's Efforts to Boost Consumption: Are They Enough?", *The Diplomat*, https://thediplomat.com/2015/05/chinas-efforts-to-boost-consumption-are-they-enough/.

International Monetary Fund, (2017), *IMF Fiscal Monitor: Tackling Inequality*, https://www.imf.org/en/Publications/FM/Issues/2017/10/05/fiscal-monitor-october-2017.

Islam, N., (2014), "Will inequality lead China to the Middle Income Trap", *Frontiers of Economics in China*, Vol.9, No.3, pp.398-437.

Kharas, H., & Kohli, H., (2011), "What Is the Middle income Trap, Why do Countries Fall into It, and How Can It Be Avoided?", *Global Journal of Emerging Market Economies*, Vol.3, No.3, pp.281–289.

Kuijs, L., & Wang, T., (2005), *China's Pattern of Growth: Moving to Sustainability and Reducing Inequality*, Washington, D. C: World Bank.

Lardy, N., (2006), "China: toward a Consumption-driven Growth Path", *Policy Briefs in International Economics*, Vol.6, pp.1–13.

Li, P., (2013), "Changes in China's Social Stratification Since 1978", in P. Li, M. K. Gorshkov, C. Scalon & K. L. Sharma, eds., *Handbook on Social Stratification in the BRIC Countries: Change and Perspective*, pp. 59-83, Singapore: World Scientific.

Li, S., (2016), "Recent changes in Income Inequality in China, in F. Caillods & M. Denis, eds., *World Social Science Report: Challenging Inequalities: Pathways to Just World*, pp. 84-89, Paris: UNESCO Publishing.

Li, W., (2013), "Stratum Consciousness and Stratum Identification in China", in P. Li, M. K. Gorshkov, C. Scalon & K. L. Sharma, eds., *Social Stratification in the BRIC Countries: Change and Perspective*, pp. 733-754, Singapore: World Scientific.

Lin, J. Y., & Treichel, V., (2012), *Learning from China's Rise to Escape the Middle-income Trap-A New Structural Economics Approach to Latin America*, Washington, D.C. World Bank.

Nassif, A., (2017), "An Analysis of Brazil's Economic Situation: 2014–2017, the Short-term Outlook and Policy Alternatives", *Brazilian Keynesian Review*, Vol.3, No.1, pp.95-108.

Ngai, P., (2003), "Subsumption or Consumption? The Phantom of Consumer Revolution in 'Globalizing'" China, *Cultural Anthropology*, Vol.18, No.4, 469–492.

O'Dougherty, M., (2002), *Consumption Intensified: The Politics of Middle-Class Daily Life in Brazil*, Durham: Duke University Press.

Piketty, T., (2017), Brasil não cresce se não reduzir sua desigualdade. *Folha de São Paulo*, http://

www1.folha.uol.com.br/mercado/2017/09/1922435–brasil-nao-cresce-se-nao-reduzir-sua-desigualdade-diz-thomas-piketty.shtml

Pinheiro-Machado, R., & Scalco, L. M., (2014), "Rolezinhos: Marcas, consumo e segregação no Brasil", *Revista Estudos Culturais*, Vol.1, No.1, pp.1-20.

Scalon, C., (2013), "Social Stratification and Its Transformation in Brazil", in P. Li, M. K. Gorshkov, C. Scalon, & K. L. Sharma, eds., *Handbook on Social Stratification in the BRIC Countries: Change and Perspective*, pp. 3–20, Singapore: World Scientific.

Tian, F., (2013), "The Stratification of Consumption among Social Classes, Occupational Groups, and Identity Groups in China", in P. Li, M. K. Gorshkov, C. Scalon, & K. L. Sharma, eds., *Handbook on Social Stratification in the BRIC Countries: Change and Perspective*, pp. 649–674, Singapore: World Scientific.

Tjong, E., (2014), *Evaluating Sino-Brazilian Economic Relations: Which Roads for Development in a Resource-Rich Country*, Shnaghai: Fudan University.

WID, (2017), Income inequality, China, 1978–2015, http://wid.world/country/china/.

WID, (2017), Income inequality, Brazil, 2001–2015, http://wid.world/country/brazil/.

Wong, C. P. W., (1991), "Central–Local Relations in an Era of Fiscal Decline: The Paradox of Fiscal Decentralization in Post-Mao China", *The China Quarterly*, Vol.128, 691-715.

World Bank, (2004), *Inequality and Economic Development in Brazil*, Washington, D.C.: World Bank.

World Bank, (2016), *Poverty and Shared Prosperity 2016: Taking on Inequality*, Washington D.C.: World Bank.

World Economic Forum, (2017), *Global Risks Report.*, http://www3.weforum.org/docs/GRR17_Report_web.pdf.

Xie, Y., & Zhou, X., (2014), "Income Inequality in Today's China", *Proceedings of the National Academy of Sciences of the United States of America, 111*(19) 6928–33.

Yuan, Y., & Xu, L., (2015), "Are Poor Able to Access the Informal Credit Market? Evidence From rural Households in China", *China Economic Review, 33* 232–246.

Zacharias, J., (2007), *Emergence of a Central Space in a New Chinese City: the Case of Shenzhen*, Paper presented at 47th ACSP Annual Conference, Milwaukee, https://doi.org/10.13140/2.1.4586.6567.

Zhigang, Y., Vercueil, J., & Boyer, R., (2017), "A Growth Model with Chinese Characteristics", *Revue de La Régulation, Capitalisme, Institutions, Pouvoirs, 21*, http://regulation.revues.org/12315.

Chapter 12. Climate Change in Brazil and China: Impacts, Political Responses and Challenges

Albuquerque, J.A. & Ferreira, (2013), *China & Brasil: desafios e oportunidades*, São Paulo: Annablume.

Basso, L. & Viola, E., (2014), "Chinese Energy Policy Progress and Challenges in the Transition to Low Carbon Development, 2006–2013", *Revista Brasileira de Política Internacional*, Vol.57, pp.14-16.

Barbi, F., (2015), "Governing Climate Change in China and Brazil: Mitigation Strategies", *Journal of Chinese Political Science*, Vol.21, No.3, pp.357–370.

Barbi, F. & Ferreira, L., (2016), "Governing Climate Change Risks: Implications for Mitigation and Adaptation", *Fudan Journal of Humanities and Social Sciences*, Vol.9, No.4, pp.589–606.

Beck, U., 2010, *Sociedade de Risco-Rumo a uma outra modernidade*, São Paulo: Editora 34.

Dewulf, A., Meijerink, S., & Runhaar, H., (2015), "Editorial: The Governance of Adaptation to Climate Change as a Multi-level, Multi-sector and Multi-actor Challenge: a European Comparative Perspective", *Journal of Water and Climate Change*, Vol.6, pp.1-8.

Ewing, S.A., Christensen, J., Shaun, T.B., Vancuren, R.A., Steven, S., & Depaolo, D.J., (2010),"Pb Isotopes as an Indicator of the Asian Contribution to Particulate Air Pollution in Urban California", *Environmental Science Technology*, Vol.44, No.23, pp.8911–8916.

Ferreira, L. & Barbi, F., (2012), Questões ambientais e prioridades políticas na China. *ComCiência*, p.*137*.

Ferreira, L., (2017), *O Desafio das Mudanças Climáticas: Os Casos Brasil e China*, Jundiaí: Paco editorial.

Gamer, R.E., (1999), *Understanding contemporary China*, Colorado: Lynne Rienner Publishers.

Gerth, K., (2010), *As China Goes, So Goes the World: How Chinese Consumers are Transforming Everything*, New York: Hill and Wang.

Governo do Brasil, (2009), "Política Nacional sobre Mudança do Clima—PNMC", http://www.brasil.gov.br/meio-ambiente/2010/11/plano-nacional-sobre-mudanca-do-clima.

Giddens, A., (2010), *A Política da mudança climática*, Rio de Janeiro: Zahar.

Guimarães, R., (2011), Política, o elo perdido na interação ciência-políticas públicas, in: Ferreira, L, ed., *A questão ambiental na América Latina*, pp. 127-139, Campinas: Unicamp; São Paulo: Fapesp.

He, Qinglian., (2006), "Who is Responsible for China's Environment?", *Big Country, Small World 37*, China Rights Forum, no 1, http://www.hrichina.org/sites/default/files/PDFs/CRF.1.2006/CRF-2006–1_Responsible.pdf.

Hu, G., (2017), *The Cost of Development in China*, Singapore: Springer.

Hsü, I., (2000), *The rise of modern China*, New York: Oxford University Press.

IEA, (2015), *World Energy Outlook 2015*, OECD/IEA.

IPCC, (2007), Climate Change 2007: Synthesis Report, in: R.K. Pachauri e A. Reisinger, eds., Contribution of Working Groups I, II and III to the Fourth Assessment Report of the Intergovernmental Panel on Climate Change, Cambridge: Cambridge University Press.

IPCC, (2013), Working Group I Contribution to the IPCC Fifth Assessment Report. Climate Change 2013: The Physical Science Basis. Summary for Policymakers, Cambridge: Cambridge University Press.

Leite, A C., (2013), *A industrialização de áreas agrícolas na China: uma consequência do recente desenvolvimento chinês.* Revista da Sociedade Brasileira de Economia Política, Vol.36, 91-116.

Liu, Zhu, (2015), *China's Carbon Emissions Report 2015*, Cambridge: Harvard Kennedy School.

Lobell, D.B., Schlenker, W. & Costa-Roberts, J., (2011), "Climate Trends and Global Crop Production since 1980", *Science*, Vol.333, No.6042, pp.616-620.

Margulis, S., Dubeux, C. & Marcovitch, J., (2011), *The Economics of Climate Change in Brazil:*

Costs and Opportunities, São Paulo: FEA/USP.

Mignolo, W., (2004), "Os esplendores e as misérias da 'ciência': Colonialidade, geopolítica do conhecimento e pruri-versalidade epistêmica", in: Santos, B., ed., *Conhecimento Prudente para uma Vida Decente: 'Um Discurso Sobre as Ciências' Revisitado*, pp. 667-709. São Paulo: Cortez.

Moreira, H.M. & Ribeiro, W., (2017), "A atuação da China no G77, Basic e Brics nas negociações internacionais do clima", in Ferreira, Leila C. *O Desafio das Mudanças Climáticas: Os Casos Brasil e China*, pp. 57-82, Jundiaí: Paco editorial.

Mortatti, C.M.; Galvão de Miranda, S.H. & Bacchi, M.R., (2011), "Determinantes do comércio Brasil-China de *commodities* e produtos industriais: uma aplicação VECM", *Economia Aplicada*, Vol.15, No.2, pp.331-335.

Moyo, D., (2013), "*O vencedor leva tudo: a corrida chinesa por recursos e seu significado para o mundo*", Rio de Janeiro: Objetiva.

Nahur, A.C., Guido, F.L., & Gildi dos Santo, J.A., (2015), *As Mudanças Climáticas: Riscos e Oportunidades*. Programa Água Brasil, http://www.bb.com.br/docs/pub/siteEsp/uds/dwn/mudclimatica.pdf.

Newell, P., Pattberg, P, & Schroeder, H., (2012), "Multiactor Governance and the Environment", *Annual Review of Environment and Resources*, Vol.37, pp.365-387.

Nobre, A.D., (2014), *O Futuro Climático da Amazônia*, Relatório de Avaliação Científica, São José dos Campos: Edição ARA, CCST-INPE e INPA.

OC—Observatório do Clima, (2017), *Emissões do Brasil sobem 9% em 2016*, Presskit, SEEG.

UNHCR-United Nations High Commissioner for Refugees., (2008), "Climate Change, Natural Disasters and Human Displacement: a UNHCR perspective", Geneva: UNHCR.

Raman, G.V., (2016), "Environmental Governance in China", *Theoretical Economics Letters*, Vol.6, pp.583-595.

Rehan, R. & Nehdi, M., (2005), "Carbon Dioxide Emissions and Climate Change: Policy Implications for the Cement Industry", *Environmental Science & Policy*, Vol.8, pp.105–114.

Liu, C., (2014), Milhões de chineses fazem seguro climático, *Scientific American Brasil*, http://www2.uol.com.br/sciam/noticias/milhoes_de_chineses_fazem_seguro_climatico.html.

Shapiro, J., (2012), *China's Environmental Challenges*. Malden: Polity Press.

Shi, H. & Zhang, L., (2006), "China's Environmental Governance of Rapid Industrilisation", *Environmental Politics*, Vol.15, No.2, pp.271-292.

Shuxiao, W., (2016), "New Study: Air Pollution from Coal a Major Source of Health Burden in China", https://www.healtheffects.org/system/files/HEI-GBD-MAPS-China-Press-Release.pdf

United Nations, Department of Economic and Social Affairs, Population Division, (2014), *World Urbanization Prospects: The 2014 Revision*, New York: United Nations.

Watts, Nick, et al. (2017), "The Lancet Countdown on Health and Climate Change: from 25 years of Inaction to a Global Transformation for Public Health, *The Lancet*, Vol.391 ,pp.581-591.

World Health Organization, (2015), *Reducing Global Health Risks Through Mitigation of Short-Lived Climate Pollutants. Scoping Report for Policy-makers*, Geneva: WHO Press.

Zhang, L. & Ong, A., (2008), *Privatizing China: Socialism from Afar*, New York: Cornell University Press.

About the Authors

Andreas M. Hartmann

Andreas M. Hartmann is an associate professor at Tecnologico de Monterrey in Monterrey, Mexico, where he is teaching in the fields of strategic management, cross-cultural management, and intercultural negotiation. His research focuses on multinational companies, knowledge-based firms, and cross-cultural aspects of management. A native German, he is fluent in English, Spanish, and French. Prior to his current position, he worked as a language teacher and as a free-lance translator and conference interpreter in Europe and Mexico. Andreas M. Hartmann holds a Ph.D. in International Business and an MBA from the Tecnologico de Monterrey as well as a double Master's degree in Translation and Conference Interpreting from the University of Heidelberg.

Andres Borquez

Andres Borquez is Ph.D. candidate in International Politics at Fudan University and Research Collaborator at Fudan Asia Pacific Center. He also is Assistant Professor at the International Business School at University of Valparaiso, Chile. Andres is the author of "Transformations of the Chinese economy post-Mao: beyond capitalism and market socialism?" (2015) and other articles that seek to analyze China's cooperation model for Latin American countries and the Political Economy of Internation.

Augusto Frederico Junqueira Schmidt

Bachelor's student in Civil Engineering at the Federal University of Technology—Paraná, Curitiba, Brazil researching on the use of wetlands as a solution to basic sanitation problems. He took part in a two-year exchange program at the College of Civil Engineering at Tongji University, Shanghai, China. He is currently a technical assistant in the research group Public Policy and Dynamics of Territorial Development at Federal University of Technology—Paraná and participated in the activities of the international pilot research Studio Cities and Biodiversity from 2012–2013, where he contributed to a UNU-IAS Policy Report on Integrating Biodiversity with Local and City Planning. He is currently also developing research on water resource governance in this project.

Bruno Binetti

Bruno Bienetti is a non-resident fellow at the Inter-American Dialogue, a think tank in Washington DC, and a guest lecturer at Torcuato Di Tella University in Buenos Aires, Argentina. He holds an MA in International Affairs from the Elliott School of International Affairs, George Washington University, where he was a Fulbright Scholar. His research interests include Latin America's relations with China and the United States, the region's role within international political economy, and Latin American politics.

Carlos Cerda

Carlos Cerda is professor of international relations at Tecnologico de Monterrey, Campus Guadalajara. His research and teaching has centered on International Development Cooperation and Mexico Foreign Policy.

Daniel Lemus Delgado

Daniel Lemus Delgado is professor of Regional Scenario of Asia Pacific at School of Social Science and Government at Tecnologico de Monterrey. He is member of the National System of Researchers (Mexico). Fields of academic interests are Regional Innovation System with special focus on the ideational structures of innovation.

Erick Tjong

Co-author of the World Bank's Doing Business report since its 2016 edition, his research is focused on the quality and efficiency of business regulations in 50 countries, particularly in Latin America and East Asia. Prior to joining the World Bank, he worked at PwC, providing consulting services for Chinese investments in Brazil, and at the Paris City Hall's international relations bureau. Erick holds a Bachelor's Degree in International Relations from the University of São Paulo-USP (Brazil) and a Dual Master's Degree in European and Asian relations from Sciences Po Paris (France) and Fudan University (China). His Master Thesis focused on the relations between development and natural resources, with a case study on the impacts brought by Chinese trade and investments on economic development in Brazil.

Fabiana Barbi

Fabiana Barbi is a postdoctoral researcher at the Center for Environmental Studies and Research (Nepam), University of Campinas (Unicamp) in Brazil. Her current research involves climate change policies in Brazil and China, concerning mitigation strategies at national and local levels. She is a research fellow of the Earth System Government Project. She is author of "Climate change and political responses in cities" (2015, published in Brazil).

Hua Zhou

Hua Zhou is a full time associate professor at School of economics and management, Tongji University. She earned a Ph.D. in World Economic from Peking university, China. Her research targets the contagion effect on the formation of FTA. She has published many articles on FTA under different free trade networks and most recently she started a research dedicated to the influence of FTA utilizing the GTAP framework.

Francisco Valderrey

Francisco Valderrey is a full-time professor at the Business Department of Tecnologico de Monterrey, Campus Leon. He earned a Ph.D. in Administration and Marketing from Universitat de Valencia, Spain. He has co-authored two textbooks about fundamentals of marketing. His research targets are marketing in China, along with negotiation strategy on multicultural environments and cross-cultural studies. He has published several book chapters and articles on the Asia Pacific, international business diplomacy and business model for the base of the pyramid. He has been a visiting professor in Asia and Europe.

Gabriel A. Zapata

Industrial engineer from the Universidad Peruana de Ciencias Aplicadas (UPC). Professional in Project Management (PMP), with more than ten years of experience in process improvement, project management and management.

Juan González García

Juan González García is professor at Colima University in the Economy Faculty, where he teaches economic development and development regional in Asia Pacific. His research has centered on comparative studies on Asia Pacific economies and Mexico. He is author of many books about comparative studies between Mexico and China. Two of the last researches are on BRI in a Global Perspective and The Chinese Dream in the Twenty Century.

Leila da Costa Ferreira

Leila da Costa Ferreira is a full professor at the Institute of Philosophy and Human Sciences and at the Center for Environmental Studies and Research (NEPAM) at the University of Campinas (UNICAMP), Brazil. She is a faculty member of the Earth System Governance Project. She is autor of "Environmental Issues in Latin American" (2011, published in Brazil) and "The Challenge of Climate Change: Brazil and China" (2017, published in Brazil).

Mariana Delgado Barbieri

Mariana Delgado Barbieri is a Ph.D. candidate at the Center for Environmental Studies and Research (NEPAM), at the University of Campinas (UNICAMP), Brazil. Her current research involves climate change and civil society in China. She has experience in Sociology, focusing on environmental sociology, environmental governance and social movement. She is a member of LABGEC (Laboratory of Social Dimensions of the Global Environmental Changes in the Global South).

Mariana Hase Ueta

Ph.D. Candidate at University of Campinas—UNICAMP (Brazil) in the Postgraduate Program in Social Sciences on China-Brazil Studies, supervisor Tom Dwyer. She holds a Bachelor's Degree from UNICAMP in Social Sciences with emphasis in Anthropology and a Master's Degree in Chinese Society and Public Policy from the School of Social Development and Public Policy of Fudan University (China). Her research focused on the analysis of intercultural communication in the Sino-Brazilian Strategic Partnership. Mariana also participated in the research team of "Shanghai Manual: A Guide for Sustainable Urban Development of the 21st Century", organized by the Shanghai Coordination Center of World Cities, UN-Habitat and International Exhibitions Bureau. She has experience in the fields of Chinese Studies, Anthropology, Sociology and International Relations. In her Ph.D. she is engaged in the development of comparative studies between China and Brazil with focus on consumption and sustainability, from the social inclusion perspective.

Mauricio Cervantes Zepeda

Full professor, specialized in Global Business, and Finance. Member of the National System of Researchers of CONACYT, SNI 1.Ph.D. in Administration specialization Finance, MBA, and Electronic Engineer. He is currently a research professor at the Center for "Strategy and Management of Organizations in Emerging Economies". Additional, he founded and directed the "Fudan-Tec de Monterrey Research Center for Studies China-Latin America". He has been a visiting professor at University of International Business and Economics in Beijing, China; Portland State University, USA; University of San Francisco at Quito, Ecuador; University ESAN, Peru. His research area is microfinance, business models, global business and emerging markets.

Miguel A. Montoya B.

Miguel A. Montoya is a professor of International Business and Economics at Tecnologico de Monterrey (Mexico). He is an expert on global Mexican firms. He has published some articles in different academic journals and participated in various academic conferences. He has written different books and chapters in Spain, UK, Mexico and Switzerland. He is member of the Academy of International Business, the National Council for Technology and Science (CONACYT-Mexico), and the editorial board of Competition and Regulation in Network Industries Journal. He was awarded a Ph.D. from Universidad Autonoma de Barcelona.

Niklas Werner Weins

Master's student at the Federal University of Technology—Paraná, Curitiba, Brazil in the Post-Graduate Program in Technology and Society (PPGTE), supervisor Prof. Christian Luiz da Silva. He holds a Bachelor of Arts in East Asian Politics & Economics from Ruhr-Universität Bochum (2015) with research stays at Tongji University, Shanghai and UAM Mexico City. He has research and practical experience in Development, Environmental Studies and International Relations with a focus on Political Economy. Since 2015 he is a research assistant at Studio Cities and Biodiversity with Prof. Tatiana Gadda and is currently a Research Assistant at the research group Public Policy and Dynamics of Territorial Development, researching on institutional arrangements of Payment for Ecosystem Services (PES) in the Metropolitan Area of Curitiba, as well as developing comparative research on PES in China and Brazil.

Paulo Roberto Feldmann

Paulo Roberto Feldmann is professor at USP-University of São Paulo where he teaches the relation between companies and the world business economic environment. He is also a researcher at USP responsible for projects related to FDI-Foreign Direct Investment and also projects about the relation between Innovation/Technology and Economics. Visiting Professor at three Hungarian Universities: Pecs, Corvinus and SZE-Széchenyi. Author of the book *Management in Latin America: Threats and opportunities in the globalized world* and two other books published in Brazil: *Management in Latin America* (2010) and, *Robot: bad with it worst without it* (1988). Former CEO of 3 companies in Brazil: Eletropaulo, Compucenter and Iron Mountain—He was also partner of Ernst & Young in Brazil.

Otto Regalado Pezúa

Associate professor of ESAN Graduated School of Business, Universidad ESAN. Doctor in Management of Organizations from the Université de Nice-Sophia Antipolis, Nice, France; Master in Quantitative Marketing from the Université Pierre Mendes France, Grenoble, France; Master in Business Administration from Universidad ESAN and a degree in Administrative Sciences from the Universidad de Lima.

Roberto Hernández Hernández

Roberto Hernández Hernández is professor at University of Guadalajara where he teaches regional integration processes, and foreign policy in Asia. His research and teaching has centered on China's modern and contemporary history, China's foreign policy, Asia-Pacific integration processes, and foreign trade between China and Mexico.

Silvia Cortés C.

Silvia Cortés works as a Research Collaborator at the University of Costa Rica's International Politics Observatory, in the elaboration of studies and analyses of current international affairs, with special emphasis on East Asia and transpacific relations. She also works as an Investment Promotion Executive at the Costa Rican Investment Promotion Agency (CINDE), focusing mostly on research in different investment sectors. She holds a B.A. degree in Political Science from the University of Costa Rica, and a M.A. degree in International Relations and International Organization from the University of Groningen, the Netherlands. Prior to her current positions, she worked as a Research Assistant at the University of Costa Rica's Center for Research and Political Studies in the design and execution of various academic projects. Her research interests include Chinese internationalization in Latin America related to economic growth, foreign direct investment, sustainable development, and public diplomacy.

复旦发展研究院

复旦发展研究院成立于1993年，是改革开放以来国内最早设立的智库之一，从早期的“基金会智库”到现在的新型高校智库，研究院25年发展史堪称中国智库的缩影。研究院在体制机制创新的道路上形成自身特色，在国内具有相当知名度——目前，研究院是复旦重点建设的综合性智库平台，拥有一支国内独创、30人规模的“智库运营团队”，聚集一支数百人的专家团队，创造性地设立“政策规划学社”为智库培养和储备下一代人才。

研究院每年举办上海论坛、中国大学智库论坛，并与高校高端智库联盟秘书处、上海高校智库研究和管理中心等合署办公。研究院围绕区域经济、科技创新、产业发展、全球城市、网络治理等五大研究领域，已建和在建数据库近20个。国际化是研究院的鲜明特色，研究院国内首创“海外中国研究中心”，在美国、丹麦、墨西哥、中亚、大洋洲布局智库分支机构；研究院国内首创“国际智库中心”，形成了涵盖37个国家78家机构的国际智库网络，两年内吸纳国际访问学者逾150人次；研究院国内首创拉美大学联盟，与6个拉美国家12所高校形成深度协同关系。复旦发展研究院是光明日报“十大影响力智库”之一，入选中国社科院“AMI核心智库”，在各类智库排名中稳居国内高校智库前十。

联系方式：

网址：http://fddi.fudan.edu.cn

邮箱：fdifudan@fudan.edu.cn

电话：86-21-55670203

传真：86-21-55670203

Fudan Development Institute

Founded in 1993, Fudan Development Institute (FDDI) has been exploring institutional innovation to build up a key comprehensive think tank of Fudan University. The Institute is operated by a staff team of 30 people, and it gathers a research team of hundreds of experts depending on the comprehensive disciplinary advantages of Fudan University in arts, science, medical science and engineering. FDDI is also a pioneer in establishing Students Consulting and Decision-making Society in order to achieve better performance on training and fostering talents. It hosts a variety of national and international conferences, including the Shanghai Forum and the China University Think Tank Forum, and undertakes daily managements and operations of several institutions including the University High-End Think Tank Alliance and the Center for Think-Tanks Research and Management in Shanghai.

FDDI conducts researches in five key areas: Regional Economics, Technology & Innovation, Industrial Economics, Urban Development and Digital Governance. It has been establishing nearly 20 databases covering these areas. FDDI takes the lead in promoting globalization of think tanks in China, and is the first domestic think tank to establish "Overseas Center for China Studies" in the United States, Denmark, Mexico, Kazakhstan and New Zealand. It establishes the "Global Think Tank Center" and has formed a global think tank network, which covers nearly 80 institutions from 37 countries, and allows the visit of over 150 international visiting scholars within two years. The Institute initiates the Fudan-Latin America University Consortium (FLAUC), which actively pursues the cooperation with 12 prestigious universities from 6 Latin American countries. FDDI is one of the TOP 10 "Key Think Tanks in China" according to Guangming Daily, and is selected as the "AMI Key Think Tanks" according to Chinese Academy of Social Sciences.

Contact:
Website: http://fddi.fudan.edu.cn
Email: fdifudan@fudan.edu.cn
Tel: 86-21-55670203
Fax: 86-21-55670203

This book is the result of a co-publication agreement between China Social Sciences Press (China) and Paths International Ltd (UK)

Title: China and Latin America: Paths to Overcoming the Middle-income Trap
Edited by Fudan Development Institute
ISBN: 978-1-84464-610-4
Ebook ISBN: 978-1-84464-611-1

Paths International Ltd
www.pathsinternational.com

Published in the United Kingdom

CPSIA information can be obtained
at www.ICGtesting.com
Printed in the USA
LVHW062024300621
691594LV00002B/9

9 781844 646104